The Rising Manipur

(Including other North-Eastern States)

The Rising Manipur

(Including other North-Eastern States)

Prof. M. Horam

Manas Publications

New Delhi-110 002 (INDIA)

MANAS PUBLICATIONS
(Publishers, Distributors, Importers & Exporters)
4402/5-A, Main Ansari Road
(Opp. HDFC Bank)
Darya Ganj, New Delhi-110 002 (INDIA)
Off. © 23260783, 23265523, Res. © 23842660
Fax: 011-23272766
E-mail: manaspublications@vsnl.com
www.manaspublications.in

ISBN 81-7049-117-7
Rs. 695

Typeset at
Manas Publications

Printed in India at
Jaico Printers, Delhi
and Published by Mrs Suman Lata for
Manas Publications, 4402/5-A, Main Ansari Road
(Opp. HDFC Bank),
Darya Ganj, New Delhi-110 002 (INDIA)

Preface

This book attempts to convey something of the social values, economic condition and feelings of the hill (tribal) people of the state of Manipur, of their aspirations, intense love for traditional values and their longings and frustrations. Fifty years have passed since India's Independence and while the world becomes more and more fast-paced, hardly any tangible economic developmental work has been achieved in the hills. The tribal people have often expressed their thoughts and desires but far too often such expressions have become meaningless cries in the wilderness. This book is an attempt to convey their age-old wants and needs.

Article 371(c) of the Indian Constitution has special provisions with respect to the state of Manipur - "to look after the interests of the hill areas in the state". Ironically, however, the ground reality is that the special provisions under Article 371(c) have been reduced to the status of other committees of the state assembly. This, I suspect, was deliberately done by certain self-interested person(s) who twisted the meaning of the Article in order to suppress and exploit the interests of the tribal people. The Manipur tribals, like any other tribal people around the world, are basically gullible and cannot fathom the ulterior motives of the ruling classes.

The Hill Areas Committee came into existence in 1972 by the then Indian president's order. I was elected Chairman of the committee by the tribal elected legislative members and took charge in 1995. When I wanted to know what the duties and functions of the chairman were, to my surprise, there were only two dilapidated files left by my predecessors. It was sad and shocking, to say the least. This, however, was not their fault but that of the system - the position of the chairman has been reduced to that of a glorified clerk.

Prompted by this ignoble situation, an attempt has been made to bring out a book that highlights the problems of the hill people. In whatever measure this book succeeds it is thanks to those who, through their writing, have taught me the qualities of development, justice and truth. As different contributors have written on topics of their own interest, overlapping is at times unavoidable; but this is only indicative of the topicality and urgency of the problems that the tribal people face today.

I must thank Professor Lal Dena of the Manipur University who has taken the trouble to go through the articles and make the work more meaningful with his careful and scientific impartiality.

My office personnel, especially the typists who painstakingly typed and re-typed every page, should be thanked profusely for their efforts and teamwork. I must also acknowledge a debt to the former chief minister, Sri Rishang Keishing who assisted and encouraged me at every step. I have great regard for his noble help and suggestions. I would also like to extend my appreciation to the Speaker of the Legislative Assembly for his support extended towards the publishing of this book.

We are extremely fortunate to have the knowledge and expertise of the Governor, Shri O.N. Srivastava who is imbued with an in-depth knowledge of the North Eastern States' problems, on merit of his long association with the region. I appreciate his humane understanding of the problems of the state and owe the greatest debt to him for his tireless involvement in solving the problems of the state at every stage.

Prof. M. Horam

Contents

PART-III

Issues on Education

PART-IV

Issues on Forest and Entrepreneurship

PART-V

ISSUES ON LAND

PART - I

GENERAL ISSUES ON DEVELOPMENT

1

Social Factors of Development in Manipur

- Prof B.K. Roy Burman

1. **There are two ways to Define the Social Factors of Development.**

   In a narrow sense, social factors mean the institutional framework and organisational measures that support the various programmes laid down in the developmental plan for the country. A broader definition encompasses not only the instrumental aspects of the successful implementation of programmes but also the social values and objectives that determine the structure of the plan as a whole and its components, as well as the planning process in all its phases. While determining the scope of the workshop, it would be worthwhile to keep in view some of the guiding principles enunciated by the Planning Commission in the draft of the Ninth Five-Year Plan on the mechanism and process of planning.

A). Planning has to be viewed not only as a periodical activity concerned with the drawing up of plan documents but a continuous process constantly engaged in (i) locating new resources, potential and technology and their translation into projects and programmes and (ii) identifying and diagnosing contingent problems.

B). Involvement of the people and their elected representatives has to be recognised as a prerequisite for effective planning.

2. In the light of the foregoing statement of the perspective of the draft of the Five-Year plan, it is felt that the

workshop on the social factors of development in Manipur, jointly sponsored by the Manipur University (former centre of JNU) at Imphal and the state government of Manipur, should aim at a synthesis of two tasks. First, it will try to make an analytical appraisal of the information available with respect to the different parts of the state "pertaining to levels of development, population and area, productivity and coverage of various social services and infrastructure". It will also take into account the aspirations and preferences of the people. At the same time, it will critically examine, in the light of the Fifth Plan, the objectives and policies, detailed decisions taken with regard to the choice or innovation of specific programmes and determination of locations, capacities, norms and techniques in the fields of agriculture, animal husbandry, irrigation and power, education, water supply, etc. at the regional, district and local levels.

For the successful performance of the two tasks, the following innovations have been envisaged.

A. (i) There will be a series of pre-workshop discussions on the objective facts of resources, land, population, infrastructure and social services, developmental programmes and projects. Attempts would also be made to identify the socio-political factors determining the choice of alternative patterns of institutional support, norms and procedures.

(ii In each district, at least one pre-workshop symposium will be organised in cooperation with various official as well as non-official forums, where an attempt will be made to gather information with regard to emergent socio-economic trends and monitor plan implementation. One such symposium was held at Komlathabi in the Chandel district.

B. For a number of aspects of development, critical appraisal will be made from the theoretical point of view. For this purpose, a number of scholars will be commissioned to prepare papers of a high academic quality. These papers will also be presented by the scholars at the workshop.

The foregoing strategy of the interwining of informed popular mobilisation and monitoring on the one hand and academic appraisal and analysis on the other is an experimental one. It is in line with the extremely perceptive statement in the approach to the Fifth Five-Year Plan: "The Fifth Plan is much more than an internally consistent mathematical exercise. It is conceived as the rally point for a supreme effort in a decisive phase of our struggle for a self-reliant economy and for social justice. In order to ensure that these are forthcoming in the required measure, there is need for active involvement of the people in the formulation and implementation of the plan. The involvement of the youth on a massive scale can bring about a qualitative improvement in its implementation. A necessary condition for such involvement is understanding and appreciation of plan objectives, strategies and programmes. In this task, plan formulation and education play an important role. High priority would be accorded towards working out and putting into practice the various modalities of peoples' involvement."

Obviously the task set before the workshop (along with the ancillary programme) is rather ambitious. It is a challenge, to say the least. But it is out of tremendous confidence in the dedication and social consciousness of the youth in Manipur and an awareness of the growing quest among the Indian intelligence is for the meaning of their knowledge in the life of the 'last man' among the people that this challenge has been taken up.

The basic concepts, facts and figures that will inform the deliberations in the workshop are briefly discussed here. It goes without saying that a number of other relevant issues are likely to be raised by the participants in the seminar or are likely to come up through the ancillary programmes at various stages.

Concept of Development

As a follow up to the United Nation's resolution, a review of the integration of social aspects in development planning in the ECAFE region has brought out that in the past per capita national income and GNP were used as indicators of development because they functioned as aggregate indexes which were identifiable, measurable and manageable and could also serve the purpose of international comparison. These indicators, however, ignored the social component and at best were only an indirect measure of the level of living possibilities and not the actual pattern of living. Therefore, though they were undoubtedly the measure of the strength of an economy, they could be considered necessary but not sufficient indicators of development.

Social development should not, however, be equated with social services; rather it relates to the "social objectives of economic growth such as redistribution of income, institutional changes, equalisation of distribution of development benefits, etc." The social and economic objectives, policies and indicators should be built into overall development strategies from the very beginning. Priorities, standards and goals should be determined after taking into consideration the social as well as economic costs and benefits within the framework of social, economic and political values."

The UN review, however, points out that while most of the developing countries have specified in great detail their developmental objectives, difficulties arise in the translation of the same into policies and programmes.

For instance, though growth with justice is accepted as the ideal for developmental planning in India, it is to be examined if in the short-term perspective there is a conflict between growth and justice; what weightage is actually given to social justice in concrete situations. In this manner, socio-economic realities and the political culture of an area would be the determining factors. Besides studying a large number of cases, bringing out the incongruous relationships, if any, can create a new political culture and help to approach the socio-economic realities from a different perspective.

It would be useful if the workshop discusses one or two concrete situations. For instance, the programme of encouraging local entrepreneurs in backward areas may, from a short-range point of view, appear to put in abeyance the overall goal of building up the institutional base of socialism in the area. At the same time, one may argue that such a strategy is indispensable for quickly correcting the regional imbalance of growth, ending traditional forms of exploitation and counteracting the danger of over-bureaucratisation.

The long-range social and political implications of the recent trend of differentiating the weaker sections among the weak as being eligible for developmental assistance may also be reviewed. It may particularly be considered whether it will not perpetuate the subservience of the weaker section as a whole to the hegemonic interests at the national and regional level.

Development Indicator

In view of the limitations of conventional economic indicators like GNP, a search for more comprehensive and integrative indicators has ensued at the international, national and local levels. These indicators are to be developed by each community depending upon its social, economic and political goals. Broadly, they should indicate the pattern of rural and urban development, resource mobilisation, quality of life, social integration, social stratification and mobility and participation of different categories of the population in the developmental process. These should also include the distribution of development benefits in space and time and also among the diverse social strata and groups and communities.

The United Nations Research Institute for Social Development (UNRISD) has chosen a set of 42 indicators for international comparison.

In India, the Indian Council for Social Science Research has taken steps to build up nationally valid indicators of development.

Within the framework accepted at the international and national levels, local adaptations are required to be made. For instance, whereas in those parts of the country where the *purdah* system prevails the conduct of trade in domestic products by females would have one social meaning, in Manipur it will have an entirely different meaning.

Adaptation of the indicators to the local context is a time-consuming exercise. Even then it would be worthwhile to make a start through discussions in the workshop.

Goals and strategies of the Five-Year Plan of the country which inform the development plan in Manipur:

The Five-Year Plan has set two major tasks before the nation: (a) removal of poverty and (b) attainment of economic self-reliance. The social platform on which the edifice of the plan is built up envisages: (a) democratic political order, (b) prevention of concentration of political power, (c) reduction of disparities in income and wealth, (d) attainment of a balanced regional development and (e) the spread of institutions, values and attitudes of a free and just society.

Under-development and inequality are considered to be the crucial factors of poverty. It is therefore envisaged that a growth-oriented strategy must have woven into it a series of redistribution measures. Besides, what is important is not just a high growth rate but also a particular composition of growth that will favour the weaker sections of society. There is also to be a policy of massive employment generation which will sustain and will be sustained by a much greater availability of goods and services of mass consumption and investment with a view to maximising efficiency and production of vast numbers as well as for improving the quality of life through the implementation of a minimum needs programme.

It has been assumed in the approach to the Five-Year Plan that there is a positive correlation between reduced equality and self-reliance, as the consumption pattern of the lower income group has a much lower import content compared to that of the middle and higher-income group. The technological characteristics of the economy as reflected in industry relationships involving input-output matrix on current account and an elaborate system of material balance are also important determining factors of the pattern of growth. The logic of redistribution of the growth process demands substantial narrowing down of consumption differentials between different strata. This involved action both at the stage of accuracy of income as well as the terms of disposition of income. In other words, the strategy should be that of maximisation of production while curtailing incremental consumption. Inducements should be given to invest savings in socially productive assets where possibilities of direct investment exist, as in case of agriculture and incorporated enterprises. There is also to be mobilisation of savings through appropriate financial intermediation into desirable areas of economic activity.

In terms of this overall strategy, the Five-Year Plan has assigned different orders of priorities to the different sectors of growth at the national level.

The workshop should address itself to the following questions concerning the strategies of development planning with particular reference to Manipur:

- In the light of the experience of the implementation of the draft plan during the past two years, whether the overall perspective, strategies and assumptions at the national level require any modification.
- To what extent are the various assumptions of the plan valid for Manipur?
- Manipur as a whole is not a backward region but is also located in an outlying area of the country. There are not only problems of disparity but also of diversity. To what extent do the overall strategies of the plan require to be modified to meet these conditions?
- How will the actual pattern of the Five-Year Plan of Manipur harmonise with the (i) spirit, (ii) scientific goals and objectives, (iii) long-range strategy and (iv) short-range process of the national plan?
- To what extent do the land reform and other measures of structural change as well as the fiscal policies of the states help in examination of production and mobilisation of the resources for socially productive purposes?
- While considering the problem of resource mobilisation, the role of the following agencies in the specific context of Manipur should be separately considered :

(i) central and state government; state non-financial departments, autonomous,
(ii) private corporate non-financial institutions,
(iii) cooperative non-credit institutions,
(iv) household (including unincorporated) enterprises,
(v) Reserve Bank of India,
(vi) commercial banks,
(vii) the Reserve Bank Corporation,
(viii) term-financing institutions,
(ix) private corporate financial institutions
(x) small savings scheme,
(xi) state provident fund,
(xii) the employees' and other provident funds and
(xiii) cooperative credit institutions.

One of the policy planks of the Five-Year Plan is to provide for the direct transfer from financial institutions to the private sector rather than through the control of state budgets. To what extent this policy has been successfully implemented requires to be examined. It is also to be examined what sections of the people have mainly benefited through the implementation of this policy.

The pattern of resource mobilisation determines and is determined by the sectional composition of domestic products. The Fifth Plan envisages the progressive reduction of the contribution of agriculture and a concomitant rise in the contributions of mining and manufacturing, electricity, construction, transport and services.

The workshop will examine the extent to which the overall national pattern is valid for Manipur and what modifications are required to suit local conditions. It will also try to identity the roles of natural endowment factors, social structural factors and adequacies or inadequacies of the planning process with respect to sectional programmes in determining the composition of gross domestic products.

Sectional Programmes

It has been reported in the draft of the Five-Year Plan that there was a tendency to formulate programmes for individual sectors at the state and national levels in an uncoordinated fashion without taking into consideration potential and properties of different areas; coverage, dimensions and thrusts of other programmes taken up in the area; overall orientation and capabilities of existing administrative and institutional structures. This led to the enforcement of exogenous priorities and impeded proper coordination and synchronized implementation of inter-related programmes.

The draft also makes a mention of a tendency to define needed efforts merely in terms of financial magnitudes.

While the workshop will consider in a general way to what extent the foregoing tendencies and lacunae still prevail in Manipur, it will concentrate more on the corrective measures that have been taken and the impact of the same. It will also try to identify the additional corrective measures that should be taken. For this purpose, it will be necessary to examine the various sectional programmes in some detail.

Agriculture: Facts and Figures with Respect to Agriculture in Manipur.

- Only about 1/10th of the area of the state is valley, the rest is forest. Out of the total area of 1,81,300 hectares in the valley 88,960 hectares were under forests/lakes/ cultivable and uncultivable waste or under non-agricultural use. In 1970, about 92,000 hectares were brought under cultivation. In the hills, about 50,000 to 60,000 hectares are brought under jhum or "slash and burn" cultivation every year.
- As observed in the agricultural census of Manipur 1970-71, agriculture contributes 48.9/- to 59.8/- in the state domestic products (S.D.P.). But the yield rate is very poor. As against the all-India yield rate of 1,280 kgs it is only 1,207 kgs per hectare in Manipur.

- Paddy is the main crop (98.17% of the gross cropped area) followed by maize. Potatoes, chilly, kharif pulse, rabbi pulse, mustard seed, sugarcane and fruits are grown to a normal extent.
- The practice of double or triple cropping was not in vogue till recently. The emergency agricultural production programme launched in 1972 has succeeded in inducing some farmers to take to cultivation as an additional crop.
- Out of 15.5% of the cultivated area with irrigation facilities, 11.1% was served by channel and 4.4% was served by other sources. During the Fifth Plan, 60,000 hectares of land were proposed to be brought under irrigation, out of which lift irrigation was to account for 24,800 hectares and the remaining area by other sources.
- Marginal farmers (upto 1 hectare of land) who constitute 40.91% of the holding own 18.9% of the land; the small farmers (1-3 hectares of land) who constitute 55.1% of the holding own 68.0% of the land. The remaining 13.1% of the land is owned by medium and large farmers and constitutes 4.08% of the total holdings.
- Whereas agricultural productivity remained almost stagnant till the beginning of the present decade, the percentage of workers engaged in agriculture has gone up from 66% in 1961 to 70% in 1971.
- In 1961, agricultural labourers constituted 0.61% of the total work force; in 1971, their percentage has gone up to 3.39%.
- Although in a halting manner, mechanisation has already started in the agricultural sector. In 1970, 16 tractors were procured for distribution. The programme has been continued since then. Besides, starting from 1972-73, power-tillers are being distributed at 50% subsidy. Selling of other devices like paddy weeding machines has also been taken up.

Issues to be considered regarding Agriculture in the workshop:

- It is noted that the area under cultivation in the valley has not increased steadily. In fact, in 1971-72 there was a considerable decline. What could be the cause? Is there reason to believe that some cultivators keep the land fallow in the valley or in the hill? In that case, who are these cultivators? Do they belong to the same category of small and marginal farmers? Do they leave the land fallow because of inadequate profits or because of the inability to mobilise adequate input?
- In this connection, it is to be noted that observation in a village in the valley shows that while most of the inhabitants of the village are cultivators they hold land under the jurisdiction of different villages. The land is held by people residing in far-flung areas. The narrow width of the valley, diverse quality of the land and more homogenous soil type on elongated strips coupled with the presence of roads along the length of the valley with few lateral feeder roads seem to have contributed to the high incidence of absentee land ownership. These rapid observations are to be first checked and verified in the various parts of the valley. If found to be generally correct, the following issues will have to be settled:

  (i) In the absence of a common focus of interest about their major productivity resource, to what extent do the villagers in the valleys function as integrated political communities?

  (ii) As the owners of different plots in the same field live in different villages, to what extent are they capable to rally together to serve as pressure groups in order to secure infrastructural facilities and other productive assistance for cultivation of their fields?

  (iii) To what extent has the dispersed nature of the ownership of land been a factor for neglect of cultivation of at least some plots by owners with a large number of plots?

(iv) To what extent has the dispersed pattern of ownership been a factor for open or concealed tenancy that has at least partly served as a depressant with regard to productivity and wage rate of the agricultural labourers?

- In the Chandel district, it has been observed that the owners of terrace land wet rice cultivation lands frequently depend on seasonal labourers from the valley for tilling, transplanting and harvesting. It has further been found that acceptance of high-yielding varieties of seeds sometimes created a condition when optimum periods of the different agricultural operations in the plains and the hills clashed with one another. It is to be examined what is the actual magnitude of the problem in the different parts of the state and also as to what extent the same is responsible for the stagnation in production.
- Coming to shifting cultivation, the following questions are to be examined:

  (i) Are there traditional systems of regulation of shifting cultivation among the different tribal communities?

  (ii) Which sections of the shifting cultivators take to terrace or wet rice cultivation and/or horticulture?

  (iii) Is the government subsidy adequate to meet the cost of switching over from jhum cultivation to permanent cultivation of horticulture? If not, would it be correct to assume that only a small number of affluent persons among the shifting cultivators take to permanent cultivation?

  (iv) If the bulk of the shifting cultivators continue the traditional mode of cultivation and if on the other hand, good portions of land normally under shifting cultivation pass under the control of a small number of permanent cultivators, what happens to the overall land-use pattern?

(v) Is it possible that the shifting cultivators tend to move to more marginal areas, which they otherwise would have avoided for the purpose of jhum cultivation?

Further, it is to be examined whether there are some positive aspects in shifting cultivation that can provide the basis for its transformation and introducing more advanced technology. For instance, in some areas the shifting cultivators put logs along the contour lines, thus constructing rudimentary contour bunds. This reduces soil erosion and augments productivity. If this practice is intensified, it will strengthen the economy of the shifting cultivators and with appropriate incentive, the surplus can be invested for switching over to permanent cultivation. It is necessary to go into some detail as to why the practice is not more widespread. Is it related to the nature of the terrain? Is it a function of cost benefit calculation of the labour input and the use of the log for the purpose indicated? The role of the customary differences in the land ownership system among the different tribal communities is also to be studied. One is also to examine why the developmental agencies have neglected this line of action. Is it the legacy of the political economy of forest developed during the colonial period?

In shifting cultivation, there are different methods of preparation of soil. While in most of the areas the soil is upturned with a hand-hoe, in some it is upturned with the spade and in recent years the plough is being used in some fields in North District. The bearing of each technique of productivity on the one hand and soil erosion on the other are to be known for appropriate administrative and legislative action and extension work. It is also necessary to know the labour-time disposition of the male and female workers in case of each technique.

The crops grown in shifting cultivation are diverse. The productivity of each in different types of soil and under different techniques is yet to be studied. The same requires to be compared with productivity in terrace cultivation under diverse conditions. This information is indispensable in order to rationally understand the frequent reluctance of shifting cultivators to take to terrace cultivation.

The different crops produced under shifting cultivation have different effects on soil erosion. This is to be carefully assessed. For instance, root crops of commercial value cause more soil erosion but because of the immediate economic benefit, root crop cultivation in shifting cultivation fields is encouraged by the government concerned. This raises a doubt as to whether the opposition to shifting cultivation is always guided by scientific considerations or if it is rooted in politico-economic considerations.

There is an impression of reluctance to carry out scientific investigation for improvement of the crop varieties in shifting cultivation. It is to be examined whether this observation is correct. Thus, we also have to find out whether this has contributed to further aggravating the harmful effects of shifting cultivation.

Where the different species of flora do not mature in harmonisation with nature and rather are determined by the jhum cycle, in cases where a disharmonic relationship prevails it is to be examined to what extent commercial exploitation of the forest is responsible for the same.

In Manipur and most other parts of the country, once a plot is cleared for shifting cultivation, it is cultivated for two years at a stretch. But in Mizoram, it is cultivated for a year. On the face of it, this does not appear to be related to the nature of the terrain. In any case, one is to examine whether the volume of soil erosion significantly varies according to the duration of cultivation. An examination of the change in the chemical composition of the soil depending on the duration of cultivation and cropping pattern would also help in appreciating the rationale of these two different processes in the adjoining areas.

The physical location of the shifting cultivation fields, particularly with reference to terrace cultivation fields is also an important issue about which information is needed. The possibility of a symbiotic relationship between the two does not appear to have been adequately exploited in policy planning in respect of hill cultivation.

- In the Five-Year Plan, soil conservation measures have been given high priority, especially with respect to terrace cultivation. It is to be examined whether some procedural norms have been laid down in this matter.

In the case of block terracing, is a process of concentration of holdings also taking place? One can probe further and find out whether the social consequence is also linked to the question of water management in terraces. In the Tangkhul Naga area, where a very intricate system of water management is practiced traditionally the recent tendency of construction of dry terraces is noticeable. It is reported that sometimes the people go in for such terraces to take advantage of the government subsidy that enables them to get employment for a short duration. As these terraces are delinked from the question of community action for water management, the chances of loosening of lineage and clan solidarity seems to be quite considerable in their case. This, however, requires to be checked. Further, what is the level of productivity in dry terrace farming? If it is not higher than that of shifting cultivation, does it not increase pressure on shifting cultivation land, leading to cultivation of marginal areas and consequent soil erosion?

In many parts of Manipur, dry terraces are found lying fallow. What is the extent of research support for dry farming in Manipur? In Mizoram, a variety of paddy called phulbuh is being tried. Has any experiment with phulbuh been done in Manipur?

In some areas of Manipur construction of terraces appears to have been taken up as a programme of special assistance to the landless labourers. It is to be examined to what extent institutional finance is available to the assignees of these terraces. Where institutional finance is not available, how do these persons, who are not likely to have any savings of their own, meet the cost of cultivation? Is it possible that they lease out the lands to others in a clandestine manner? It is reported that in several cases migrants from the valley have virtually taken over land, taking advantage of this situation. Thus confusion in the ownership of tribal lands is reported to be taking place. What is its magnitude? What is its impact on the solidarity of the traditional community? And what are the consequences on other aspects of development and the functioning of the cooperative institutions?

In the hills, there are a large number of narrow strips of plain land. It seems that in many cases ground water is available at a depth of 8-10 ft. It is reported that while the water is not enough.to irrigate large tracts of land, it is possible to irrigate 2-3 acres of land from each well that may be dug in these fields. In some parts of Orissa, cultivation in the hill seems to have been tremendously influenced by this strategy. How far is this the case? Has any attempt been made in this direction in Manipur: if so, what is the result?

- In the valley, there appears to be a positive correlation between the size-class of holding and fragmentation of holdings. In the size-class 0.5-1 hectare, there are 1.05 parcels; in the size class 10.0-20.0 hectares there are 9.5 parcels. In the size class 30.0-40.0 hectares there are 16.3 parcels. This extreme fragmentation of holdings is not unlikely to have adversely affected the efficiency of many of the large farms, particularly in the matter of adoption of high-yielding varieties of paddy seeds like ratna, jaya, etc. In the case of these varieties, to obtain the minimum output there must be optimum balancing of (a) the time of the various operations in conformity with the climatic conditions and (b) flow and logging of water. All these require close supervision. Where the holding is parcelled out into a large number of fragments, such supervision is not possible. The logic of the situation suggests that a class of skilled entrepreneurs may come into existence, reflecting a capitalist type of social relationship of agricultural operation. The socialist system of relationship is ruled out by the act of extreme fragmentation of holdings. In case of failure of emergence of an entrepreneur class or a corporate sector, the level of production in large holdings is likely to be comparatively low. The available data shows that it is actually low. This indirect evidence of the failure of an entrepreneur class in agriculture raises a number of questions. Is it because of the presence of other attractions for the prospective entrepreneurial class? Is it because of inadequate infrastructural support including that of institutional finance? Or again, is it linked up with the problem of tenancy reform?

The changes in the cropping pattern and in the adoption of early and late maturing varieties of seeds to suit the requirements of mechanised farming and multiple cropping on irrigated lands also require to be examined.

One of the major policy planks of the Five-Year Plan with respect to agricultural development is the maximisation of the productive roles of small and marginal farmers and agricultural labourers. To what extent have these objectives been fulfilled in Manipur? It appears that in many states the progress of S.F.D.A. and M.F.A.L. schemes have not been satisfactory. One of the main hurdles centres on the problems of identification of the small and marginal farmers. How correct are the records in Manipur? Another bottleneck is the credit policy of the cooperatives and commercial banks. The draft of the Five-Year Plan has, inter alias, envisaged the following measures:

(a) Investment policies and procedures of financing institutions are to be suitably modified to ensure flow of credit to small farmers, marginal farmers and other weaker sections of society;

(b) With regard to villages, adoption and such other specific measures that are to be taken by commercial banks, stress will be laid on areas where the effect of commercial bank finance on agriculture has been comparatively weak;

(c) Apart from administrative and legislative measures that have been recommended by the Talwar Committee for adoption by the state government, measures will have to be taken to rationalise some of the laws relating to alienation of land in favour of financing agencies. To

> maintain up-to-date land records, introduce agricultural holding credit cards for all individual farmers, ensure better rural communication, better means of storage and transport and of agricultural commodities, arrange for adequate and timely supply of inputs and ensure purposeful support with institutional credit agencies at all levels.

The workshop will update itself to the extent of which the measures envisaged at the national policy level have been implemented in Manipur. It will also examine the concrete form of the procedural and other changes introduced by the various financial institutions including banks and assess their suitability or adequacy for the specific social structural conditions prevailing in Manipur. With respect to the other measures as well, the difficulties, if any, in their implementation, the phase and process through which they should be implemented, would be considered by the workshop.

The draft of the Five-Year Plan has provided consultancy service in the eastern region that would assist in formation, implementation and appraisal of agricultural finance corporation schemes. What is the progress in this matter and what is its impact? What are the factors determining the progress and impact?

A comparative study of the assumptions, provisions and trends of planned development in the state, all-India and regional contexts helps to see them in perspective. (i) During the Five-Year Plan, the anticipated annual growth rate in the production of food grain in India as a whole in the '70s and '80s was 4.2, in Manipur it was 5.8. The corresponding figures in the other states and union territories (UTS) of North East India are as follows: Assam (6.0), Meghalaya (3.3), Nagaland (96.6), Tripura (3.9). The validity of these figures regarding Manipur in particular will have to be examined. Assuming they are correct, the wide variations in the anticipated growth rate cannot be explained by the variations in the natural endowment factors only; in that case, Meghalaya and Nagaland should not be at two ends of the scale. Infrastructural development and institutional factors might have played a role. Faculty statistics might as well have been the final arbitrator. The workshop would try to locate the relevant factor. This will help in sharpening the tools of planning in all the states and UTS of the region. (ii) In the Five-Year Plan, whereas in India as a whole Rs 1496.37 crores were proposed to be invested in long-term agricultural loan by development banks, in Manipur it was only Rs 0.50 crores. The corresponding figures for the other states of the region were: Assam (14.00), Meghalaya (0.50), Nagaland (1.00), Tripura (2.00). It is obvious that while the region as a whole is under-served by long-term loans, within the region also there are wide disparities in per capita availability of loans. If the figures for medium-term advanced by co-operatives are examined, Manipur with Rs 0.5 crores investment is at the bottom of the ladder. The workshop will address itself to the identification of the institutional factors for this dismal picture and will try to suggest remedial measures.

Soil Conservation

In the Five-Year Plan of the states, it has been visualised that one of the principal reasons for the productivity in agriculture, especially in the hill areas is the progressive deterioration of soil due to erosion caused by shifting cultivation, indiscriminate cutting of forests, etc. As a remedial measure, protective afforestation of over 640 hectares of barren and eroded lands and the terracing of over 7,600 hectares of agricultural land have been proposed.

The adequacy of the remedial measures would depend on a realistic assessment of the relative role of the contributory factors. A rapid survey in the Chandel district suggests that in some of the roadside villages near the valley there is more denudation of forests due to the combined effects of commercial exploitation of timber, cutting down of trees for supply of firewood to the local community and to Imphal and for housing material rather than due to shifting cultivation.

A more detailed study is necessary to find out to what extent this pattern holds good for the other areas of the state.

The workshop will have to address itself to find out the remedial measures with reference to each of these contributory factors.

Forestry

The Five-Year Plan envisages the following objectives of forestry development at the national level:

A. Initiate measures for increasing production of industrial wood and other forest products by changing over from conservation-oriented forestry to a dynamic programme of production forestry.

B. Develop farm forestry and improve degraded forests to increase the fuel and timber supply in rural areas.

C. Introduce a system of meaningful forest survey to assess the present growing stock, increments and potential increments by forest division, natural regions, etc.

At the programming level, the Five-Year Plan includes - (a) economic plantations like teak, sal, shir, devdar, fir, spruce, semal and other matchwood and plywood species, (b) quick-growing species, i.e. mainly eucalyptus hybrid and (c) social forestry, mainly aiming at supplying firewood needed by the community.

With this broad framework of policy perspectives at the national level, the workshop will have to examine whether there are sub-goals and objectives which are specific to Manipur and which require to be spelled out.

The economic and social implications of the policy perspective become clearer when the actual priorities assigned to the various operational aspects are examined.

At the end of the Fourth Plan in India as a whole, while 8,59,000 hectares were covered by economic plantations, 5,10,000 hectares were covered by quick-growing species and 2,20,000 hectares were covered by farm forestry.

The draft mentions that in a number of states the programme of quick-growing species was converted into a programme of plantations of economic and commercial use. This seems to confirm the suspicion that many forest officers are more concerned about raising revenue from the forest than about the overall social purpose of forests.

The workshop will have to consider whether the target set for the Five-Year Plan at the all-India level reflects any radical change of approach.

It was estimated that in 1978-79 economic plantations would cover 150,000 hectares of land, on the other hand quick-growing species would cover 860,000 hectares and farm forestry only 400,000 hectares.

In drawing its conclusion, the workshop will have to take note of the firewood requirements of the country.

In the context of the all-India trend, the position in Manipur will be examined. To some extent the position in the neighbouring states and UTS will also be considered. At the end of the Fourth Plan, 3,000 hectares of land were under economic forestry in Manipur. Farm forestry was introduced by the forest department to a next to negligible extent and there was hardly any programme regarding quick-growing species. During the Five-Year Plan while economic plantations will cover 7,000 hectares, farm forestry will continue to be negligible and quick growing species will not far better. More or less the same trend is noticeable in the adjoining states of North-East India, except Assam, where a programme of planting quick growing species has been proposed to be taken up in a big way.

In view of the fact that the large-scale denunciation of forestland, particularly in order to meeting the demands of firewood, is sometimes a more important factor for causing soil erosion, it is difficult to see the justification of the priorities assigned by the forest department in Manipur. This also holds true for other states of North-East India in their forest production programme. The workshop will dispassionately examine as to what extent the priorities have been derived out of scientific considerations in forest management and to what extent these have been acquitted by the traditional modes of thinking and functioning of the department. It is understood that of late there has been a wind of change. The workshop should take note of the same too.

The workshop may also examine the need for democratisation of the system of forest management in keeping with the progressive democratisation of industrial management and agrarian structure.

No realistic plan for forest development and management can be drawn up in Manipur if the fact that vast tracts of forestland are owned by the tribals is ignored.

It is obvious that while the legal status of the forests may differ, there must be functional inter-linkage and interdependence.

It seems that integrated planning encompassing state forest and private forest has been inhibited by a mistaken notion among many that all tribal forests are owned by their chiefs. In fact, it is only among those tribes who claim to be Kuki that the chiefs are recognised as the owners of the lands which have not been specifically assigned to individuals.

In recent years, the question of the chief's right of ownership over the community land has become the crucial focus of ethnic polarisation among the tribes.

There are those who reject the special prerogative of the chief on ideological grounds. They move towards Naga identity and claim that the land belongs to the community as a whole and not the chief. Then again, there are those tribes that retain the special prerogative of the chief not because of his strategic position in the internal power structure of the community but because of his symbolic position in the inter-ethnic historical prestige structure.

It is to be examined as to what extent this wrong notion (entertained by many in the administration) that the chief is the owner of the lands associated with the tribal communities is responsible for perpetuating rights or creating new rights, where such rights did not exist in the past.

In this matter, community-by-community definite information is necessary for issue of permits for the marketing of forest products.

It appears that some of the tribal villages informally regulate the use of their forest resources so as to be able to finance some of their community activities like running a school or building a church through the sale proceeds of the surplus. In this matter, it is necessary to have empirical data for the different parts of the state as it may lead to far-reaching policy decisions.

The workshop might like to suggest certain legal, administrative and historical relations with constructive orientation towards the forest that can be harnessed for development purposes.

Particularly, the workshop may examine whether modernisation of the land-use pattern in the hills can be effected through recognition of corporate rights and the introduction of an efficient management system in conformity with the same.

The workshop may also examine as to what extent and through what process codification and/or authentication of the customary laws of the tribals should be done so as to facilitate the flow of institutional finance for the development of community-based forestry in the hills.

Animal Husbandry

In the Five-Year Plan, great emphasis has been laid at the national level on an integrated approach to animal husbandry. Attempts will be made to augment poultry, sheep and pig production through requisite assistance to small and marginal farmers. The scientific breeding programme at the state poultry farms aims at developing an indigenous high-producing strain capable of laying about 220 eggs per annum. It also aims at developing a better meat strain which will attain over 1 kg body weight within eight weeks.

In cattle development, the emphasis is on crossbreeds. Buffalo development is also to receive attention. Simultaneously, feed and fodder development programmes are to be taken up. Besides, development of forestland for grazing is envisaged at the national level. Research is also to be taken up on the best combination of feeds, fodder and nutritional supplements that will enable cattle to produce optimum quantity of milk.

It is to be examined as to what extent the state plan in the development of animal husbandry conforms to the policy and perspective formulated at the national level. An examination of the state Five-Year Plan shows that almost all the items envisaged at the national level have been included. But it is not the aggregation of items, but their integration in a specific order of priorities and spatial distribution and temporal sequence that is important if one is to achieve results.

In the absence of a statement of perspective in the state Five-Year Plan, it is difficult to say what pattern of integrated development as regards poultry has been kept in mind by the planning authority at the conceptual level. It is expected that an authoritative paper on the subject will be available to the workshop for its appraisal. Particularly, one would like to know as to what extent poultry, pig and goat production programmes have been linked up with the diversification and improvement of the economy of small and marginal farmers. In this matter, the norms and procedures adopted by the promoting agencies and the financial institutions are of particular importance. Frequently, the norms and procedures insisted upon by financial institutions, particularly the norms relating to viable production units, are derived from the experience of urban middle class. These are thoroughly unsuitable for small marginal farmers. As a result, it becomes difficult to persuade them to take advantage of the programme. The workshop will have to address itself to this problem in great detail.

The workshop will also have to examine the strategic importance of poultry, pig and goat rearing of the marginal farmers and agricultural labourers in the political economy. If covered by institutional finance and an appropriate marketing agency, these schemes go a long way in reducing the dependence of marginal farmers and agricultural labourers on wealthy farmers. Thus a condition congenial to correct preparation of the records of rights and implementation of land reform measures is created. If these processes and developments are not taking place in Manipur it will be necessary to examine (a) whether the magnitude of the input and output is adequate to make any impact and (b) what is the pattern of distribution of the efforts in spaces? Is it too scattered to render ancillary services and to make any impact economically or politically? Or is it so highly concentrated in space and among a small number of beneficiaries that while it promotes economics it completely ignores the larger objective of structural change?

Fishery

The strategy that the Five-Year Plan adopts in the case of fishery at the national level consists of (a) adoption of intensive fish culture method, (b) seed production by fish farmers development agencies, (c) induced breeding, (d) self-employment by educated youth with reclaimed fresh water areas and (e) fish processing, marketing and transport.

At present in Manipur, about 1,000 tonnes of fish is available and fishery contributes to about 2% of the aggregate income of the state. So there seems to be adequate scope for the development of fisheries in the state. It is to be examined as to what extent the proposed outlay in the Five-Year Plan would be able to attain self-sufficiency in this field? Further, it is to be examined as to what extent there are conflicting choices in the matter of change of land use pattern? It seems that the extensive swampy and marshy lands can be reclaimed either for cultivation or for fishery: there would be limited areas where these can be developed as fishery-cum-irrigation tanks. One would like to know how the choice is actually made and which sections of the community would benefit more from each of the alternative choices? Are there some rational principles by which an optimum balance can be obtained? For policy decisions it would be necessary to have information on the system of stratification and role-differentiation among the fishermen. To what extent would the programmes of fish seed-cum-fry distribution, encouragement to commercial seed farms, assistance to pisciculturists, reduce or reinforce the system of stratification and role-differentiation? To what extent would the changes or reiteration of the existing social structure, in their turn, impede or promote technological and economic development of modern fishery?

Transport

Road transport is practically the only means of transport in Manipur as the state is not connected by railway and there is hardly any waterway for the purpose of trade and commerce. There are, however, regular Indian Airlines flights connecting Imphal with Silchar, Guwahati and Calcutta.

The road system in Manipur is questionable. It is obvious that till recently the National Highway dominated the entire transport system. This implies that the transport system was basically oriented towards the external market and security considerations rather than to the requirements of internal mobilisation. In other words, external relations determined the pattern of functional specialisation of space and growth of internal linkages. With the needs of the traditional, economic and social structure and with the political cost, what was the system that emerged? Can some of the political turmoil of the 60s at least partially be attributed to these factors? It is found that the state highway expanded quite considerably during 1971-75. But even then the headquarters of one of the districts remains to be connected by travel worthy road with Imphal; there are still 12 sub-divisions out of a total of 17 hill sub-divisions which are not yet connected with the district headquarters.

The workshop would like to discuss the order of priorities and norms that have been laid down by the state government in the matter of construction of roads.

It would also be necessary to examine as to the extent to which the distortions in the regionalisation process that might have come into existence through the domination of the National Highway have been corrected or are being corrected through the construction of the other systems of roads during the past years.

Going into the details of the district and village road systems, it appears that until recently there was no internal road network connecting various areas with the district headquarters. Whatever connections existed were generally with Imphal. The situation has been rapidly changing during the past few years.

Is there any data to substantiate the changes in the settlement pattern, in the flow of commodities and productive forces and pattern of production and consumption in the wake of the new roads?

In the Five-Year Plan, Rs 500 crores were earmarked at the national level for the construction of rural roads under the minimum needs programme. It has been envisaged that rural roads will be suitably dovetailed with the rest of the roads network and that their alignments will be framed in such a manner so as to secure optimum benefits. It has also been proposed to develop suitable machinery for the implementation and monitoring of this programme.

The approach to the Five-Year Plan visualises that all villages with a population of 1,500 persons and above would be provided with all-weather roads. In the hill areas all weather link roads will be provided to a cluster of villages.

The workshop will study the Five-Year Plan outlay in the state for the construction of village roads under the minimum needs programme. It will also discuss how the efficient and effective functioning of the monitoring agency as envisaged in the plan is to be strengthened.

The efficiency of the transport system for social planning is to be seen not only in terms of the distribution of the transport facilities in space but also in terms of organisational efficiency, rationality of procedure, availability of capital, optimum use of raw materials and impact on the labour market.

It is to be examined as to what extent there is a delay in the construction of roads due to lack of advance investigative action on an approved scheme. In case of delay, is it due to deficiency in the staffing pattern? To what extent can the implementation of scheme be expedited by procedural reforms including greater decentralisation of power and advance payment for the preparing of projects. The employment generation potential of different types of roads is also to be examined. The more sophisticated the roads system, less will be the direct employment for construction and maintenance of the roads. Is it possible to integrate a plan of absorption of construction workers in socially useful production after the construction phase is over or after the existing system is transformed into a more sophisticated one?

The efficiency of the road system is also to be seen in the context of an overall transport system.

The workshop will also have to address itself to the question of developing waterways and connecting the state with railways.

The problem of vehicular traffic is inextricably linked up with the transport system. In this connection the licensing policies for road transport, availability of public transport facilities, freight and fare rates and availability of finance on reasonable terms for road transport industry are matters that will deserve close attention.

It seems that the availability of power is not keeping pace with the extension of the transport network in Manipur. The politico-economic implication of this lacuna is to be examined.

Power

The per capita power consumption in the state is only 7km against 25km for Assam, and 93 for all-India. The installed capacity for the generation of power is only 6,510 km though Manipur is rich in hydel power potential.

At present, the state is banking on the Loktak project. It is a multi-purpose project to provide 70,000km of cheap power, irrigation over 24,000 hectares of fields in Bishenpur, Churachandpur and Imphal west sub-division and reclamation of 17,000 hectares of reclaimable land.

At the national level, the Five-Year Plan envisages (a) carrying out a detailed year-by-year examination of the position of power supply to priority industries, (b) orienting the rural electrification programme for supporting agricultural production through energising of irrigation pump sets and; (c) providing benefits of electricity in backward and hill areas under the minimum needs programme.

The workshop would like to examine, in the light of the foregoing perspective at the national level, the strategy actually accepted in the state as far as transmission of power is concerned. Of particular significance is the shift from power for domestic use to power for productive use. The difficulties, if any, faced in the state in implementing the policy because of the pattern of dispersal of the settlements and the agricultural fields, may be discussed and remedies sought.

The policy programme of generation of power would also merit some discussion. The workshop would like to know whether there are other potential sources of hydel power in the state. In that case the factors determining macrohydel project or micro-hydel project will have to be considered in terms of the bearing of the same on the total eco-system, quality of life of the population affected and pattern of regional cooperation involving the adjoining states.

Irrigation

The Five-Year Plan strategy at the national level is to have a comprehensive approach to the problem of irrigation by simultaneously taking up all the relevant aspects like engineering safety, better regulation, augmentation of supplies, making up efficiencies, efficiency in conveyance of water, scientific application of water crops, maximising benefits by changing the cropping pattern.

Introduction of irrigation in an area should be a catalyst in the agricultural and economic development of the area resulting in a major change in the cropping pattern, land development, availability of marketing facility and mechanisation of certain farm operations.

For so many years there has been under-utilisation of irrigation potential due to the following reasons: (i) non-availability of assured and regular supplies in certain irrigation systems, (ii) need for land levelling, (iii) non-existence of proper drainage systems leading to problems of water logging, salinity and alkalinity and (iv) non-adoption of the rostering system of irrigation.

There is a need for more coordinated work by the department of irrigation, soil and agriculture to make the best use of the irrigation system with its modernisation and the adjustment of the cropping pattern to the soil and agro-climatic conditions of the command area.

In the major irrigation commands, a mere coordinating agency may not be able to bring in cohesion at the various levels of operation. The organisation will have to be a unified agency with a centre of direction and radiating organisations in the various disciplines up to the field level.

It has further been envisaged that there should be a board for each command area with non-official representatives to supervise the preparation of various programmes and ensure implementation by removing bottlenecks through periodic reviews of progress. The board may be structured as a company under company law for the limited purpose of ensuring flow of institutional credit to farmers. It has also been stipulated that funds on matching basis will be provided for surveys, designs and preparation of plans on farm works, supervision of its execution and consultancy services to farmers.

In the light of the foregoing perspective and programme formulated at the national level, the workshop will examine the position in Manipur.

In the Fourth Plan, stress was laid on construction of diversion weirs and head regulators across the streams for shortfall during good rains of lands already under cultivation. An estimated area of 24,000 hectares had been covered. During the Five-Year Plan, the scheme of providing water to an area of 15,000 acres through 30 lift irrigation systems and schemes under the minor irrigation section had been formulated. Besides, the Loktak hydro-electric project will feed about 60,000 acres of total cultivable area. It is estimated that surface water flowing down the main rivers of the state will be of the order of 1.3 million acres, which, if harnessed properly, will be more than sufficient to serve the purpose of irrigating the valley area.

While the state plan provides considerable information on the outlay and physical target, there is no information on organisational and management planning. This has been found to be of crucial importance at the national level.

The Five-Year Plan at the national level has even considered the question of legal cover for the optimum utilisation of the irrigation potential. It has suggested the following: (i) beyond the outlets, distribution of water should not be left completely to the initiative of the farmers, (ii) the state should have the power to (a) make the beneficiaries construct and maintain field channels and field drains, (b) carry out land levelling and land shaping operations, (c) undertake such works if the beneficiaries fail to do so, with the costs being recovered as arrears of land revenue and (ii) canal officers should have power to deal effectively in case of wastage, unauthorised use and obstruction to the flow of water.

The workshop will discuss as to what extent these are relevant problems in Manipur, and with what concomitant actions requisite legislations should be introduced.

Industry

Manipur also has mineral resources like copper, lignite, and limestone. It gets an annual output of approximately 68 lakh tonnes of bamboo, 25,000 tonnes of firewood in forest-based industries. About 1 lakh acres of forest area are covered by oak trees which can well serve as a host for the tasar industry. Orange, pineapple and maize grown in the state make it possible to develop an agro-based industry. In the state plan, it has been mentioned in a general way that industrialisation could not progress much due to pathetic infrastructure. The workshop may like to identify the specific responsibility of each of the major infrastructural facilities like transport and communication, institutional finance power, skilled manpower and machinery to ensure the continued supply of raw material.

Among the factors retarding the progress of the industrialisation programme during the Fourth Plan, the following have been found to be particularly important (a) incomplete feasibility report, (b) incomplete investigation and (c) maintenance and design deficiency.

In one state in North-East India, it has been observed that reputed consultancy organisations commissioned to prepare feasibility reports had failed to adequately take note of the local conditions, with particular reference to the following aspects:

(i) Political consequence of the choice of a particular design which will involve an inordinately long time gap between the starting of the factory and the availability of minimum proportion of skilled manpower

(ii) The problem of inter-ethnic relations of a large number of unskilled labour recruited from different tribal communities

(iii) Existing system of ownership of resources and economic and political consequence of disturbing the same beyond the essential minimum extent when the area as a whole is passing through a phase of political transition

(iv) Problem of setting up ancillary enterprises for the purpose of rendering supportive services

(v) Traditional system of social control and problems of industrial relation.

If the feasibility reports for the various industrial projects in Manipur have already been prepared, the same require to be examined with an awareness of the local socio-economic setting and political culture and with knowledge of the technical aspects when preparing a project report.

The industrial policy as laid down in the Five-Year Plan visualises appropriate share of the public, private and cooperative sectors. It also lays down the aspects to be taken into consideration for preferring large and medium-size and small and village industries in the manufacture of various industrial goods.

To what extent and in what manner the policy guidelines at the national level are reflected in the industrialisation programme of Manipur will be discussed in the workshop on the basis of a few case studies (e.g. Khandsari sugar mills already functioning). The following questions will be put forward - (a) factors determining choice of sector (public, private, cooperative), (b) factors determining the choice of location and size, (c) assessment of infrastructural facility with particular reference to transport and communication, freight, power, institutional finance at a concession, (d) raw material planning, (e) organisational structure, (f) industrial relations with particular reference to reward structure of industrial employees in terms of wage. and non-wage benefit and participation of the employee in production planning, (g) production with reference to installed capacity and factors for under-utilisation if any, (h) micro-regionalisation process as a sequel to the establishment of the factory with particular reference to the change in land-use pattern (i.e. more area being put under sugarcane cultivation) and the growth of ancillary industries and establishments; inflow of skilled and unskilled manpower.

Coming to the village and small industrial sector, it has been found that during the Five-Year Plan, an estimated amount of Rs 131.15 lakhs has been spent in place of the targeted amount of Rs 71.22 lakhs. During the Five-Year Plan, the proposed outlay is Rs 465.00 lakhs. The factors conducive to the upward revision during the Five-Year Plan and the upsurge during the Five-Year Plan require to be identified.

It is the general experience that growth of village and small industries is ordinarily inhibited by (i) outmoded skill and technique, (ii) shortage of raw materials, credit facilities and market facilities, (iii) unorganised and widely dispersed nature of industry and (iv) shortage of power.

The workshop would like to discuss as to what extent these factors play a role with respect to the village and small industrial sector and what are the remedial measures.

It is generally assumed that village and small industries have the potential for providing increasingly larger employment opportunities with a relatively smaller capital investment, shorter gestation period and satisfaction of the substantial part of the essential and other requirements of the masses.

To what extent are these assumptions valid for Manipur? If in some aspects these are not found to be valid, what could be the reasons? Should any corrective measures be adopted? Or should more far-reaching adjustments be made in the overall industrialisation programme? The workshop will address itself to these questions.

Cooperation

The Five-Year Plan sets the following objectives in respect of Cooperative Institutions in the country - (a) strengthen network of agricultural cooperatives dealing with credit supply, marketing and processing; (b) build up viable consumer movement; (c) correct regional imbalances at the level of cooperative development, particularly in the sphere of agricultural credit; (d) restructure and reorient cooperatives so as to shift the focus of their activities increasingly in favour of small and marginal farmers and other under-privileged section of. the people.

In operational terms, the following programme has been formulated (i) organisation of farmers' service cooperative which while keeping the cooperative frame substantially intact will act as a guided institution focusing mainly on the economy of small and marginal farmers and agricultural labour. One of the highlights of these cooperatives is the provision for professional management, generally under the supervision of a commercial bank; (ii) organisation of large-sized credit-cum-marketing societies in tribal areas as recommended by an expert group; (iii) structural reform of a large number of non-viable primary agricultural credit societies and weak district central cooperative banks and (iv) reorganisation of a large number of consumer cooperative stores.

Other aspects deserving special mention are: (a) reliance chiefly on professional management within cooperatives; (b) building up of a cadre of cooperative managers; (c) growing collaboration between public sectors, commercial banks and primary credit societies; (d) intimate working relationship between public sector undertakings like Food Corporation of India, Cotton Corporation of India, and marketing and processing cooperatives dealing in relevant commodities.

As the Five-Year Plan marks a radical change in the structure and organisation of cooperatives, it is desirable to examine the underlying assumptions and philosophy in some detail.

One may first question whether the reliance mainly on specialised professional management rather than popular initiative is in conformity with the echoes of the Five-Year Plan, which in the draft has been claimed to be a peoples' plan? The unsatisfactory functioning of the existing cooperative institutions seems to be because of what some may consider a bureaucratic takeover of the movement. This seems to suggest that till now the cooperatives were by and large free from official control. But is this true? It seems that there had always been official control and guidance of some sort or the other in varying degrees in different parts of the country. It is not unlikely that a dispassionate study will show that the areas where the cooperative movement has grown through acceptance of the norms and constraints of the social structure they have done better; where they have grown according to the dictates of the officialdoms, they have failed. One need not be dogmatic but one requires to be sure that a course of action that has far-reaching consequences has been taken on a sound empirical and theoretical basis.

Secondly, it is to be seen as to what extent and in what manner operational norms and procedures can evolve in favour of small and marginal farmers under the guidance of commercial banks. Ideally, the cooperative system is a synthesis of three sub-systems—the moral sub-system of the society, legal sub-system of the state and rationality of the economic sub-system. The new dispensation seems to be based on lack of confidence in the first, accentuation of the second and mythical ideas about the third. One is to examine whether there is any abstract rationality of the economic sub-system. Is it linked up with the attitudes and values relating to production, consumption habit, and management experience and decision-making process about investment, among the people concerned? Is there any rational ground to consider that commercial banks have the necessary insight and expertise in these matters?

Thirdly, with regard to jumps (large-sized multi-purpose cooperative societies) envisaged for the tribal areas, an argument is advanced that tribals would like to have all kinds of credit from a single source; and as small primary credit societies are not viable for such purposes, it is better to go in for large multi-purpose cooperative institutions. Which category of tribals is this argument valid for and what is their proportion to the total population of the tribal societies? The bulk of the tribals do not have the resources to go in for long-term credit; they are interested in short-term credit. Hence the organisational structure should be such as to suit their convenience. Is a large cooperative, which will increase the distance of the centre of decision-making, more compatible with the need of the marginal and small farmers among tribals? Is there not a danger they will react to the new set up by simply withdrawing from the cooperative fold? The large farmers among the tribals will, of course, be interested in not only in short-term loans but also in long-term loans; they will naturally like to have both from the same source. On the face of it, does it not appear that the large tribal farmers have been equated with the entire tribal society and that the new organisational pattern will benefit only them?

Again in operational terms, there are certain problems that deserve consideration. The tribal villages are generally widely dispersed and communication is undeveloped in their area. Does it not pose a problem even for the board of management to meet as frequently as is required? Are there opportunities for the members living in widely dispersed areas to interact among themselves, mobilise their moral consensus in the functioning of the cooperative? In the absence of the same, will not the cooperative depend only on the coercive power of the state for its successful functioning?

These are the questions about the new strategy of the Five-Year Plan which logically arise. What is the empirical reality? It is quite possible that, notwithstanding the incongruities of the formal structure, there is much elasticity in the functioning of the institutions. In that case in each specific context specific answers might have been found to the questions raised here. The workshop would like to discuss them in the light of actual experience in Manipur.

The analysis of the logical incongruities of the new strategy should not, however, take the attention away from the generally unsatisfactory functioning of the existing cooperatives. In Manipur, there are now even forest cooperatives, labour cooperatives, marketing cooperatives and so on. It appears they do not always functioning very satisfactorily. Why? Are there systematic studies of their structure and functions? For instance, has it been carefully examined what categories of persons become their members? What controls them? If undesirable elements (like professional contractors using forest cooperatives as a cover) have been able to establish a hold over the cooperatives, is it possible that faulty laws and organisational strategies are responsible for the same to a large extent? Has anybody in the academic arena made a study of the problem in Manipur or in the North-Eastern region of India? It is not unlikely that it would be possible to gain fresh insight about the problems of cooperatives. Rather than treating them as homogeneous institutional complexes, they are looked upon as highly different structural types each having a distinct meaning in the economic, social and political systems in the region. The pre-working symposia at the district level and in the colleges will perhaps provide considerable useful data in this connection.

Education

In the field of education, the thrust of the Five-Year Plan is visualised to have taken place along four directions: (a) equality of educational opportunities as part of overall plan of ensuring social justice; (b) closer links between the pattern of education on the one hand and the employment market on the other; (c) improvement of the quality of education imparted; and (d) involvement of the academic community including students in the tasks of social and economic development.

Equality of opportunity requires increased emphasis on primary and adult education; incentives to help enrolment and the retention of weaker sections in schools; provision of informal education to enable those who are forced to enter life early to improve their prospects.

Linkage of employment and development envisage introduction of vocational courses as a part of general education at the university stage; also linkage of professional and adult education estimated manpower needs, both quantitatively and qualitatively for various development programmes; reorientation of the curriculum to bring it into closer relationship with developmental needs and utilisation of the resources of educational institutions for developmental tasks.

Quality improvement centres around the questions of curriculum and examination reform; improvement of text books, the increased use of mass media, development of research and training institutions and their linkage with institutions at the base level; encouragement of talent through scholarship and so on.

Linkage with social environment requires the curriculum to be brought down to the level of practical application at various stages and social education and social services need to be made an essential part of the curriculum at every stage.

From the foregoing perspective at the national level, the Five-Year Plan outlay for primary, secondary and post-secondary education require to be examined. Particularly, the problems of wastage and stagnation are of considerable importance.

The problem of employment and wastage in the primary stage can be seen in perspective if comparative statistics of the different states and UTS of the North-East region are considered together.

According to the data furnished in the Five-Year Plan, the boys and girls enrolled in the primary schools in Manipur in

1973-74 constituted 115% of the children of the age group 6-11. The corresponding figures for India as a whole and the states and UTS of the North-East region were as follows: India 84%; Assam 78%; Meghalaya 80%; Nagaland 100%; Tripura 77%; Arunachal 50%; and Mizoram 73%.

The boys and girls enrolled in the middle classes VI-VIII in 1973-74 in Manipur constituted 44% of the children of the age group 11-14. The corresponding figures for India as a whole and the states and UTS of North-East region are as follows: India 36%; Assam 40%, Meghalaya 30%; Nagaland 52%; Arunachal 14%; Mizoram 39%.

When the two sets of figures are compared, a number of important issues come to light. Why is it that Manipur, which has the leading position in enrolment in the primary schools in the region, has to trail behind Nagaland when it comes to secondary education? Does it mean there is greater wastage at the primary stage in Manipur? Or is it possible that the highest enrolment rate in the primary stage in the state conceals certain weaknesses of its education system? The 115% enrolment obviously means that a large number of boys and girls not quite around the age of 11 study in primary schools; perhaps there are a much larger number of late starters than early starters. But these sets of statistics do not say how many boys and girls of the age-group 6-11 do not study in school. Can this be checked and verified with the assistance of the North-East Council or the ICSSR? Incidentally, contrary to the general impression, the Khasis seem to be lagging behind both in the primary as well as the secondary stage.

The fact that Manipur had to concede rank to Nagaland in the matter of secondary education may perhaps be linked up with one or more of the following factors: (a) wastage and stagnation among the children, particularly girls of a higher age-group who start primary education late in Manipur; (b) better distribution in space of secondary schools in Nagaland; (c) language policy in respect of primary and secondary education of the tribals in Nagaland; (d) more facilities for secondary education in Nagaland; (e) less of a motivation factor for secondary education in Manipur; (f) comparative weakness of the social structure in Manipur to sustain a higher rate of secondary education and (g) more job opportunities for persons who have gone in for higher education in Nagaland.

Whatever information is available regarding these matters should receive the workshop's close and careful attention.

The problem of informal education of those who had to begin life early will have to be discussed with reference to (a) categories of persons requiring such education, (b) context and (c) method of imparting education and role of various agencies. Perhaps in this matter the experience gained by the department of continuing education, North East Hill University, Shillong will be useful.

The linkage of education to the developmental needs consists of two components - social service and training components and employment components.

The social service and training component would require the students to take up studies of the resources, including human resources, of their respective communities on a voluntary basis. Each year they could take up some problem of topical importance like area under cultivation of a particular variety of crop and problem of adoption of improved technology; functioning of the applied nutrition programme, child-rearing practices among different rural communities; indigenous beliefs and practices about various diseases. If standardised schedules are given, the secondary students can carry out the survey. On the basis of such survey, programmes can be initiated by post-graduate students under N.S.S. Besides, post-graduate students can take up soil analysis on a large scale to guide the cultivators. The life sciences department can establish close liaison with the rice-research centres, seed multiplication farms and other field organisations of agriculture, animal husbandry and sericulture departments. They could take up collaborative studies for a systematic analysis of the records maintained at the field level.

The feasibility of preparing a glossary of all flora and fauna found in Manipur, giving local names and English equivalent and scientific names, should be examined.

These ancillary matters should be examined in great detail at the workshop.

With regard to teaching and learning methodologies, the question of creating an organic link with the community will have to be examined in detail. The workshop might like to consider the role of the institutions of community resource persons in the social sciences and community reference service in the natural sciences.

Health

The Five-Year Plan objectives as regards to health are: (a) minimum public health facilities integrated with family planning and nutrition for vulnerable groups, i.e. children, pregnant women and lactating mothers, (b) accent on (i) increasing accessibility of health services to rural areas, (ii) correcting regional imbalance, (iii) development of referral services by removing deficiencies in district and sub-divisional hospitals, (iv) intensification of control and eradication of communicable diseases especially malaria and small pox, (v) qualitative improvement in education and training of health personnel and (vi) development of referral services by providing specialists' attention to common diseases in rural areas.

At the programme level, the following have been visualised: Minimum needs (i) one primary health centre (PHC) for each CD block, (ii) one sub-centre for 1,000 persons, (iii) drugs at the rate of Rs 12,000 per annum per P.H.C. and Rs 2,000 per sub-centre, (iv) Upgradation of one in 4 PHC to a 30-bed rural hospital.

i) Under-graduate education is to be reoriented to the need of the country and emphasis is to be on community centre rather than on hospital care, (ii) district hospitals, integrated with the activities of the medical colleges, (iii) health education is to be woven into a general education system.

Integrated childcare service with emphasis on immunisation, health check-ups and supplementary nutrition is to be built up.

Indigenous systems of medicines and homeopathy are to be developed and integrated in the medical system.

It is found that in Manipur the outlay for primary health centres has gone up from 38.06 lakhs to 152 lakhs in the Five-Year Plan. The corresponding figures for hospital and dispensary are 66.04 lakhs and 93.00 lakhs respectively. These seem to indicate a certain shift in emphasis in the direction required by the Five-Year Plan at the national level. It is to be examined whether the ancillary changes in the education of the medical and paramedical personnel and in the health education of the population are also taking place. Such changes pose a number of social and cultural issues - (a) attitude and values of the population concerning different types of medical aid, (b) social and cultural consequences of acceptance of positive health as a way of life, (c) shifts in the status of medical profession within the prestige system of occupation in the country and (d) shifts in the relative status of various specialisations within the medical profession.

The integrated childcare service requires minimal acquaintance among the concerned medical personnel of the feeding, weaning and the indigenous methods of treatment of infants and children as found in different areas. The workshop will address itself to the confident and cheapest methods of treatment of documentation of these practices and to the problem of making use of the implementation of the childcare programme.

Family Welfare Planning

The components of the family welfare planning during the Five-Year Plan are mainly as follows:

i) Increasingly integrated FP service with those for health and maternity and child welfare and nutrition to be extended to other fields like functional literacy, workers' education, health education etc.

ii) Efforts are to be concentrated on healthy family life, education before marriage, intensive motivation of high parity couples in the 25-35 age group and the recently married ones.

iii) More emphasis is to be given on community involvement. While compensation for acceptance is to be continued, payment to doctors, etc. is to be gradually discontinued, converting the same into community award.

iv) Involvement of voluntary agencies and practitioners of the indigenous system of medicines.

The Manipur population growth has been 37.53% during 1961-71 as compared to 24.80% at the all-India level. In the Five-Year Plan of the state it has been observed that the moderate rate of growth of the economy was largely offset by the phenomenal increase in the population. The family welfare programme is, therefore, of particular importance for the state. The validity and efficiency of the strategy developed at the all-India level and the different categories of population in the state will be keenly discussed in the workshop. The crucial issue is whether there is any shortcut to structural change and socio-economic development for family welfare planning? In this connection, such demographic and socio-cultural data as the trends in birth and death rates, reproductive index, age at marriage, incidence of divorce and widow marriage, incidence of different types of family, role differentiation among family members, child rearing practices, incidence of child labour, trend in female participation in primary sector of economy, role of women in the decision-making process, incidence of marriage payment in different forms, preference for male or female child, family size norm as defined by the culture of the community, religious beliefs and practices impeding or promoting birth control measures require to be discussed in detail. An annotated bibliography of the research done in this field in Manipur should be available. A paper analysing the magnitude of the problem and suggesting the steps to be taken to impart to the family welfare planning, the dimensions of a peoples' movement and not merely a state programme is expected.

Development of the Backward Classes

The Five-Year Plan defined the objectives of the development of the backward classes as follows: (a) to improve the quality of life among the backward classes and narrow the gap with the rest of the population, (b) to formulate a time-bound programme to eliminate exploitation and (c) to speed up the process of economic development.

The strategy of development envisages the following: (i) greater emphasis to be laid on the role of the general sector in providing major thrust to the development of backward classes; (ii) basic infrastructure in terms of growth centres, network of communication, school, rural health centre, rural electrification to be provided; (iii) integrated credit cum marketing structure to be organised; (iv) legal and institutional framework is to be created for realising the social and economic objectives; (v) integrated area development plan is to be drawn up by providing for: (a) separate sub-plans for areas with large concentration of scheduled tribes within respective state plans; (b) T.D. Blocks, T.D. Agencies and other projects set up by central ministries in various states to be integrated with area plans; (c) taking into consideration the concentration of tribal population as the criteria, compact areas to be demarcated at district, taluk and block levels and core programmes to be drawn up which will be related to credit, marketing, completion of land records and records of rights, debt redemption, development of medium and minor irrigation, provision of improved practices in agriculture and horticulture, tackling the problem of shifting cultivation, establishment of agro and forest-based processing industries, artificial roads linking up tribal huts and forests, transport and communication facilities, strengthening of administrative structure; (vi) special attention is to be paid to tribal pockets scattered throughout the country; (vii) state resources for sub-plans for the development of tribal areas are to be supplemented by suitable financial support from the centre, which will be in addition to the provisions on supplementary as well as sector-wise programmes; (viii) in other areas with a dispersed population, backward classes sector is to assume a coordinating role providing critical inputs where necessary and (ix) the more backward among the Scheduled Castes and Scheduled Tribes are to be identified and special programmes are to be formulated.

Before discussing the specific provisions and programmes in Manipur, the workshop may like to examine some of the concepts and assumptions underlying the strategy at the national level.

a) It has been envisaged that the general sector will provide the major thrust in the development of the backward classes. The crucial question is how to ensure in operational terms that it does not degenerate into merely earmarking a portion of the funds for the welfare of the backward classes. Can the general sector provide a major thrust in the development of the backward classes without bringing about a qualitative change in the general sector itself? In other words, how is one to ensure that the general sector as a whole is oriented in such a way that the interests of the backward classes automatically take first place? Perhaps the 20-point programme of the prime minister may be considered to have introduced the necessary corrective. In that case, is it not necessary for the planners to embark upon a rethink? Why is it that the lacuna, which was perceived in the planning process, has been carried out merely as a technical exercise without adequate appreciation of the role of the political process? In the present context it becomes a pertinent question. The whole approach to the problem of backward classes development seems to be based on techno-bureaucratic management. There is no indication of the role of the peoples' forums in the formulation, monitoring and execution of the plan and programmes;

(b) growth centre has been considered to be basic infrastructure but is it a correct assumption particularly for the tribal areas both on theoretical grounds and in the light of empirical experience?

(c) What is actually meant by integrated credit cum marketing structure? Does a structure become integrated simply by aggregation of functions? The two functions of operation of credit and marketing of commodities require skill. Integration of these two functions does not take place automatically. Detailed organisational, operational, procedural intelligence and communication planning is necessary. The nature and quality of orientation training imparted to the cooperative functionaries also require to be examined;

(d) A long list of services has been drawn up as the core programme in the context of tribal blocks; and the whole approach has been termed as an integrated area development plan. Again, one would ask whether it is correct to equate aggregation with integration of too many functions without right phasing and appropriate balance, which may have just the opposite effect. Are there clear guidelines on these matters? Also in view of the long list of items, one wonders what has been meant by core programme? What is the concept of core in social planning? Obviously it requires that society be looked upon as a unified field. In that case, are there enough guidelines in the plan to identify the parameters and the contours of the social fields for various tribal areas? Again, is it scientific and precise to anticipate the core?

(e) Lastly, it has been visualised that in areas with a dispersed population, the backward classes sector is to assume a coordinating role, providing critical inputs where necessary. It is by no means clear what is meant by coordinating role; the emphasis seems to be on supplementing the financial outlay. The various models of coordination of the tribal sector and the strong and weak points of each have been discussed in several reports of the commissioner for Scheduled Castes and Scheduled Tribes. In the light of the same, perhaps a clear guideline can be given in the plan itself.

The workshop would like to examine all these questions and give suggestions.

Coming to the problem of the backward classes in Manipur, it is to be noticed that in the state, 32% of the population consists of Scheduled Tribes and 2% are Scheduled Caste. Out of the six districts in the state, tribals form the majority in five of them. During the Five-Year Plan, the outlay for the backward classes sector was Rs 121.50 lakhs; in the Fifth Plan it is Rs 180 lakhs (Rs 170 lakhs for Scheduled Tribes and Rs 10 lakhs for Scheduled Castes). It is to be examined whether the outlay is adequate even to meet the minimum needs of the tribals who inhabit 9/10ths of the territory of the state.

The schemes for backward classes welfare are divided into three major heads, viz, education, economic development, health and housing.

The workshop would like to discuss the principles on which the various items of development are assigned to the general special sectors; it will also like to go into the method of calculating the share of benefits actually enjoyed by the backward classes and others.

Development of the Backward Areas

In the statement of perspective of the Five-Year Plan, it has been observed that each backward area represents a unique combination of factors and as such an essential pre-requisite for accelerated development is evolution of appropriate location-specific strategies.

The Five-Year Plan has divided the backward areas broadly in two categories: (a) areas with unfavourable geographic conditions, terrain, climate and regions inhabited by people with typical cultural characteristics (hill areas, drought-prone areas and tribal areas) and (b) economically backward areas marked by adverse land-man ratio, lack of infrastructure, inadequate development of resource potential.

As regards the approach to the problem of the backward areas, the Five-Year Plan envisages the following:

(i) Allocation of adequate financial resources is only one of the many steps necessary for accelerated development of the area. Other essential measures include (a) evolution of locally-oriented integrated strategies; (b) development of suitable programmes with appropriate norms, procedures and technologies; (c) strengthening and coordinated functioning of financing, promotional and consultancy institutions; (d) reorientation and, where necessary, restructuring of field organisation to suit functional requirements of identified development programmes;

(ii) The main responsibility for the development of the backward areas pertaining to the state though central government will participate by - (a) making special allocations; (b) providing technical support in respect of planning as well as programme development; (c) channelling institutional resources on a priority basis; (d) continuing and further extending liberal patterns of central assistance; (e) providing special incentives for the flow of private investment to the identified backward areas.

Manipur as a whole is considered a backward area. One is to know what the parameters of backwardness are. Besides, as in the case of development, backwardness also causes a particular pattern of inter-dependence with the rest of the country and with other states in the region. Development does not mean only a creation of certain material or social traits; it is also implied in the pattern of relationship.

The development perspective for Manipur should clearly indicate the new pattern of relationship within the North-East, and with the rest of the country. If the requisite work has already been done in this matter, the workshop should like to receive an appraisal of the same; it should be the starting point for initiating work in collaboration with other states and UTS and with the assistance of the North-East Council.

Within Manipur, the hill areas as a whole are considered to be backward. One is to consider whether such an approach is in conformity with the perspective of the Five-Year Plan; and whether it would not be more useful to go in for specific classification. For instance, Ukhrul district with its wonderful system of water management of the terrace fields cannot be considered as agriculturally backward in the same sense as Tengnoupal district. There is also a massive gap in the intensity of communication with the rest of the nation, particularly at the symbolic level. On the other hand while Tengnoupal district is comparatively more backward in agriculture and education, it seems to be in an advantageous position with respect to transport and communication. In the field of institutional preparedness for modern technology and services it seems to lag behind. But, for historical reasons, the communication gap with the rest of the nation doesn't seem as wide as is case with the people of Ukhrul district. These are but impressionistic observations. But after carefully establishing the specific indicators of arrested development and ecological non-adaptation, the strategies and programmes for each area are to be drawn up. One may for instance consider whether it would not be more useful to persuade the people of Ukhrul to invest a part of their savings from the agricultural sector in the diversification of their economy with more emphasis on forest-based industries and animal husbandry. On the other hand, would it not be more useful to persuade the tribals of Chandel district to go in for modernisation of the land-use pattern on the basis of recognition of the corporate nature of ownership. Once the basic strategies for the respective areas are decided, the core programmes and linked-up ancillary programmes can easily be identified.

Along with the characterisation of the region in terms of specific attributes, it would also be useful to delineate the agro-climatic micro-regions within Manipur. At the present level of technology and with the limited availability of investible resources, the physical environment will certainly be the next important limiting factor, though not necessarily the sole determining factor for the pace and direction of development.

2

Problems of Development of Tribal Areas of Manipur

• - *Prof Gangmumei Kamei*

Development: Its Implications

Development can be defined as the process of change in order to progress. It is a holistic concept. Development implies that not only economic growth be measured in terms of per capita GNP (Gross National Product) of a country but that it should also cover social development. These two aspects of development are inseparable. Social development is concerned with man and society while economic development deals with material resources. Economic growth is essentially the quantitative change in the economy. Therefore, development covers qualitative change in both economic and non-economic aspects of human life. Social development is linked to social quality, social justice and freedom from exploitation, the absence of which will lead to poverty and consequent powerlessness. This is based on the key concepts of social solidarity, distributive justice and peoples' organisation to bring about a change from the existing exploitation-ridden social and economic order.

What are the indicators of development in a country?

. Many people do not accept the theory that the GNP of a country is the sole indicator of development. The physical quality of life index (PQLI) method has the indicator - life expectancy, literacy level and standard of living. The UN in its various pronouncements has linked development with the following features.

(i) Extent and nature of the independence or autonomy of a nation.

(ii) Extent and nature of popular (democratic) participation in the developmental process.

(iii) Level of developmental technologies and social control as the means of production.

(iv) The level and nature of the distribution of the fruits (achievements) of development and the mechanism for redistribution.

(v) The encouragement or discouragement of a specific form of individual or collective consumption of goods and services.

(vi) The extent and nature of production of the human environment.

(vii) Extent and nature of protection of human relationships contributing to solidarity, security, self-realisation and freedom.

1.2 India's planning philosophy is conducive to such a universal conceptual framework. In the context of tribal area of Manipur it implies - (1) the integration of economic development with social development based on social egalitarianism, (2) the people's control over different developmental processes, (3) development of the capacity of the local people to manage means of production, especially modern agricultural practices, agro-industries and commerce, (4) apart from people's representatives in the democratic political powers of the state, to see that development does not disturb the cultural heritage and social egalitarianism and does not lead to division of the people into the haves and have-nots with concentration of wealth in the hands of the few. It is heartening that the planners of our country have discarded the idea of tribal welfare and adopted the concept of tribal development instead.

Demographic Profile:

The total area of Manipur is 22,456 sq. kms. The hills cover an area of 20,126 sq. kms. and the valley area is 2,230 sq. kms. The hills are inhabited by the tribal communities broadly divided into Nagas and the Kuki-Chins-Mizos. There are five districts in the hill areas - Senapati, Ukhrul, Chandel, Churachandpur and Tamenglong and there are four valley districts - Imphal East & West, Bishenpur and Thoubal. The inhabitants of the valley districts are the Meiteis, the Muslims and other Indian immigrant communities with some tribes. The hill tribes, according to the order of the President of India, are 29 scheduled tribes of which some tribes like Angami, Sema and Sahte are not domiciled tribes. The following table shows the trend of the growth of population among the tribal people.

TABLE NO. I

Population of Manipur

(1981-1991)

Year	*Total Population*	*Tribal Population*	*Percentage*
1881	2,21,070	85,288	38.57
1891	1,53,563	-	-
1901	2,44,455	-	-
1911	5,46,323	-	-
1921	3,84,016	-	-
1931	4,45,606	1,54,804	34.77
1941	5,12,069	1,52,805	29.84
1951	5,77,635	1,94,239	3.63
1961	7,80,037	2,49,049	31.93
1971	10,72,753	3,34,466	31.18
1981	14,20,953	3,87,977	27.30
1991	18,26,714		

TABLE NO. II

The following table shows the population growth in each tribe of Manipur from 1961-1981.

	Name of tribe	*1961*	*1971*	*1981*
1	Aimol	108	836	1862
2	Anal	4868	6670	9349
3	Angami	632	70	560
4	Chiru	1809	2785	3743
5	Chothe	1035	1905	1687
6	Gangte	4856	6307	7891
7	Hmar	15365	23312	29216
8	Kabui	29218	40257	26006
9	Kacha Naga	9734	13026	12753
10	Koirao	406	1620	919
11	Koireng	631	458	949
12	Kom	5477	6550	9830
13	Langang	1866	2622	3452
14	AnyMizo	2746	7483	6126
15	Maram	4928	4539	6544
16	Maring	7745	9825	11910
17	Mao	28810	33379	50716
18	Monsang	1342	931	1139
19	Moyon	647	1360	1642
20	Paite	17029	24755	50716
21	Purum	82	-	447
22	Rale	80	154	107
23	Sema	4	3	24
24	Simte	2818	4177	5035
25	Sahte	-	3	283
26	Tangkhul	43943	57851	79029
27	Thadou	47994	59955	55466
28	Vaiphei	8215	12347	15462
29	Zou.	6761	10060	12576

* *Tribe-wise population of 1991 has not yet been published.*

TABLE NO. III

District-wise distribution of tribes in 1981

Name of tribe	*Central*	*Sena-pati*	*CC Pur*	*Ukh-rul*	*Tameng-long*	*Chan-del*
1. Aimol	306	86	269	1	4	1196
2. Anal	230	5	328	2	3	8780
3. Angami	30	18	511	-	-	7
4. Chiru	316	2069	401	1	959	2
5. Chothe	45	3	208	1	-	1429
6. Gangle	471	347	5417	5	1225	424
7. Hmar	2492	138	25650	14	632	390
8. Kabui	8158	·3703	2484	14	11638	9
9. Kacha Naga	69	3266	10	-	9408	1
10. Koireng	184	762	-	-	-	1
11. Kom	2751	2602	3310	-	169	999
12. Langang	39	-	-	-	-	3412
13. Mao	697	49942	6	41	12	17
14. Maram	61	6464	8	-	1	6
15. Maring	619	1359	67	3	1	9863
16. AnyMizo	367	297	4608	20	17	833
17. Monsang	23	3	-	-	-	1119
18. Moyon	79	2	-	-	1	1559
19. Paite	1045	201	39156	109	17	432
20. Purum	6	418	17	3	2	3
21. Ralte	1	2	-	-	1	-
22. Sema	4	1	10	3	4	2
23. Simte	62	200	4527	-	207	38
24. Sante	2	4	269	1	-	8
25. Tangkhul	3330	6566	317	68339	27	450
26. Thadou	1502	2306	17196	5116	4359	5233
27. Vaiphei	350	3057	11036	296	581	152
28. Zou	760	1	9707	7	3	2150
29. Koirao	1	908	-	-		-

Source: Census of India (Data for 1991 has not yet been published).

The Administrative Structure

During the pre-colonial era, the hill villages of Manipur were autonomous units. There was the occasional military and political control by the kings of Manipur. The genesis of the hill administration may be traced to the establishment of the Hao Macha Loisang (Department of Hill Tribes) during the last days of King Charairongba (1706-1709) when his long lost son Pamheiba (Garibaniwaz) was found from Thangal village and restored to the throne. In 1735, Garibaniwaz introduced the *lallup* system in hill areas and recognised the hill chiefs as *'khullakpas'*. However, regular administration was not carried out and no taxes were imposed, only tribute and service were given to the monarch. The hill villages were responsible for their own administration. After the British conquest of Manipur in 1891, they did not disturb the hill villages whose headmen were recognised and entrusted with village-level administration. The British divided the Manipur hills into five divisions. To each division was appointed one *lamsubedar* who was assisted by seven *lambus*. They were under the overall administrative supervision of the political agent. In 1906, the hill office was established. In 1907, the Manipur state *darbar* was established with Raja Churachand Singh as the president. The *darbar* was not given the jurisdiction of the hills. In 1913, when the *darbar* was re-formed, the president of the *darbar* was one British ICS officer. The president of the Manipur state *darbar* (popularly known as PMSD) was entrusted with the hill administration under the supervision of the political agent. After the Kuki rebellion for an intensive administration, two subdivisions, i.e. North-West with Tamenglong as the headquarters, North-East with Ukhrul as the headquarters; were established. In 1930, due to the non-availability of Anglo-Indian officers to man the subdivisions, the headquarters were shifted to Imphal. And so, the hill office under the president of the Manipur state *darbar* became the sole authority of hill administration. With the outbreak and suppression of rebellion of Jadonang and Rani Gaidinliu (1930-33), the British once again decided to open the headquarters of the subdivision at Tamenglong and Ukhrul. In 1933, the Sadar subdivision was created to administer to the hill areas which were a one-day journey from Imphal. A new rule for the management of the hill tribes was also adopted.

On the eve of Independence, 10th August 1947, the government introduced the Manipur Hill People's (Administration) Regulation. This regulation is one of the well-formulated local government systems of the hill areas. The *darbar* was abolished and the Manipur State Council was established. Under the new Manipur Constitution Act of 1947, Manipur became a constitutional monarchy. Major R. Khathing was appointed as minister of hill affairs. On 15th October 1949, Manipur was made part 'C' state under a Chief Commissioner and later on a union territory of India. On 26th January 1950, Manipur was made one district territory with a chief commissioner, a deputy commissioner and sub-divisions noted below were created.

1. ***Sadar sub-division:***

a) Whole of Imphal West tehsil

b) Whole of Imphal East tehsil

c) 18 villages of Thoubal tehsil

d) *Ahallup* circle No.I and *ahallup* circle No. IV of Mayang Imphal.

e) Whole of Sadar hill circles except 23 villages.

2. ***Thoubal:***

a) Whole of Thoubal tehsil except 18 villages

b) Whole of Bishenpur tehsil

c) Whole of Mayang Imphal except *ahallup* circle No.I & IV

d) 28 villages of the hill Sadar circle

3. ***Ukhrul:*** Circles of Ukhrul and Phaisat

4. ***Churachandpur:*** Circles of Churachandpur and Thanlon

5. ***Tamenglong:*** Circles of Tamenglong and Aimol

6. ***Mao:*** Mao circle

7. ***Tengnoupal:*** Tenoupal circle

8. ***Jiribam:*** Jiribam mauza

After the creation of the hill subdivisions, the hill bench was abolished on 19th January 1950. The Mao subdivision was amalgamated with the Sadar subdivision on 31st August 1950. After almost two decades, Manipur was divided into five districts in November 1969 as follows:

1. Manipur Central
2. Manipur West
3. Manipur North District with 3 administrative units:
   (I) Sadar hills
   (ii) Mao West and
   (iii) Mao East with 305 villages.
4. Manipur East
5. Manipur South

Out of the Manipur Central district, two more districts - Thoubal and Bishenpur districts were carved out on 29th October 1970. The remaining areas of Manipur Central were constituted into the central district. However, further modifications were made on 21st January 1972 after statehood, affecting the subdivisions of Manipur north district with headquarters at Karong which were as follows:

i) Mao Maram subidivision consisting of 95 villages with headquarters at Tadubi.

ii) Sadar hills east subdivision consisting of 175 villages with headquarters at Saikul.

iii) Sadar hills west subdivision consisting of 147 villages with headquarters at Kangpokpi.

Note*: Paomata subdivision was created on 21st November 1983.

On 15th July 1983, the names of the districts were changed to the following:

Sl.No.	*Old Name*	*New Name*
01.	Manipur North	Senapati
02.	Bishnupur	Bishenpur
03.	Tengnoupal	Chandel
04.	Manipur East	Ukhrul
05.	Manipur South	Churachandpur
06.	Manipur West	Tamenglong
07.	Central District	Imphal
08.	Thoubal	Thoubal

Formation of the District Council

With the grant of statehood in 1972, the hill districts were granted the autonomous district council. There are six district councils for five districts:

1. Manipur North Autonomous District Council, Karong.
2. Sadar Hills Autonomous District Council, Kangpokpi
3. Manipur East Autonomous District Council, Ukhrul
4. Manipur South Autonomous District Council, Churachandpur
5. Tengnoupal Autonomous District Council, Chandel
6. Manipur West Autonomous District Council, Tamenglong

Village Authorities

The Manipur (Hill Areas) Village Authorities Act, 1956, provided the local-level government in the form of village authorities to those villages that had at least 20 tax-paying households. The office of the *khullakpa* and the chief has been institutionalised in the statute. The deputy commissioner, the SDO/SDC and district level departments, the district councils and the village authorities looked after the administration of the hill areas. At the state level, it was the hill commissioner (hill administration) in addition to the other departmental network of the government.

Problems of Development

The Manipur hills, which were isolated for centuries by an unfavourable geographical position, are now on the threshold of a great march towards progress and development. The process of modernisation, which was started by the British with the advent of Christianity and western education followed by a massive developmental programme by the government of India, is a continuing phenomenon. The economy of the tribes has outgrown the subsistence level and is now in the market economy with all its good and bad effects. The urge to improve the quality of life, have a better standard of living and ensure the dignity and freedom of man has been reflected in the recent methods of development among the hill people. Yet, it is not that easy. The political, economic and social changes that have come to the tribal community are not wholly a blessing but, on the whole, are far better. The hill people face a number of basic problems. The poverty of the hill people is reflected in several forms — illiteracy, ill health, unemployment, failure of commercial development and general development. This dissatisfaction is reflected in complex political agitations including insurgencies organised by different ethno-political groups. Policy planners, academicians and social leaders have now identified the problems of development among tribals. These include:

(i) Absence of infrastructural communication system like good roads, transport and postal service and mass media;

(ii) Uncertain tribal land ownership system;

(iii) Unproductivity of the tribal agriculture;

(iv) Lack of good educational facilities;

(v) Lack of power supply;

(vi) Lack of marketing facilities;

(vii) Absence of adequate social services like medical and health, water supply and housing; and

(viii) The absence of well organised bodies for people's direct participation in the developmental works.

Communication

Isolation has to be broken with improving the accessibility to hill areas. The existing roads, the two national highways, No. 39 and No. 53, which are the lifelines of Manipur, the state highways and district roads, are not adequate. The philosophy of road making should not only be to link up with the administrative and marketing centres but to reach out to every village in the state. Construction, maintenance of roads and supervision by the state P.W.D. is not satisfactory. The transport network, which has expanded tremendously with private enterprises, has linked up with the centres on the highways. Newspapers and T.V. have not reached the hill villages while radio has penetrated into the interior. A massive road network will facilitate the mobility of People, trade and commerce and better administration.

Tribal land-ownership system

The state accepts that all the land and forests of hill areas belong to the state, while the tribals think and assert that they are the owners of the land. This hiatus in perception persists due to historical reasons. The normal land laws requiring the payment of land revenues have not been introduced by the government. Only hill house tax which is levied on households of a hill village exists. The Manipur Land Reforms and Land Revenue Act, 1960, has still not been properly introduced. There are two systems of land ownership among the tribals. Among the Nagas, there exists a three-tier land ownership system: the village community land, the clan land and the individual land. Among the Kukis, the chiefs claim the ownership of village land and the villagers who till the land are his tenants. There is a scope for investigating into the Kuki chiefs' claim for land ownership. There is currently a strong resistance to the introduction of the MLR & LR Act in the hill areas. However, privatisation of landed property has now come to tribal communities and the record of rights on their lands will surely come. Due to the absence of the authorised record of right establishing the title to the land, no *patta* system exists in the hill areas. As a result, financial institutions are unwilling to give loans to the tribals, who are now desirous of acquiring it. Under the circumstances, land ownership is to be settled recognising the tribal communal right on village land along with the clan and individual rights.

Tribal Agriculture - Shifting Cultivation

There are two systems of agriculture in the hill areas of Manipur; Shifting cultivation (pam lou) and terrace cultivation. In Senapati and Ukhrul districts, the Maos and Tangkhuls developed terrace cultivation long ago. Other tribes are catching up. But the lands available for terrace cultivation are limited. Shifting cultivation cannot be easily discarded. It has been blamed for destroying the forest and causing soil erosion. But commercial exploitation of forest causes more destruction to forest and soil erosion than shifting cultivation. Moreover, there is not enough land for terrace fields and it is not easy to give up the system. This system is linked to their right to use forests that have been the livelihood of the tribals for centuries. The government's attempts at the jhum control programme have raised awareness among the tribal people. The tribals are hunting for new lands for terrace cultivation. They also realise that the alternative to shifting cultivation is horticulture and cash crops plantation for which they require capital which is unavailable. These realisations and motivations are difficult to be translated into action. But looking into the ecological hazards caused by shifting cultivation, we cannot allow it to continue for perpetuity. Yet it is not possible immediately. This dilemma of the tribal people will be a temporary one and should be settled within a few decades.

Education

It is a well-known fact that the government school system has not produced the desired results. Only private and missionary schools function effectively. Educational problems, large-scale failure of students in the examination, school drop-outs, absence of the teachers, lack of school amenities, lack of interest of the local people in the school, politicisation of appointments inadequacy or absence of proper supervision by the education department are extremely problematic issues. This should be tackled both by the government as well as by the people.

Lack of Power and Marketing Centres

There is no power plant in the hill areas of Manipur except the Loktak project and a few incomplete micro-hydel projects. The marketing centres are to be developed; trade and commerce have to be promoted in order generate more income.

Forests

The forests are the domain of the tribal people. There is a symbolic relationship between the tribals and the forests. The forest management and afforestation programme can only be successful with the support and participation of the hill people.

Problems of Implementation

Well-formulated programmes are to be implemented through the government bureaucracy. There is a nexus between the politicians and administrators at the local-level programme implementation. If plans are to be successful, the district and the sub-divisional officers are to do their job honestly and they should not be interfered by the political leaders.

Some Thoughts on Developmental Strategy

The United Nations Declaration on Social progress envisages the following:

(i) Effective participation of all sections of society in the preparation and execution of national plans;

(ii) Equitable distribution of national income;

(iii) Acceleration of the process of industrialisation with due regard to social aspects;

(iv) Legislative and administrative measures to ensure political and civil rights and full utilisation of economic, social and cultural rights;

(v) Democratically-based and institutional reforms including land reforms; and

(vi) Protection and improvement of the human environment.

With regard to planning in Manipur, especially the tribal areas, the following considerations should be kept in mind:

(1) While trying to satisfy the minimum needs of the population, the poverty alleviation programmes should be the core concern of planning as far as possible. An attempt should be made to satisfy the same through the process of development itself and not through mere welfare measures. In other words, the production activities of each mini-micro, micro-region should be oriented to satisfy the basic consumption needs at the first instance, and the surplus obtaining goods and services of a progressively higher order.

(2) Introduction of cash crops and commercialisation of resources in other forms should be at par with the creation of a requisite infrastructure and commensurate development of indigenous institutions and entrepreneurship.

(3) Currently dislodged from their habitats in the wake of the implementation of major projects, the people are given compensation. It is to be considered whether this practice should not be replaced by rehabilitation subsidy and equity share and partnership in the new economy on a regular basis. Other feasible forms of partnership are also to be considered in this connection.

(4) In the development of the transport and communication systems, over-emphasis is laid on linking up the administrative and marketing centres. Intra-valley and intro-range communication and transport network should be planned keeping in mind the needs of functional specialisations and linkages in harmony with the growing democratisation of the social and cultural process and also the egalitarian aspirations of the diverse social formation in the region.

(5) The village authorities in the hills should be recognised as legal authorities for the purpose of extension of institutional finance to them for creating public convenience and other specified services.

(6) In those areas where the communal system of ownership/ access to resources exist, the village authorities should be enabled by law to certify the share of the individuals subsumed within the communal rights so that on the basis of such certification authenticated by the state revenue officials institutional finance can be obtained by the individuals concerned.

(7) Appropriate legislation should be enacted so that the communally owned/managed resources can attract institutional finance through creation of an appropriate management structure without the fragmentation of the system for the development of resources for common good.

(8) While planning for the establishment of industries, plantations and other major enterprises, the potential of the same in generating employment for the indigenous population keeping in view their skill levels, tradition of social and physical mobility and cultural values should be carefully considered.

(9) Keeping in view the cost factor and other problems of generation and transmission of electricity in rural areas, greater emphasis should be on micro-hydel projects and other forms of generation of power in outlying settlements.

3

Problems and Prospects of Development in the Hills of Manipur Revenue

- Prof. (Dr.) M. Horam

Introduction

The state of Manipur is situated between 23.50 and 25.41N and 93.2 and 94.47E and it covers an area of 22,327 sq. kms. To the north lies Nagaland, on the east lies Myanmar (Burma), to the west is Cachar and at the south is Mizoram.

The greater part of the state consists of ranges of hill areas covering more than 20,000 sq. kms. In the centre of the state is the tiny valley of Manipur. It covers an area of 2,000 sq. kms. It must be said, however, that the people who are living in the valley are much more developed economically and educationally. Even in the political arena, of the total 60 Member Assembly seats, 40 seats are allotted to the valley, 19 for the tribals and 1 for Scheduled Caste.

The state has nine districts, 4 valley districts and 5 hills districts.

Valley

Name	*Area (in sq. kms.)*
1. Imphal (West)	1,708
2. Thoubal	
3. Bishenput	530
4. Imphal (East)	

Hills

1.	Ukhrul	4,544
2.	Senapati	3,271
3.	Tamenglong	4,391
4.	Chandel	3,313
5.	Churachandpur	4,570

Prior to British arrival, Manipur was ruled by kings and administration was highly centralised; the king's administration was mainly concentrated in the valley. His administration centred on the Meiteis community who lived in and around 10 sq. miles.

After the Anglo-Manipur war of 1891, the state of Manipur was taken over by British Agents. Even during the British rule, the tribals were left to themselves except for collection of Rs. 3/- house tax annually. Manipur is now governed under the Indian Parliamentary system like any other state in India. Historically it is clearly proved that the tribals of Manipur were kept out from the mainstream of modern developmental process for centuries. Even today, with all the tall talk of planners and policy makers, the hill tribals are not given their due and remain economically backward.

Objectives

In this brief write-up, I would like to concentrate only on the hill tribals' problems in order to avoid confusion. It is intended to do so because of the following reasons:

1. For clarity to the approach of tribals' problems while making plans and policies.
2. To pinpoint the nature of the problems faced by the tribals.
3. To find out alternative agro-based technology for future tribal development.

Scheduled Tribes

There are as many as 29 recognised Scheduled Tribes. Besides, there are also smaller tribes who are not recognised by the constitution of India. These tribes are again divided broadly into two groups:

(i) The Nagas

(ii) The Chin-Kuki-Mizo group

As there are different tribes, there are also varied social habits and customs and, therefore, one cannot study the problems of scheduled tribes with uniform norms and apply the same yardsticks. I have chosen only the common problem faced by these gullible people.

During the past 50 years or so, the tribals of Manipur have undergone several changes almost in all areas of life socially, economically, and politically. Some changes are good, others are bad. The tribals are, by and large, well-organised social groups having their own well-defined polity, administration and mode of life. In the days of yore, the village council was very effective: disputes could be settled peacefully and decisions were honoured. Indeed, the village council acted as a judge, lawgiver and dispensing agency of administration. But this basic foundation has been shaken today; if there is a village council system in the tribal areas, it is more a mere symbol.

One of the main factors that brought about a change in the tribal society is the sudden exposure to the outside world. Till the British came around 80 years ago, the tribes lived peacefully almost oblivious to the world around them.

Even after the British came, they were not interested in the development and progress of the tribes but were mainly concerned with collecting house-taxes. Their motivation was to check the tribals' sporadic raids into the valley. Except for constructing a few footpaths and seasonal unmotorable roads, its administration did not leave any lasting impact.

The slight twist in the administration began only when the First World War broke out. When the British tried to recruit tribals into the Labour Corps; many went to the War front. As a sign of gratitude, the British showed some interest in the development of the tribes, and thus a few primary schools were opened; a few dispensaries were built. The actual exposure began only during the Second World War. Many thousands of soldiers, Japanese as well as Allied Arms landed in the tribal areas and in fact, the hill areas of Manipur became the battlefield of the Second World War where these areas were used as a springboard which Marshall Slim aptly described as "Defeat into Victory".

The Second World War was for the tribals of Manipur a turning point in many respects; they came in contact with various forces, which was a novel experience in their lives. This contact left remarkable imprints on their lifestyle and habits. Needs of the tribes began to change. One of the most important outcomes of the war was the sudden realisation of ethnic assertion - an identity crisis that came in the form of a political awakening. It must be mentioned here that in the earlier period, at least for 20 years or so, the administration did not realise the gravity of the socio-economic problems of the tribes. It was thought that the problems of this region were like any one of those prevalent in the other parts of India. The administrators, therefore, handled the areas with a nonchalant attitude. They imposed their ways on the tribals without trying to understand the customs and ways of tribal life. Secondly, most of the administrators, especially the bureaucrats, ruled the tribes with a "holier than thou" attitude. For the tribes it was nothing but another masters' rule handed down from the British. The frustration of the tribes, especially the youths only increased. The struggle goes on and continues even today.

Developmental work slowed down, more money was spent on maintaining law and order rather than on developmental work. Tribal life was filled with fear and suspicion and this situation dragged on. No meaningful dialogue was conducted between the men at the helm of administration and the people concerned. Taking advantage of this situation, so-called public leaders and middlemen exploited both the ignorant people and the Government.

Any-meaningful progress and development must come from the grassroots; any development must percolate into the bulk of the society. But at the moment it is a far cry from becoming an actuality.

The Manipur tribals, like many of the tribals of India, are egalitarian and their livelihood depends on farming and agriculture. Not so long ago, land among the tribals was not a problem. Every household could cultivate any size of land and the yield was enough for a year. But the situation has changed immensely due to rapid growth of population. Demand of land has multiplied and there is, almost, in every community scarcity of cultivable land. This has resulted in a number of problems; first disputes over land have increased every year, the annual yield has become scanty and meagre; many a villager has left his original village in search of other cultivable land; a few tribes have even migrated to Imphal.

Mode of Land Ownership

Broadly speaking, there are three forms of land ownership among the hill tribes:

1. Lands owned by the villagers collectively.
2. Lands owned by the clans.
3. Lands owned by individuals.

A tribe has a well-defined boundary separating it from neighbouring tribes. Within the tribe there are numerous villages that in turn have their own well-demarcated land. A particular village may be either owned by the community as a whole or owned by the individual families.

The concept of exercising authority and control over an area originates from tradition. Group control and collective authority has arisen out of the habit of corporate tribal life where every household enjoys the right of cultivating that much of land which is needed by a particular family. Conflicts arising out of claims and counter-claims are usually settled through the mediation of certain groups or persons. But the concept of tribal land ownership of this region cannot be understood in the modern land tenure and judicial systems.

Concept of tribal land may, therefore, be divided into the following categories:

1. Land for village site;
2. Land for cultivation, both shifting and terrace cultivation;
3. Forests, for housing materials, fuel, hunting, and collection of wild fruits, roots;
4. Land for public utility such as burial grounds, bachelors' houses and cattle grounds, etc.

Recently, the State Government tried to take over the forests as reserved but this has been strongly opposed by the tribals. The tribals depend on shifting (slash-and-burn) cultivation and this is a part of their culture and way of life.

AGRICULTURE

1.a. Jhum (Slash-and-burn):

By this practice, the jungle growing on the hillside is cut down and burned between January and March. The seeds of hill rice, millet, etc. are dibbled in amongst the ashes, and while the crop is growing, it is weeded once or thrice.

The history of Jhum cultivation is as old as man himself, and it is indeed a matter of great interest to us that the age-old pre-historic methods and techniques of food production are still in use as the principal mode of subsistence among the tribals of this region.

The method of shifting cultivation includes:

1. Selecting the forested hilly land;
2. Clearing the forests by indiscriminate cutting of trees;
3. Burning the dried forests into ashes;
4. Worship and sacrifices;
5. Dibbling and sowing of seeds;
6. Weeding;
7. Watching and protecting the crops; and
8. Harvesting.

The above process speaks well about the most simple and primordial nature of cultivation. The process demands the selection of a plot in the jungle. In winter it is cleared by felling the trees and lopping off the undergrowth. Shortly, dry leaves and bushes are burned. Simple implements like digging sticks of iron hooks are used to make holes for the seeds. No animal is put to use, there is no artificial irrigation system. No manure is used. Investment in this procedure is minimal therefore.

After cultivating the same plot once or twice, the plot is shifted to another place due to loss of fertility of the soil. The cycle of recovery of the same plot varies from place to place. In early days, it ranged between 10-20 years or more, but today, due to rapid population growth, the pressure on land use has increased tremendously and thus it ranges only from 4-5 years.

Effects

The system of 'jhum' cultivation has its drawbacks. The crops are entirely dependent on rainfall. Much time and trouble is expended in the clearing of the Jhum and the amount of land required is very large. After the second year,. the yield tapers off and weeds spring up and choke the crop. A village thus requires cultivable land about five times the area actually under cultivation at any given time and the outlying jhums of large communities must of necessity be sometimes situated at a considerable distance from the village site.

This primitive type of cultivation is the main cause of deforestation in Manipur. About 13,845 sq. kms. of forest area is utilised for shifting cultivation. The rate of clearance of forest has increased from 900 sq. kms. per year to 1,880 sq. kms. per year. The demand for a wider area and quicker jhum cycle by shifting cultivation are due to:

1. Increasing population because of birth and migration;
2. Construction of roads and buildings in the hilly areas;
3. Lack of an alternative method of cultivation;
4. Tremendous increasing pressure on land; and
5. Occupation of large areas by the Armed Forces in different hill areas.

The population of Manipur has increased from 14,11,375 to 18,27,000, according to the 1991 census. The density of population varies between hills and valley; it is 33% persons per sq. km. in the hills while it is 501 persons per sq. km. in the valley as per the 1991 census. The growth rate of Manipur with 2.9% per year is higher than the all-India average of 2.1% as per the 1991 census.

The increasing population exerts pressure on land for settlement area and cultivable land. Again, due to the expansion of the district administrative machinery in the hills, there are structural changes in the socio-cultural system of the tribal people. Money-based activities are replacing traditional community-based economic activities. This change forces the tribals to produce more agro-products to meet their ever-increasing daily demands. But, the traditional method of jhum cultivation cannot meet the demands. Over and above this, valley middlemen control trading activities. So, the tribal people's economy goes from bad to worse; several villagers are living below the poverty line. In short, the jhum (slash-and-bund) mode of cultivation:

a) Destroys forests;
b) Is wasteful;
c) Dries up springs;
d) Causes soil waste-erosion;
e) Affects ecological imbalances;
f) Adversely affects rainfall and even;
g) Deprives the people of forest products; and
h) Destroys flora and fauna.

As shifting cultivation plays a vital and dominant role in both the eco-system and the social system, the replacement by another alternative method is not an easy task and it cannot be solved by piecemeal arrangements. The process needs serious planning and systematic implementation.

To overcome all hurdles and to re-establish an ecological and social equilibrium, alternative technology supported by massive in-flow of money ought to be adopted. This can be done through two-pronged agencies viz: State Government and Non-Government Organisations.

Side by side, the crops other than the traditional cereal crops are to be replaced by high yielding varieties of cereals: cash-crops, horticulture, tea, rubber, bamboo and teak plantations, in a big way. This needs capital and manpower. There is a glaring absence of a marketing system in the tribal areas and, therefore, a tolerable marketing system based on modern method must be supplied. To do so, all-weather motorable roads and transportation facilities are necessary.

On the other hand, the liberals consider that the practice of shifting cultivation is not as bad as we think because.

This method of cultivation is simple and inexpensive,
It is a way of life of the people and above all the
soil-erosion can be checked effectively by some methods.

This school of thought even goes to the extent of saying that shifting cultivation does not create ecological imbalances as much as the modern technological erosion on the land by way of construction of roads, dams and canals, instituting modern industries and multi-storied buildings that cause pollution.

But new technology and techniques of agriculture may not meet all the needs and may not be easily be accepted by the tribals. Traditions die hard after all. In order to support my argument, I would like to cite an example: Under th rehabilitation programme, the Assam Government provided model villages to the Karbi Anglong tribe of Assam. Many tribal families left for these model villages hoping it would be a better arrangement. But families soon abandoned these model villages and come back to their old villages. Families re-constructed their traditional houses and started the same shifting cultivation.

The tribals then realised they now face opposition from the Government. Besides, the abolition of shifting cultivation in some areas renders them helpless and suspicious. The Government has failed to provide appropriate alternatives to the tribals. These factors have discouraged the tribals from participating in certain developmental schemes with zeal and enthusiasm.

Assuming the growth rates for the North Eastern Region of India remain unchanged, the tribal population of this area alone will itself reach 40 million by the end of this century, much above the sustaining capacity of the present resources of the area. This will inevitably lead to massive migration to towns, to substantial educated and semi-educated unemployment, and even greater general under-employment. The food crops potential of the area will be totally inadequate to meet the minimum essential needs of the people. The resultant sinking of the tribal population into the role of "the sewers of wood and the drawers of water", and the sharpened contrasts between the affluence of essential alien commercial elements and the local people will cause considerable social unrest, bitterness and even conflict. The erosion of the authority of village elders and of the tribal councils, and the absence of real adjustment to the civil and criminal laws of the land will result in considerable breakdown of the law and order situation.

However, any projection of the future of tribal societies in India will be on the assumption that every effort will be made to draw them into the mainstream of national life without destroying the individual characteristics and traditions of the different tribal groups. The richness and variety, and, indeed, the vitality of Indian culture rests on this capacity to find overall unity amidst incredible diversity. It also emphasises the inalienable right of these people to retain their individual identities.

There is no more moving statement than the one made by the American Indian Director of the Indian Treaty Council demanding the abandonment of a project which would inundate his homeland. It is entirely applicable to our country particularly to all tribals and therefore, I would like to quote it in its totality:

> "I am a Cherokee, in the language of my people ... there is a word for land: Eloheh. This same word also means history, culture and religion. We cannot separate our place on the

earth from our lives on the earth nor from our vision and our meaning as a people. We are taught from childhood that the animals and even the trees and plants that we share a place with are our brothers and sisters.

So, when we speak of land, we are not speaking of property, territory, or even a piece of ground upon which our houses stand and our crops are grown. We are speaking of something truly sacred.

Is there a people anywhere in the world that does not revere its homeland? Is there a human being who does not revere his homeland, even if he may not return? We say that reverence for ancestral lands, no matter how insignificant in our own daily affairs or how far from our own homes, is vitally important to the whole of humanity.

The Cherokee people lived for thousands of years in what is now Tennessee, Georgia, and Carolina. In our own history we teach that we were created there, which is truer than anthropological truth because it was there that we were given our vision as the Cherokee people. But President Jackson illegally drove us out of that land, Rom Echota, the centre of our world.

There is no Cherokee alive who does not remember that Trail of Tears, who does not remember and revere that sacred land and Echota.

Today the Tennessee Valley Authority plans to flood the sacred valley that hold our two principal cities, Echota and Tenasi, after which that state is named. The Tellico project would destroy an area of great religious importance, many settlement cities, cemeteries, rich farmlands, forests, and the river itself. This is an unneeded dam which can, at the whimsy of TVA, wipe out thousands of years of history of a great and currently oppressed people. To do so will be an insult not only to the Cherokee, but to all the people in the US and to all humanity. Yes, I am proud enough to state that the history and vision of my people are important to humanity".

We are all parts of the same entity, and the sum total of the parts is greater than the whole. Future trends point to absorption - meaning a loss of identity and the emergence of another group to broaden the poverty base. It has already happened in tribal areas where there are the labourers exploited by employers, shopkeepers, and moneylenders. This need not happen. In North Eastern India, we are considering an area larger than Switzerland with greater intrinsic wealth. We have the technological means to bring about a dynamic and dramatic change in the time span considered, but is a gigantic task of co-operation and communication.

The majority of the people are scattered in tiny remote villages perched amid thick jungles on inaccessible hilltops. Audio-visual equipment has to be taken to them, along with specially designed programmes for them in consultation with peoples' representatives, their chiefs and village councils. The diversity is so great that no centrally planned general programme can hope to be either applicable or properly understood by all.

Terrace (Rice Cultivation)

In some areas of the hill tribes, scattered terrace cultivation is practised. However, compared to jhum cultivation, terrace cultivation is in those slopes of the hills below the villages that are cut out into succession of terraces and are irrigated from the hill streams, whose water is carefully distributed through little channels over every step in the series. Where the slope is fairly gentle, these terraces are sometimes nearly twenty yards in breadth. The average terrace is more than three feet high and is not more than three or four yards wide, and is often built up with stone retaining walls. In some places these stones walls are as much as five feet wide.

An ample supply of water is an absolute necessity for terrace cultivation, and where this is to be had, fields are cut on slopes that are almost precipitous in their steepness. The initial labour required to make these terrace fields is very great, but once made they give less trouble than a jhum.

Terrace cultivation is practised on a large scale, and owing to non-availability of sufficient wet cultivable flat land, terraces are fragmented and the annual yield is minimal, not even enough for the yearly consumption of the villagers. To top it all, there is no proper modern irrigation system in these areas and most of this type of cultivation depends on rainfall.

Paddy is the principal crop of the tribal people and the entire economy depends on the annual produce of paddy. This is because rice is the staple food of the hill people. Besides paddy, there are several items like maize, millet, yams, potatoes and other varieties of vegetables.

Causes of Poverty

Causes of tribal economic backwardness and poverty may briefly be examined. These are:

a) Perpetual Economic Exploitation

From early history till date, the simple hill folk have been exploited economically. Exploitation takes place in several forms; no effective measure was introduced to ease economic backwardness before and during the British rule in the tribal areas of Manipur. There was no financial assistance to the tribal communities to develop their agricultural products.

After India's Independence, at least on paper, many new steps are indicated to ameliorate the economic backwardness of the tribals; however it must be said that the so-called development schemes adopted by the State Government does not percolate to the masses.

b) Absence of Modern Methods of Cultivation and Technology:

For centuries the tribals depended on their simple mode of cultivation. There has been no modernisation in the method of cultivation. The old method of cultivation still continues. Forests products are not enough now. Besides, the forests have been destroyed indiscriminately by a few sections of tribal businessmen for petty financial profits at the expense of the ignorant villagers.

Also tribal agriculture is a gamble of the monsoons. Once crops fail in the hills, there is no other substitute. The Government has not taken up any major step to tackle such an eventuality.

No fertilisers are used. No modern and scientific technology is applied to the tribal areas to take up land irrigation works for cultivation. Double cropping system is a failure in the hill areas. Projects taken up in the tribal areas have all been on paper alone.

c) Absence of Good and Motorable Roads

Even today, there are many villages that cannot be reached by buses and other vehicles. It may be mentioned that the road system in Manipur is one of the worst in North-East India despite the fact that Manipur attained statehood early and is an erstwhile princely state. The condition of communication is just as appalling to put it mildly. Besides, there is no balanced development in the state; rural and hill areas are totally neglected. The brunt of all this shall be borne by the young generation. We have to realise that all social issues spring from exploitation and imbalanced economic development.

d) Absence of Industries

In the tribal areas, there are no industries worth mentioning. The old practice of cottage industries such as weaving and handicrafts are dying out. There are two reasons for this:

i) Lack of capital

ii) Uneconomical mode of production.

The State Government has not taken any effective steps to promote cottage industries in the tribal areas. No financial assistance is forthcoming. Also since the cost of production is high, tribal goods cannot compete with cheap qualities produced in the valley.

Besides, the tribals who live in the hill areas cannot take loans from banks on the plea that the hill men do not have land *patta*. This is ridiculous considering that all other tribals living in North-East India, except for the Manipur tribals, can tak loans. While the tribals in Nagaland, Mizoram, Arunachal and Meghalaya do not have a patta system and can still take loans, why not the Manipur tribals? Why can't the men at the helm of affairs change this policy? The so-called district council is most ineffective. The Government has to review the preva ing system in the State if a healthy society is to be maintained

e) Lack of People's Involvement

In any developmental work people should be involved but as far as Manipur is concerned there is a glaring absence of people's involvement. There is no link between the locals and the Government machinery. Whenever work is taken up in the tribal areas, it centres on the interest of a few individuals. There is too often an unholy alliance between the men at the helm of affairs and individuals. The money to be spent for the villagers is somehow pocketed by people with selfish interests rather than for the public. As long as this practice continues, no substantial work can be taken up in the tribal areas.

f) Political Interference

There is undue pressure and interference from the local politicians and public leaders. Tribal leaders and politicians do not go by issues but by their own immediate needs. All policies are made for gains as well as for the benefit of their close friends and associates.

g) Absence of Peoples' Awareness

Often even the educated tribals become complacent to the existing situation and turn into victims of circumstance. Tribals are not united and every tribe sees to its own selfish ends. Collectively, the tribals do not ask for their share. The Centre gives a number of facilities to the tribals but these do not reach them.

A few Remedial Measures:

- Sense of awareness among the tribals must be created;
- All reservations and facilities given by the Centre must be implemented fully for the tribals and tribals alone;
- There must be time-bound schemes;
- There must be peoples' participation and involvement in implementing tribal schemes and projects. As developmental work must be rooted through the village level and village authorities, beneficiaries must be the deserving families.

- The present agricultural method of cultivation must be improved. The Government must be able to provide alternative technology.

1. Need for Grass-root Planning

Planning is a complex and technical exercise; it involves several stages such as identification of problems, formulation of objectives, determination of strategy and priorities, taxation of targets, allocation of resources, formulation of programmes and projects and their evaluation.

The Constitution of India gives an important role to the State Government in the planning process. The subject of "Social and Economic Planning", for instance, is included in the current list of the Constitution. However, such planning is often more oratory and less realistic. National leaders have attempted several times to introduce planning at the district levels. The Third plan emphasised the role of peoples' participation in local level planning under the framework of democratic decentralisation. But, this practice is non-existent in the tribal areas of Manipur. The district and block planning is non-operational. The State Government does not give any importance to this and there is absolutely no directive from the State Government. Thus progress and development in the tribal areas is slow and funds allocated for the tribals do not percolate to them.

There are several reasons why the Manipur tribals do not get enough share of their own. The followings are the main reasons for poverty of the hill tribals:

1. Total absence of grass-root planning.
2. Central schemes meant for poor villagers are siphoned off and appropriated by Middlemen in connivance with bureaucrats.

2. To Encourage People's Participation

The state/district planning body should include members from local bodies and the existing system be recast. Before finalising any programme or project of the area, it is necessary to take the views:

- of the local people.
- of the village councillors.
- of people with knowledge of the area as well as professional experts.
- of the women.
- of the youth.
- their views should be examined for decisions and implementation.

People's participation should be in every stage of planning - identification of problems, scheme formulation, strategy setting, monitoring and review and not only at the time of plan finalisation.

3. *No Faculty Fund Allocation*

Only a meagre share of the state funds is allocated for the hill tribals. Of the total state yearly budget outlay, a mere 27% goes to the development of the tribal areas. Supposedly keeping in mind the density of the population, 73% of the Annual State Budget outlay is spent entirely for the valley people who live in and around 10 sq. miles.

4. *To Remove Ignorance of the Tribals*

No serious effort to eradicate the ignorance of the tribals has been conducted. Mass education and awareness camps in the tribal areas are urgently needed, especially in the interior villages. Such programmes in the form of seminars, awareness camps and education need not be confined only to the headquarters of the district but must penetrate into the tribal villages.

5. *Need for Political Will*

There is a glaring absence of political will. Political leaders because of various reasons do not take steps in this direction. Reasons could be partly due to the selfish motives of certain communities or severe political myopia.

6. *Need-based Planning*

To make any programme and policy meaningful, a systematic need-based planning is very essential especially for the backward areas. The plan can have several time frames: one year, three years, five years and even 10 years. The plan should concentrate on those areas which need to be tackled first and plan accordingly. Grass-root problems can be identified in the meetings of the villagers, village council or from the views given by the social workers or political parties. Most importantly, it is necessary to ascertain the views and opinions of the weaker sections of society as the aim of any planning is to alleviate the needs and poverty of the villagers.

7. *Objectives*

Formulation of objectives is an important aspect of any planning and for this purpose, diagnosis of village problems at the grass-root level is of immense importance. While taking the clues from the State and National planning target, the duty of grass-root planning is to formulate the additional objectives based on the peculiarities of local conditions and area. Though it is the aim of planners to solve all problems, it is not feasible to do so because of financial and organisational constraints. Hence the need for grass-root level planners. They should decide as to what problems need to be tackled and solved. At the village level: poverty, unemployment, improvised cultivation, illiteracy, etc. should be tackled first. Objectives should also be more specific like rehabilitation of the jhumies, housing scheme, horticulture, cash-crops, minimum marketing facilities and proper land use, water management and supplying of improved and alternative technology.

8. *Time Phasing*

All objectives, however well meant, shall not be able to solve problems at the same time because of various reasons. It is therefore, necessary to determine certain problems on priority basis. Certain objectives can be tackled in the long term whereas the others can be solved in the short term; priority selection is, however, not an easy task. It needs prudent and meticulous judgement based on the immediate needs of the local people.

9. *Review*

Planners should review the earlier plans to find out if they were properly implemented or not. If not implemented when necessary, they have to diagnose the causes of failure. In addition, some of the schemes and programmes which were included in the plan but not taken up should also be reviewed for necessary implementation. Together with these, the on-going programmes must be reviewed as an essential part of planning. This will enable planners to record progress, evaluate it, find out the success or failure of schemes and projects and suggest to take up appropriate follow-up action.

10. *Importance of Non-government Organisations (NGOs)*

In other parts of Indian states there are many voluntary organisations that are doing some commendable work. In the North East Indian states, however, the works of the agencies is not as prominent though there are few agencies which have been working in certain areas of the region. Some of the reasons why the NGOs cannot and do not function effectively could be due to:

a) Local peoples' ignorance;

b) Absence and apathy of the funding agencies, both national and foreign;

c) The irrational and unnecessary interference of government & bureaucrats.

The wrong impression given to the men on the job is that the North Eastern Region, particularly Nagaland and Manipur, are insurgency-prone areas and therefore, foreign and national agencies are discouraged and misled. Often, Government machinery, especially the bureaucrats, suspects that such funds, if given, are likely to be diverted to anti-national activities. These assumptions amount to dangerous and unhealthy propaganda.

In order to be at par with the rest of the countrymen and also to partake in an equal share of the mainstream of the country, NGOs should and must be given an opportunity to avail of funds from national and international agencies.

Therefore, the North-East should be opened to both national and international tourists without any restrictions. This will bring about not only humane understanding but also help in the upliftment of the local economy.

As far as the question of Manipur goes, though there are apparently a number of NGOs (particularly in the valley) their presence is not felt in the hills. This could be either due to lack of communication or sheer apathy with respect to tribal interests. The few NGOs working in the tribal areas and hills need to be encouraged to participate more actively.

4

Planning for the Hill Areas of Manipur : A Perspective

- *Dr. E. Bijoykumar Singh*

The mere mention of hills conjures up the image of the natural beauty of forests and its flora and fauna in the undulating hill ranges. It also reminds us of our helplessness in ensuring an uninterrupted flow of benefits of development planning to the hills, be it in the form of development infrastructure even after nearly five decades of planning. As a consequence of this shortcoming, the way of life of the tribals has remained vulnerable to the steady on slaught of exogenous changes over which they have little control. Their vulnerability has increased and the voice of protest has been reverberating in our hills.

This paper seeks to discuss three aspects of policies pertaining to development of the tribal areas that are synonymous with hill area development in Manipur. First, the broad outline of tribal policy will be highlighted. Second, an attempt will be made to describe the current environment in terms of development of the tribal areas. Finally, the broad outline of plans for tribal areas will be spelt out.

Policy

The five basics propounded by *Jawaharlal Nehru*, the architect of modern India which have guided the direction and content of tribal administration and development are:

1 People should develop along the lines of their own genius and we should avoid imposing anything on them. We should try to encourage in every way their own traditional arts and culture.

2. Tribal rights in land and forest should be respected.
3. We should try to train and build up a team of their own people to carry out the work of administration and development. Some technical personnel from outside, no doubt, will be needed, especially in the beginning but we should avoid introducing too many outsiders into the tribal territory.
4. We should not over-administer these areas or overwhelm them with a multiplicity of schemes. We should work through and not against their own social and cultural institutions.
5. We should judge results not by statistics or the amount of money spent but by the quality of human character that in evolved."[1]

It has been a gigantic task to help the people in order that they may be ready to face the challenges unleashed by the process of development. It has never been clear how people should be made to develop along the lines of their own genius. The genius of the tribal people was invoked to help them to solve their own problems. Unfortunately, no significant dent could be made on their way of life, which proved to be incompatible with economic development. According to the Approach paper of the Ninth Five-Year Plan, efforts are to be made to protect the tribal economy against threats from the external markets.[2] The paper also talks of the need of formulating a national policy for tribal development. The emphasis now is on education, health and employment. Education will be given top priority, as it is the most effective instrument in empowering them. However, the kind of education that needs to be imparted to them should be consistent with their milieu, their genius and special needs. These statements, even after five decades of planning amount to admission of our failure in arousing tribal genius. Nehru's vision of tribal India has remained a dream. The crux of the problem has remained untouched.

1 Dube, S.C. (1989): PP 1-2

2 Planning Commission (1997): p. 94

An important characteristic of tribal societies is their non-competitiveness, where each person has a certain mode of living and standard of life that cannot be changed at the expense of other members of the group. Calculations based on market values are alien to their production decisions.[3]

Development Environment

As per the 1991 Census, Scheduled Tribes constitute 34.41% of Manipur's population. If we go by the results of the 44th round of the National Sample Survey (July 1988-June 1989), 36.3% of the tribal population can be termed as poor with a monthly per capita of Rs 125 in 1998-89.[4] Since this norm is based on calorie intake only, it does not mean affluence sufficient enough to meet the non-calorie requirements of life. Work-force-participation-rate (WFPR) of males is 47.5% while that of females is 37.5%. Their unemployment rates are 2% and 3% respectively.[5]

It has often been argued that the concept of unemployment used in the NSS does not adequately reflect the job market. However, in the absence of any alternative and for the sake of comparability, NSS data has to be used. This may be contrasted with the main source of livelihood of tribal households. The primary source of the livelihood of 56% of tribal households remains agricultural activity. 91% of them are self-employed in primitive agricultural activities, modern agriculture and non-agricultural pursuits.[6] Shifting cultivation constitutes 87% of the primitive agricultural activities. Their dependence on forests can be measured by the percentage of households reporting collection of minor forest produce during the preceding 30 days. 79% of tribal households reported collection from forest with an average value of collection per household equivalent to Rs 121.58. 6% of households reported wage employment in forests during the last 30 days.[7]

3 Planning Commission (1981): p. 5

4 Department of Statistics (1994b), p. 42

5 Ibid; p. 46

6 Ibid; p. 50

7 Ibid; p. 63

The average area per household is 0.91 hectares with 93% of ownership holdings concentrated in the 0.01 hectares -2.02 hectares size class. Here, ownership of land means not only permanent heritable possession of land but also long-term possession of land distributed by the local chieftain or village council.[8] The average value of assets per tribal household is Rs. 27,700. Only 0.5% of households reported outstanding dues and the average amount of dues outstanding per household works out to Rs. 9.00[9].

The asset base, sources of livelihood and unemployment rates indicate that tribals in Manipur are trapped in a low-level equilibrium. They are marginally above the poverty line and have no investible resource with which they can escape from this trap.

What have we done to improve their lot? The following table gives an idea of the infrastructural developments in the tribal areas.

TABLE - 1

Percentage of villages reporting specified infrastructural development during the past 5 years.

Sl. No.	*Infrastructure*	*Tribal Majority village*	*Non-tribal majority village*
01..	School buildings	53.5	47.7
02.	Dispensaries	6.5	2.5
03.	Link Roads	30.8	42.2
04.	Electrical connections	12.3	14.4
05.	Drinking water	25.9	20.3
06.	Irrigation (medium/minor)	0.9	2.5

Source : Department of Statistics (1994a), p. 42.

8 Ibid; p. 67

9 Ibid; p. 75

The index of infrastructural development in tribal majority village is 1.99 and non-tribal majority village is 1.296. Our ranks among Indian States are 16 and 17 respectively.[10] Sikkim with 3.856 and Gujarat with 3.671 has the highest index among tribal majority villages and non-tribal majority villages respectively.

TABLE - 2

Gives the nature of availability of important facilities within the specified distance.

Facility	*Tribal majority villages*	*Non-tribal villages*
1 All weather road *(2 km)*	33.4	56.8
2 Post Office *(2 km)*	11.1	37.3
3 Market *(2 km)*	3.0	16.0
4 Fair Price Shop (within village)	7.9	10.7
5 Supply depot of agricultural input *(5 km)*	40.5	12.0
6 Primary School *(2 km)*	91.2	53.6
7 Veterinary dispensary *(5 km)*	53.1	41.3
8 Primary health centre/Sub-centre *(2 km)*	2.9	29.0
9 Child feeding nutrition center	11.5	15.0

Source : Department of Statistics (1994a), p-35.

The index of availability of facilities works out to 2.546 for tribal majority villages and 2.737 non-tribal majority villages. The corresponding ranks are 14 and 16. The highest figures are 4.885 for Gujarat and 5.914 for Sikkim respectively.[11]

Land constitutes the core of tribal assets. However there has been a gradual reduction in community land, i.e. land put to common use for the entire village community such as land for

10 Department of Statistics (1994b), p. 43

11 Department of Statistics (1994a), p. 36.

grazing, playgrounds, *panchayatghar*, etc. 40% of the tribal majority villages in Manipur reported a decrease in community land during past 5 years. It was the highest in India. Tribal households accounted for 12.8% of the decrease and the rest was attributed to government/public/private bodies.[12]

Regarding shifting cultivation, which is the dominant mode of cultivation in the tribal areas of Manipur, 86.35% of tribal majority villages reported shifting cultivation and in 77.3% of the tribal majority villages, the majority of the households were not practising settled cultivation.[13] It is interesting to note that 98.4% of tribal majority villages not practising settled cultivation (by majority of households) reported that the government has not taken any step to introduce settled cultivation.[14]

Those who continue to support shifting cultivation in tribal areas claim that the tribals take measures against soil erosion as a result of which the system can regenerate itself. However, the survey found that 99.3% of the tribal majority villages practising shifting cultivation do not take any anti-soil erosion measures. Only 0.7% took measures other than terracing and contour bunding.[15]

What have we done in the field of education? 5% of the tribal majority villages have no schools. There are primary schools in 53.8% of the villages. Middle schools are only available in 1.3% Higher Secondary schools are available in 10.5%. Only 1% of the villages have all three - primary, middle and higher secondary schooling facilities.[16]

The findings of the 44th round of the NSS indicate that not much has been done in the hill areas of Manipur. The people's perception of government as a supportive agency, rather than an interfering agency, has not emerged. Basically, we have a system that has been completely bypassed by planning. The limited

12 Ibid; p. 39.

13 Ibid; p. 40

14 Ibid; p. 41

15 Ibid; p. 41

16 Dept. of Statistics (1994a), p.; 5218.

interaction with the market has been able to abort the diffusion process. Liberalisation has generated more challenges.

Outlines of Development Policy

The one major defect of our policies for tribal area development has been our obsession with technocratic options. Decisions made by tribal households are influenced by deep-rooted social customs. Social bonds are much stronger than their urbanised counterparts. Decisions that appear to be inefficient and counter-intuitive may not be so if the bigger social matrix is taken into consideration. Unless we understand this matrix, it will be almost impossible to influence the way of living among tribal households. One such example is the apparent failure of policies made to control shifting cultivation. There is a bigger socio-economic decision matrix that makes a village opt for shifting cultivation as the dominant mode of cultivation.

Technical aspects like unsuitability of soil, slope of the fields, etc. form only a smaller subset of the decision matrix. Not all villages have the same propensity to opt for this mode of cultivation. The intensity of this propensity will have significant influence on the success or otherwise of anti-shifting cultivation policies. The offshoot of this argument is that it will be more productive to invest the resources in villages with a higher propensity for going in for shifting cultivation as the dominant mode of cultivation. The argument in favour of a more comprehensive analysis can be extended to all decisions made by tribal households.

In this context, no other policy has as much potential as education because education will be a key input in the decision matrix. The tribals are the best judges of their own development. Education can dovetail their developmental inspirations in the national perspective. This process of dovetailing is essential for the smooth implementation of policy programmes.

The bifurcation of tribal areas into smaller States/UTs is definitely not the answer. Bifurcation simply duplicates. The planning process has failed to deliver the goods and this is not because of the inaccessibility of tribal areas. It is likely to fail even when planning is brought to their doorstep simply because planning still cannot incorporate the bigger dimensions of the tribal decision matrix. Bifurcation need not change this matrix and its internal structure.

There is also a sense of urgency because of the threat to the federal structure of the nation. We cannot afford more failure on this front. Besides, it may be ages before we can awaken the tribal genius. Hence with the emphasis on education, every possible effort should be made to understand the multi-dimensional decision matrix of tribals. Until this is done, everything else will seem like a mere scratch on the surface. Planning for the development of tribals in the hill areas can be considered a challenge for developmental economists.

References

1. Department of Statistics (1994a): *"A Note on Some Important Characteristics of villages in Tribal areas"* Sarvekshana Vol. XVIII, No.1, Ministry of Planning & Programme Implementation, Govt. of India.

2. Department of Statistics (1994b): *"A Note on Survey of Life and Economy of Scheduled Tribes in India: NSS 44th Round (July 1988 - June 1989)"* Sarvekshana Vol. XVII, No.4, Ministry of Planning, Government of India.

3. Dube, S.C. (1989): *"Nehru and Tribal India"* Paper presented in "A Conference on Nehru & Tribal Wealth", March 16th & 17th, Ministry of Welfare, Government of India.

4. Planning Commission (1981): *"Report on Development of North-Eastern Region" National Committee on the Development of Backward Areas"*, Government of India.

5. Planning Commission (1997): *"Approach paper to the Ninth Five-Year Plan (1997-2002)"*, Government of India.

5

Annual Tribal Sub-Plan (TSP): Its Salient Features

The Tribal Sub-Plan area of Manipur covers more than 90% of the total geographical area of the state. Out of total eight districts in the state, five are in the hills, occupying 20,089 sq. kms. The tribal population of 6,32,173 persons distributed in the five hill districts and in the three valley districts are as indicated in the table below. According to the 1991 population census, the Scheduled Tribe population in the state increased by 62.94% over the 1981 population figures. The Scheduled Tribe population constitutes 34.41% of the total state's population of 18,37,149 persons according to the 1991 population census. The table shown below indicates the distribution of population in districts as per the 1991 census.

Valley

Name of the District	*Area in sq. km*	*POPULATION*			*Total State*
		S.C.	*S.T.*	*General*	
1	*2*	*3*	*4*	*5*	*6*
Imphal	1299(p)	22,764	33,900	6,54,597	7,11,261
Thoubal	409(p)	11,044	2,844	2,80,070	2,93,958
Bishenpur	530	2,333	9,575	1,68,865	1,80,773
TOTAL	**2,238**	**36,141**	**46,319**	**11,03,532**	**11,85,992**

Source: Directorate for Development of Tribals and Backward Classes, Government of Manipur.

Hills

Name of District	Area in sq. km.	POPULATION			Total State
		S.C.	S.T.	General	
1	2	3	4	5	6
Senapati	3,271	172	1,75,206	33,028	2,08,406
Tamenglong	4,391	33	83,332	. 2,913	86,278
Churachandpur	4,570	301	1,64,709	11,174	1,76,184
Chandel	3,313	237	50,729	10,048	71,014
Ukhrul	4,544	221	1,01,878	7,176	1,09,275
TOTAL	20,089	968	5,85,854	64,339	6,51,157
GRAND TOTAL	22,327	37,105	6,32,173	11,67,871	18,37,149

The main occupation of most of the tribal people is cultivation. 92% of the total scheduled tribe families living in the TSP area are cultivators and about 72% of them still depend on jhum cultivation. Out of the total 22,237 sq. kms. in the state, an area of about 1,800 sq. kms. is reported to be under jhum cultivation. With the increase in population, the jhum cycle has come down to 3/4 years in comparison to last cycling of 5/6 years.

The TSP area of the state is still marked by lack of communication facilities and other amenities conducive to generating a stable economy for its inhabitants, i.e. the tribal people. As a result of which, despite the best efforts of the government during the past Five-Year plans, a large number of tribal families are still living below the poverty line. According to a survey conducted all over the state in the latter half of 1988, it was observed that 45.06% of the total population was below the poverty line. In so far as the Scheduled Tribe people are concerned, the incidence of poverty among them is 56.88%. Therefore, more emphasis needs to be laid on the speedy development of the Scheduled Tribe families in the field of education, social and economic status to enable them to be on par with the mainstream.

Objectives and Strategies

Facts and factors enumerated in the preceding pages determined the objectives and strategies to be adopted for the development of the TSP areas and the tribal people, with due regard to the general strategies adopted during the Ninth Five-Year Plan. The basic objective remains acceleration of socio-economic development of the tribal people, taking into account the existing environment and socio-economic situation prevalent in these areas. The main strategy to be adopted is creation of amenities through infrastructure development schemes, poverty alleviation programmes through income-generating and family-oriented schemes and the encouragement of required resources and amenities.

It is also to be ascertained that more flow of funds are earmarked for the TSP area to achieve the targets. The present flow of fund to the TSP areas is slightly higher than the percentage of population of the Scheduled Tribe people of the state. Furthermore, out of the earmarked amount of cash flow to the TSP areas, a huge sum is kept aside for administrative and overhead charges, thereby leaving only a nominal fund for the implementation of developmental schemes for the hill areas. Moreover, a coordinating body in the state to monitor the activities of the hill areas is yet to be established in the state, without which the progress of hill areas cannot be assessed. Emphasis will be given to the setting up of a coordinating body in the state to monitor all developmental activities that will consist of representatives of all development departments. This will be to ensure the proper implementation of developmental programmes.

Planning Process

Though stress is laid on grass-root level planning, the same is yet to be achieved. One district planning office is posted in each of the five hill districts with a nucleus of supporting staff. Proper reinforcement of staff is essential in order to monitor progress for quicker development of the TSP and tribal people.

District level offices of the tribal development department in the five hill districts were recently opened under the charge of an officer of the rank of deputy director in the department. They have a small supporting staff at their disposal as well. These district officers are entrusted with the implementation of the T.D. programmes for their respective districts and also their periodical monitoring.

The administration of the TSP areas are carried out by the deputy commissioners concerned who on the other hand act as district magistrate. Most of the district level schemes/programmes are implemented by the deputy commissioner concerned, in collusion with the district level officers of the concerned departments along with the block development officers. At the state level, the hill commissioner is the nodal authority who looks after the developmental process of the hill areas.

Since the flow of funds for the TSP areas is still controlled by the concerned development departments, developmental schemes are implemented independently and in isolation in the hill areas. Because of this, there is need for coordination among development departments in order to get a clear picture of the entire developmental activities carried out in the hill areas.

At the village level, there are village authorities and at the district level, there are district councils. The role of these statutory bodies is yet to be brought forward in practical terms though they do carry out some developmental activities. There is a need for coordination between the district councils/village authorities and development departments. At the state level, there is the Hill Areas Committee consisting of all MLAs elected from the hill areas as its members. This is the highest legislative body in the state to oversee the planning and implementati process of developmental schemes/programmes for the hill areas.

Shifting (jhum) cultivation is still practised in the TSP area. This is one of the major factors responsible for the deterioration of forests and upsetting the ecological balance. Every year, about 900 sq. kms. is cut and burnt because of jhum cultivation. With the increase in population and reduction of soil fertility, the jhum cycle is reduced to 3-4 years from the earlier 5-6 years. Subsequently, the intensity of cultivation is on the increase leading to severe degradation of the environment itself. Though, several schemes have been taken up by the state government for the rehabilitation of jhumia families, the outcome is unsatisfactory. Assistance from the Centre is needed to set up a time-bound programme. Although necessary steps are taken by the horticulture, agriculture, forest and other related departments to tackle this problem, because of too few available resources, such a big problem could not be solved. The absence of individual ownership of land in the hill areas adds to the problem. A suitable land tenure system has to be introduced to bring in individual ownership to improve the land.

Credit and Marketing

The lack of proper marketing facilities for the tribal deprives the tribal farmers from getting their fair share of produce. Different measures are taken by the State Government through concerned departments to create suitable marketing facilities for the produce but the desired result is yet to be achieved. During the Eighth Five-Year Plan, the state government proposed to open regulated markets in each district to ensure remunerative prices to the farmers. The Manipur Tribal Development Corporation Limited, a state government undertaking, is also being entrusted with the marketing of some agricultural produce from the hill areas. The tribal development department will provide the funds for this.

Though branches of commercial banks and state-level cooperative banks have been opened in the hill areas, credit flow to the hill areas is still not satisfactory. There are certain reasons for this. First, from the borrower's point of view, the tribal people are unable to get a higher loan since they cannot provide collateral security. Land in the sub-plan area is yet to be surveyed and people are unable to make good use of their only property, i.e. land. On the other hand, due to the low rate of repayment of loans earlier extended to the tribal people, banks are reluctant to extend fresh loans to them. The only possible suggestion that could be made is for financial institutions to relax the lending rules as far as the Scheduled Caste and Scheduled Tribe people are concerned.

Protective and Anti-exploitative Measures

Article 16 of the Constitution emphasises the special responsibility of promotion with care for the educational and economic interests of the weaker sections of society, particularly Scheduled Castes and Scheduled Tribes to protect them from social injustice and exploitation. The Constitution provides adequate authority to a state in order that they do indeed achieve these objectives.

Tribal development is based on a two-dimensional approach. (i) Protection of SC/STs through legal and administrative support, and (ii) Promotion of developmental programmes through planned efforts. The following are carried out by the State Government as protective and anti-exploitative measures for the SC/ST in the state.

For the protection of SC/ST through legal and administrative support, the state government has set up special courts under the provision of the SC and ST (Prevention of Atrocities) Act, 1989 even though there has been no case of atrocity in the state so far. Manipur is probably one of the few states in the country that is not plagued by such a social evil. Atrocity on SC/STs by the non-SC/STs in the true sense of the term is practically nil in Manipur. There are stray incidences of crime among the SCs and STs that are commissioned not on caste considerations. However, as mentioned above, the state government under section 14 of the said Act, has declared the court of district sessions judges, Manipur East, as the special court that covers the districts of Imphal and Ukhrul and appointed additional public prosecutor for special court, Manipur East. Similarly, the court of district and sessions judges, Manipur West has been declared as the special court for Manipur West that covers the Senapati, Tamenglong, Churachandpur, Chandel, Thoubal and Bishenpur districts of Manipur and appointed public prosecutor as the special public prosecutor for special court, Manipur West to try cases under the said Act. The District Magistrate and the district superintendent of police have been suitably instructed to take protective measures if there is any immanent threat of atrocities on STs and SCs. Suitable measures are taken on all the religious and social functions held in the SC and ST areas and in various elections. Further, the provisions of the Act are translated into the five major tribal dialects and published in the local dailies for the ST and SC communities in order to publicise the provisions of the Act. This is to make them avail of the facilities provided to the victims/relatives under this Act. The department has made a provision in its budget in the form of funds to provide financial assistance to the victims.

As mentioned earlier, most of the tribal people reside in the five hill districts in concentrated blocks, except for a small tribal population that is in the valley. Out of the total tribal population of 6,32,137 persons, 5,85,854 STs people reside in the tribal sub-plan areas and the remaining 46,319 ST persons reside in the three valley districts. In most of the cases, the land belongs to the tribal chiefs. There are restrictions on transfer of land by a tribal to a non-tribal. There is a provision in Section 158 of the MLR & LR Act, 1960, restricting the transfer of land belonging to tribals to a non-tribal.

Money-lending is a common practice in the tribal areas. But most of the borrowing is usually in the form of food grain within the village itself that is similarly returned in kind after the harvest.

The tribals are allowed to brew their traditional liquor for social and religious purposes. This practice is kept outside the preview of the prohibition. No country liquor distillery has been introduced in the state so far. Distillation and sale of country liquor and Indian-made foreign liquor have been completely banned in the tribal areas.

The forest policy is still given emphasis as is laid down in the Seventh Five-Year Plan. Development of Minor Forest Produce (MFP) both indigenous and exotic have also been given due importance. Out of total area of 22,327 sq. kms. of the state, the hill areas of the state covers 20.089 sq. kms. The area covered by forest is 15,154 sq. kms. Of this, 1,463 sq. kms. are reserved forests, 4,171 sq. kms. are protected forests and the remaining 9,520 sq. kms. are not in any classified area. The tribal population mostly spreads over the five hill districts where the terrain in general is inhospitable and less productive. Shifting cultivation is traditionally the most important source of livelihood for most of the tribal people. The people living in the hill areas mainly rely on forests for their livelihood. Sustenance by way of food, housing material, cooking fuel, cattle fodder, etc. is all drawn from the forest. They also satisfy their deep-rooted sentiments and in times of distress like famine or floods, the forest is their last hope. The problem of forest conservation and protection cannot be separated from the lives of forest dwellers and the local population. Therefore, the forest policy adopted by the state government emphasises the safeguarding of the customary rights and interests of the tribal people. Forestry programmes pay special attention to the following points:-

i. Protection, regeneration and optimum collection of MFP along with institutional arrangements for the making of such products;
ii. Taking up departmental logging to wean away the middlemen and improve the lot of the tribals and the condition of the forests;
iii. Department of forest villages on par with the revenue villages;
iv. The taking up of more family-oriented schemes to improve the lot of the tribal people;
v. Understanding integrated area development programmes to meet the needs of the tribal economy in and around forest areas including the provision of alternative sources of domestic energy on a subsidy basis to reduce the pressure on the existing forest area;
vi. Taking up of forestry schemes which would give top priority to poverty alleviation programmes with ecological requirements; and
vii. To increase awareness among school-going children and villagers by adopting the school nursery and village nursery.

The existing pattern of reservation of 31% of vacancies in both direct recruitment and for promotion in government offices and semi-government institutions for the Scheduled Tribes will continue. All heads of departments/officers are instructed to strictly follow rules of reservation. By and large, the tribal population of Manipur is well represented in government and semi-government institutions.

Financial Framework

During the Eighth Five-Year Plan, 1992-97, the total state plan outlay was agreed at Rs 979 crores out of which Rs 433.17 crores was the identified flow of funds to the TSP areas. This accounted for 44.25%. The allocation of funds for the TSP areas during the Eighth Five-Year Plan was on the higher side considering the need for quicker development of the TSP areas and tribal people. During the year 1992-93, the actual flow of funds to the tribal sub-plan areas was Rs 52.25 crores, which was 38.47% of the total state expenditure on plans. Special assistance from the Centre to the TSP areas during the same year was Rs 434.48 lakhs. During the year 1993-94, the flow of funds to the tribal sub-plan areas was Rs 66.78 crores as against the total actual expenditure on state plans of Rs 184.78 crores. This accounts for 36.19% of the total expenditure. During the year 1994-95, the anticipated expenditure under the state plan was Rs 214.50 crores of which the anticipated expenditure in the tribal sub-plan areas was Rs 82.25 crores. This accounts for 38.34% of the total anticipated expenditure. During 1995-96, an amount of Rs 300 crores was agreed to for the state plan outlay out of which Rs 116.86 crores will be the identified flow of funds to the tribal sub-plan areas. This accounts for 38.95%.

The approved outlay/expenditure under the state plan and under the flow of funds to the tribal sub-plan areas during the Eighth Five-Year Plan along with the outlay/expenditure under special central assistance for the tribal sub-plan during this period were as indicated in the table below :

STATEMENT SHOWING SECTOR-WISE FLOW OF FUNDS TO THE TRIBAL SUB-PLAN AREAS DURING THE 8TH PLAN 1992-97

Sl.	Sector of Development	8th Plan 1992-1997		1992 - 1993		1993 - 1994		1994 - 1995		1995 - 1996	
		Total State Plan	*Flow to T.S.P.*	*Total State Plan*	*Flow to T.S.P.*	*Total State Plan*	*Flow to T.S.P.*	*Total State Plan*	*Flow to T.S.P.*	*Total State Plan*	*Flow to T.S.P.*
1.	Agriculture and allied services	91.49	44.49	19.47	8.08	18.88	8.35	21.06	9.12	26.63	13.05
2.	Rural Development	15.30	5.25	3.66	1.10	3.68	1.27	4.55	1.52	12.97	6.90
3.	Special area Programme	-	-	-	-	-	-	-	-	-	-
4	Irrigation & flood Control	177.00	45.62	28.61	7.76	39.92	12.13	41.63	14.17	52.52	31.08
5.	Energy	186.65	142.24	20.27	13.13	32.16	20.84	35.78	25.43	50.00	23.16
6.	Industries & Minerals	39.80	5.19	6.92	1.14	8.20	1.20	9.58	1.54	9.41	2.27
7.	Transport	160.60	94.25	20.65	8.05	25.20	9.76	33.69	14.08	43.28	23.61
8.	Communication	-	-	-	-	-	-	-	-	-	-
9.	Science, Tech. & Environment	5.00	1.00	0.86	0.17	0.84	0.20	1.04	0.26	1.20	0.30
10.	General Economic services	16.94	8.83	3.62	2.04	3.26	1.69	3.79	2.81	13.58	2.39
11.	Social services	260.40	77.85	26.99	10.40	46.83	10.38	56.55	12.15	80.52	12.40
12.	General services	25.82	7.45	4.75	0.38	5.55	0.96	6.83	1.90	8.39	1.58
13.	Special Development Fund	-	-	-	-	-	-	-	-	1.50	-
	GRAND TOTAL	**979.00**	**433.17**	**135.80**	**52.25**	**184.53**	**66.78**	**214.50**	**82.25**	**300.00**	**166.86**

Statement Showing Sector-wise Special Central Assistance to Tribal Sub-plan (TSP), 1992-1997.

Sl.	*Sector Development*	*8th Plan 1992-97 outlay*	*1992 -93 actual expn.*	*1993 -94 actual expn.*	*1994 -95 antici-pated expn.*	*1995 -96 prop-osed outlay*
1	2	3	4	5	6	7
01.	Agriculture & allied services	680.00	78.35	68.20	155.70	159.00
02.	Village & small industries	145.00	22.60	7.76	16.74	25.90
03.	Education (including Ashram school)	495.00	125.63	153.69	76.15	111.00
04.	Water Supply	25.00	5.33	2.00	30.24	20.00
05.	Medical & Public Health	137.00	36.24	32.08	20.85	21.00
06.	Housing	335.00	80.01	75.08	83.74	32.00
07.	Communication	205.00	19.37	27.33	63.67	40.21
08.	Others	253.00	66.95	45.59	35.72	57.89
	Grand Total	**2275.00**	**434.48**	**411.73**	**432.81**	**467.00**

Sector-wise scheme details are shown below. The total approved outlay and the flow of funds to the sun-plan areas during the Eighth Plan were as follows:

AGRICULTURE

The main crops in the state are rice, wheat, pulses, oilseed, etc. and the thrust is on scientific production of crops. Maize is the second major crop after rice that is cultivated in the hill areas and the importance of its production has been emphasised during the 8th plan period. Augmenting agricultural production and achieving the target for food grain production can be achieved through:

- A slight shift in the strategy of agriculture production.
- By pumping in a requisite quantum of inputs.

- By making sure that upto-date technology in the hill areas is extended.

During the Eighth Plan, an amount equivalent to Rs 18.80 crores was agreed to under this sector of development of which the estimated flow of fund to the tribal sub-plan areas was Rs 4.85 crores which accounts for 25.79% to the total agreed outlay under this sector.

HORTICULTURE

Under this sector of development, the main thrust is on the increase of horticultural production in order to improve the economic condition of the tribal people in the hill areas. The vast area covering the hill areas of the state would be suitable for the cultivation of tropical and sub-tropical and also for temperate fruit production. The targeted fruit production by the end of the Eighth Five-Year Plan, was 1.00 lakh M.T.

During the Eighth Plan period, an amount of Rs 4.68 crores was earmarked as the flow of funds towards the tribal sub-plan areas against the total outlay of Rs 5.20 crores under this sector, which accounts for 90% of the total agreed outlay of the sector.

SOIL CONSERVATION

(a) Horticulture:

The tribal sub-plan area covers about 9/10th of the total geographical area of the state where jhum cultivation is still practised. The target of the Seventh plan was to treat 10,000 hectares of jhum land under the soil conservation programmes, against which only 4,630 hectares could be treated.

During the Eighth Plan, an amount of Rs 6.32 crores was the estimate flow of funds to the tribal sub-plan areas against the total agreed outlay of Rs 7.02 crores which accounts for 90.03% of the total agreed outlay under this sector.

(b) Forest:

Large-scale deforestation because of jhum cultivation, non-scientific agricultural use and over-grazing of the hill slopes has resulted in ecological breakdown. This over-exploitation has resulted in a loss of soil productivity, drought conditions, flood and siltation, etc. To check these, afforestation of 8940 hectares in the hill areas was carried out during the Seventh Plan. Under this programme, 270 jhumia families were rehabilitated.

During the Eighth Five-Year Plan, an amount of Rs 4.75 crores was earmarked as the flow of funds to the tribal sub-plan areas as against an agreed outlay of Rs 4.98 crores of this sector.

ANIMAL HUSBANDRY AND DAIRY

The programmes taken up under this sector of development for the hill areas are, (i) strengthening of A.I. centres, (ii) subsidy to tribal families for poultry, piggery programmes, etc. (iii) animal healthcare, (iv) self-employment programmes, etc. For the implementation of these programmes in the hill areas, an amount of Rs 5.17 crores was earmarked against the total agreed outlay of Rs 12.80 crores under this sector, which accounts for 40.39% of the total agreed outlay.

FISHERIES

Major programmes taken up in the hill areas under this sector of development are, (i) assistance to tribal pisciculturists, (ii) establishment of FFDAS, (iii) development of cold-water fisheries, etc. For the implementation of the above programmes in the hill areas, an amount of Rs 3.25 crores was earmarked as the flow of funds against the total agreed outlay of Rs 8 crores, which accounts for 40.62% of the total agreed outlay under this sector of development.

FORESTRY AND WILDLIFE

Major features under this sector of development are, (i) increasing in the tree coverage in the state to a minimum of 66.6% of the geographical area especially on denuded and unproductive lands, (ii) meeting the requirements of fuel wood, fodder, minor forest produce and small timber by launching massive social forestry programmes with an emphasis on motivating the tribal people, (iii) controlling of shifting cultivation without hurting the sentiments of the tribal people, and (iv) ensuring a close linkage between the forestry programmes and welfare programmes for the tribals and other communities traditionally dependent on forests.

During the Eighth Plan, an amount of Rs 10.30 crores was earmarked for the tribal sub-plan areas as against the total agreed outlay of Rs 23 crores which works out to 44.78% of the total agreed outlay.

CO-OPERATION

Under this sector of development, programmes to provide assistance to various tribal co-operative societies like handloom cooperative, cotton cooperative, sugarcane cooperative societies etc, are chalked out. During the Eighth Plan, Rs 1.75 crores was earmarked for the implementation of the above programme in the hill areas against a total agreed outlay of Rs 5 crores, which is 35% of the total agreed outlay.

RURAL DEVELOPMENT

Under the sector of development, IRDP is taken up. The DWCRA and TRYSEM schemes are sub-schemes of IRDP programmes. Taken up under this scheme are training, A.H., agriculture, M.I., etc. with an objective to assist the selected families of the target group in rural areas to enable them to cross the poverty line by taking up self-employment ventures. The concurrent evaluation report reveals that the assets created under the IRDP are not properly maintained. The immediate reason being the shortage of funds. In the state, there are more than 1.40 lakhs families living below the poverty line of which 0.42 lakhs are tribal families. In order to assist them, Rs 14 crores will be required at the minimum. It is also worth mentioning that credit facilities in the hill areas are inadequate. In fact, the banks are quite reluctant to participate in the implementation of the programmes under IRDP. Hence, implementing agencies are compelled to implement the schemes without loan component. For this reason, the subsidy component has to be increased. During the 8th Five-Year Plan, 1992-97, the target was to cover

26,500 tribal families with an allocation of Rs 1.96 crores against the total agreed outlay of Rs 4.50 crores.

MINOR IRRIGATION

Minor irrigation plays a very important role in the development process especially for the hill areas. During the 8th Plan, more emphasis was laid on the extension of minor irrigation activities in the hill areas as follows:

i) To reduce heavy soil erosion in the hills, the practice of jhum cultivation was to be discouraged and more area under permanent cultivation would be created with assured irrigation facilities.

ii) By constructing permanent diversion structure and lift irrigation scheme facilities for the implementation of multiple cropping and revitalisation of the permanent irrigation terraces already constructed would be taken up. Assured irrigation would be provided for the introduction of HYV crops in the terrace fields with proper inputs i.e. fertilisers, pesticides and capital for land development etc.

An amount of Rs 9.25 crores was earmarked for the hill areas as the flow of funds as against the total agreed outlay of Rs 25 crores under this sector of development, which accounts for 37% of the agreed outlay during the Eighth Plan.

POWER

Under this sector, providing electricity to rural areas was taken up. During the Eighth Five-Year Plan period, it was proposed to cover all the remaining tribal villages for achieving 100% village electrification in the hill areas and as well as for the state as a whole. To achieve this, an amount of Rs 141.09 crores was earmarked for the tribal sub-plan areas against a total agreed outlay of Rs 185.35 crores, which accounts for 76.12% of the total. **Detailed financial outlay and expenditures and physical targets and achievements in the tribal sub-plan areas are shown respectively in the statement TSP-I and TSP-II.**

VILLAGE AND SMALL INDUSTRIES

Under this sector of development, programmes like incentive to SSI units, handloom units, handicrafts units, etc. are taken up in the hill areas. In the handloom sector, 209 societies in the hill areas were given various assistance like share capital, managerial subsidies, modernisation of handlooms, construction of work sheds, etc. Besides, individual weavers were also provided with assistance in kind, training programmes, etc. Under this sector of development, the divisible outlay as agreed to during the Eighth Five-Year Plan was Rs 6.94 crores of which the flow of funds to the tribal sub-plan areas was Rs 1.67 crores, which accounts for 24.06% of the total agreed outlay of this sector.

SERICULTURE

There is plenty scope for sericulture in the hill areas of the state and for this purpose adequate emphasis is laid on the development of this sector in the tribal sub-plan areas. Extensive culture of oak tussar, mullberry, eri was proposed to be taken up during the Eighth Plan. For the implementation of all these programmes, an amount of Rs 3.52 crores was earmarked for the tribal sub-plan areas against a total agreed outlay of Rs 8.80 crores in this sector, which is 40% of the total agreed outlay.

ROADS AND BRIDGES

Road communication plays a very vital role in the developmental process, particularly in the hill areas. A good network of road communication system is required for the socio-economic development of the tribal people, a task that is yet to be achieved. The road length per 100 sq. kms. in the hill areas varies from district to district. The table below indicates the same for the tribal sub-plan areas:

i)	Ukhrul	-	9 kms.
ii)	Tamenglong	-	8 kms.
iii)	Senapati	-	13 kms.
iv)	Churachandpur	-	13 kms.
v)	Chandel	-	10 kms.

The road length in the state as a whole is 25 kms per 100 sq. kms. of area which when compared to 70 kms per 100 sq. kms. of area of the national average is poor. So there is a need for greater emphasis to be laid on the development of the road network in the hill areas. During the 8th Plan, an amount of Rs 93.24 crores was earmarked for the tribal sub-plan areas against Rs 150 crores, which is 62.16% of the total agreed outlay of this sector.

EDUCATION

As per the 1991 population census, the literacy rate in the state is 59.89% against the all India average of 52.11%. Though the literacy rate in the state as a whole in higher than the national average, in the hill districts it varies from 34.8% to 51.57%. As such, a lot has to be done for the educational development of the tribal people.

Various developmental programmes are implemented in the hill areas for the tribal students such as, (i) supply of textbooks and stationery to ST students, (ii) strengthening of existing book banks, etc.

During the Eighth Plan, Rs 17 crores was earmarked for the hill areas against the total agreed outlay of Rs 42 crores under this sector, which accounts for 40.48% of the total agreed outlay.

ADULT EDUCATION

Under this sector of development, programmes for the eradication of adult illiteracy in the age group of 15-35 years are taken up. State adult education project (SAEP) and Rural Functional Literacy Project (RFLP) are set up in the hill areas of the state for the implementation of the adult literacy programmes.

During the Eighth Plan, an amount of Rs 1 crore was earmarked for the hill areas against the total agreed outlay of Rs 2 crores under this sector, which accounts for 50% of the total outlay of this sector.

STATEMENT SHOWING DISTRICT-WISE LITERACY RATE IN THE HILL AREAS

(as per the 1991 population census)

DISTRICT	*TOTAL POPULATION*			*POPULATION IN THE AGE GROUP OF (0 - 6 YEARS)*			*LITERATES*			*LITERACY RATE*		
	Person 2	*Male* 3	*Female* 4	*Person* 5	*Male* 6	*Female* 7	*Person* 8	*Male* 9	*Female* 10	*Person* 11	*Male* 12	*Female* 13
MANIPUR	1837149	938359	898790	306617	155308	151309	916692	560884	355808	59.89	71.63	47.60
SENAPATI	208406	107310	101096	32382	16100	16182	81047	50404	30643	46.04	55.26	36.13
TAMENG-LONG	86278	44593	41685	14427	7398	7029	36039	22289	13750	50.16	59.92	39.67
CHURA-CHANDPURA	176184	91218	84966	29153	14993	14460	85355	50597	34758	58.05	66.38	49.30
CHANDEL	71014	37118	33896	11650	5892	5758	27711	17920	9791	46.68	57.39	34.80
UKHRUL	109275	57997	51278	19106	9842	9264	56391	34724	21667	62.54	72.11	5157

SPORTS AND YOUTH AFFAIRS

Physical education is an important part of a school curriculum. It has been made a compulsory subject from standards - I to X and optional in standards - XI to XII in school. For the effective implementation of the physical education programme in educational institutions, P.E.T. teachers are required. But out of the required number of 776 P.E.Ts, so far only 297 posts have been created and these are posted in selected schools only.

For the implementation of physical education programmes in the hill areas, Rs 3.18 crores was earmarked for the TSP areas against an agreed outlay of Rs 15.50 crores, which is 20.52% of the total agreed outlay in the sector.

MEDICAL AND PUBLIC HEALTH

The approach adopted by the department during the Eighth Five-Year Plan was as follows:

i) Top priority will continue to be accorded to primary healthcare in the context of the national commitment to achieve the goal of "health for all by 2000 AD".

ii) Emphasis will be laid on the consolidation of the infrastructure already in existence rather than on the creation of additional infrastructure.

iii) The prevention and control of AIDS will be taken up on a massive scale with adequate support from the Central Government.

iv) Special emphasis will be laid on the construction of sub-centres, PHCs, CHCs and state hospital buildings and the strengthening and equipping of these institutions in order to ensure their efficient functioning.

v) The main thrust will be on schemes connecting with the prevention and control of diseases through immunisation, school health, etc. During the Eighth Plan, Rs. 6.61 crores was earmarked as the flow of funds to the TSP region against a total agreed outlay of Rs 21 crores under this sector of development, which accounts for 36.24% of the total agreed outlay.

WATER SUPPLY AND SANITATION

Out of the total number of 1,545 tribal villages in the hill areas, 1,344 of them were covered under the safe drinking water programme till the end of the Seventh Plan period. The remaining 201 tribal villages were to be covered during the Eighth Plan. For the implementation of water supply and sanitation programmes in the hill areas, Rs 26.79 crores was earmarked as the flow of funds to the TSP areas against the total agreed outlay of Rs 85 crores, which accounts for 31.52% of the total agreed outlay.

HOUSING

Under this sector of development, three programmes are implemented viz. (i) P.W.D. housing (ii) Police housing and (iii) LSG housing. Under LSG housing, the houses are constructed by the DRDA/PDA and are allotted on a hire-purchase basis. The unit cost of LIG and EWS houses are Rs 20,000/- and Rs 12,000/- respectively. During the Eighth Plan, 500 houses under the LIG and another 750 houses under the EWS scheme were to be constructed for the tribal people. Rs 1.90 crores was earmarked for the TSP areas against the agreed outlay of Rs 4 crores, which accounts for 47.5% of the total outlay under this sector of development.

SOCIAL WELFARE

Programmes like child welfare, the welfare of women and handicapped persons are concentrated on under this sector of development. During the 8th Plan period, the target was to set up 50 and 125 vocational training cum production centres for the handicapped and women respectively. For the implementation of various other developmental programmes under this sector, Rs 0.61 crores was earmarked for the hill areas against a total agreed outlay of Rs 2.50 crores, which accounts for 24.4% of the agreed outlay.

WELFARE OF SC/STS AND OBCS

The programmes implemented under this sector of development are all supplemental in nature to the primary developmental programmes in order to achieve quicker development of the scheduled tribe people in the state. During the Eighth Plan, Rs 3.30 crores was earmarked as the flow of funds to the TSP areas, which accounts for 41.21% of the total agreed outlay under this sector. In fact, out of the total Rs 8 crores, Rs 1.20 crores was earmarked for direction and administration and Rs 1.24 crores for the development of the Scheduled Castes. The remaining Rs 5.56 crores was meant for the development of the Scheduled Tribes. Of this, Rs 3.30 crores went to the TSP areas and the balance of Rs 2.26 crores were used in state-level schemes for the scheduled tribe people.

The major programmes taken up under this sector are

(i) construction of one combined SC/ST girls' hostel at Imphal,

(ii) construction of one combined SC/ST boys' hostel at Imphal and

(iii) construction of one tribal research institute-cum-museum at Imphal.

Each of the girls' and boys' hostels were to have 150 seats of which 105 seats will be reserved for the scheduled tribe students and the remaining 45 seats for the scheduled caste students. Due to scarcity of land in and around the Imphal area, the decision to have a multi-storied building instead for the hostel was taken. Because of financial constraints, these buildings could not be completed within the stipulated time.

NOTES ON SPECIAL CENTRAL ASSISTANCE TO TRIBAL SUB-PLAN

Under the special central assistance to tribal sub-plan, Rs. 22.75 crores was tentatively earmarked during the Eighth Plan for the implementation of various developmental programmes for the scheduled tribe people living in the state. Under economic development schemes, programmes like agriculture/horticulture development programmes, animal husbandry, village and small industries programmes are implemented. For infrastructural development programmes, there were schemes for construction/repair of suspension bridges, wooden bridges, inter-village roads, school/hostel buildings, community halls, etc. Under welfare schemes, programmes like pipe water scheme, financial assistance for medical treatment, conducting of training for tribal youths, etc. are also implemented. The table below indicates the sector-wise outlay/expenditures incurred under special central assistance to the tribal sub-plan areas during the Eighth Plan period, 1992-97:

Sl.	*Sector of*	*8th Plan 1992-97*	*Actuals 1993-94*	*Anti-exp. 1994-1995*	*Proposed 1995-1996*
1	2	3	4	5	6
1.	Agriculture & allied services	6.50	0.482	1.38	1.51
2.	Minor Irrigation	0.30		0.18	0.20
3.	Village & Small Industries	1.45	0.078	0.167	0.26
4.	Education/Art and Culture	4.95	1.139	0.317	0.40
5.	Water Supply	0.25	0.02	0.302	0.25
6.	Medical & Public Health	1.37	0.32	0.208	0.21
7.	Housing	3.35	0.75	0.337	0.32
8.	Communication	2.05	0.273	0.637	0.402
9.	Others	2.53	1.054	0.802	1.068
	TOTAL	22.75	4.116	4.33	4.62

6

Development in the North East Constraints and Prospects

- Rev. (Dr.) J.H. Thumra

I would like to state at the beginning that I shall be writing from the developmental point of view and while concentrating on the constraints and problems and prospects of development in the North-East, I shall try to keep the overall perspective in mind.

Arguably the most important reason for the lack of proper development in the North-East has been the lack of awareness among the people with regard to the basic parameters of development. People here are unaware of developmental processes and of the ideology of development that is currently practiced in this country. They are also unaware of the various government schemes for rural development and of their own abilities and capabilities regarding both of the above.

It may be said this came about because of the imposition, adoption or adaptation (in various forms) of an alien method of government i.e. the Westminster model of parliamentary democracy - as opposed to traditional and indigenous methods of governance. While the rest of the country has had plenty of time not only to adopt this method of government but also to abuse it, we in the North-East have not. We have, so to speak, fast-forwarded from primitive tribal socialism to a perverted form of democracy.

A very obvious reason for under-development in the North-East is the geography of the land. The physical distance from the political, financial and industrial heartland of the country, i.e.

the 'mainland', has had its repercussions. The difficult terrain in these states has not helped matters either.

One resultant factor is the absence or paucity of proper roads, rail, air and water transport and communication facilities. This applies both to links between the North-East and the rest of the country and to links within the region itself. Over and above this are local factors like the fact that the construction of roads and their maintenance in states like Arunachal Pradesh, Nagaland and the hilly areas of Manipur is a much more expensive proposition than it is in the plains.

This results in a vicious circle. Industries are not set up because of the lack of transport and communications and transport and communications are not given priority because of a lack of "economic viability".

Adding to the constraints is the all-pervading sense among the ruling elite of the North-East of trying to "join the national mainstream". There is an unholy trinity that consists of the politician-bureaucrat-businessmen/contractor nexus. Despite the many developmental schemes, the benefits are not percolating to the masses because of this corruption that is prevalent at all levels.

Barring Assam, there is a fallacy that the per capita governmental expenditure in the region is far higher than elsewhere. As a rebuttal, it may be stated: first, there is a vast gap between these states and others that needs to be filled in by paying some extra attention. Second, the Government is never willing to specify exactly how much of this expenditure is for the purpose of security, anti-insurgency, etc.

The unsettled political situation all over the North-East and its strategic position for the country's defence are two additional causes of poor development. What is required is political stabilisation of the situation, both internally and externally. Otherwise, development will continue to suffer while this country continues to wage wars in the Himalayas or the states try to put out bush fires in their own backyards.

One aspect of this instability (internally) is the neglect of the tribals in states where non-tribals constitute a majority of the population, for e.g. Assam and Manipur. This not only hampers their development but can also lead to dire consequences of the sort that is at present occurring in the Bodo areas of Assam.

Another major developmental constraint is the lack of trained manpower to utilise properly the skills of the local people and resources of the region. The entire educational system is in shambles and needs to be overhauled. To take one example: there is the inability of the youth (especially in the tribal-majority states like Nagaland, Arunachal, Mizoram and Meghalaya) to achieve a minimum standard. This minimum standard is required for admission or entrance into higher academic or educational institutions, especially in technical fields. This is happening despite reservations for our people. We do not have to look far for the reasons. At the lower levels, students are weak in English (in most states) and in Mathematics (in all states). This leads to difficulty later on. Those local youths who are proficient in these subjects are lost to the teaching profession as they take up careers in either the Central Services or in the many available technical fields.

A hidden constraint is the moral decline in general of the people. They are unable to either continue the (moral) traditions of the old way of life nor can they conform to the precepts of the "new" religions, e.g. Christianity. This is especially true of the younger generation, who have no worthwhile role models for them to look up to. The result is an identity crisis.

It may be studied as to how far this is true of any society that is in transition from one stage to another society that is in a constant state of flux, whether willingly or unwillingly.

Planning for development in the North-East has also not been sufficient or properly organised. Where planning is undertaken more or less correctly, the implementation has been faulty.

The state governments are more interested in fulfilling the "desires" of the Centre than in properly evaluating their own requirements. As a result, money is spent on 'schemes' and 'projects' that are currently popular at the Centre and not on what is really needed.

The feedback from the people is practically nil and they are not involved in the developmental process. They are not consulted at any stage: be it formulation, implementation, monitoring or evaluation. Traditional village-based authorities have been shunted out or (where made use of, either in original or adapted form, as with the village development boards in Nagaland) they have usually been co-opted into the prevailing structure, which is a non-productive one in any case.

Also in need of examination in this context is the question of how far the political importance of the North-East at the national level and its financial dependence on the Centre have led to warped developmental priorities.

People in the North-East are, by now, used to natural calamities like earthquakes and recurring disasters like floods, but what should be kept in mind is that these are also a major cause of the region's under-development.

A major ecological problem facing the region is deforestation, and this is often the cause of more problems like floods. A slow but steady process of 'eco-cide' seems to have been set in motion, fuelled by ambitious plans for large hydro-electric projects and the like.

Requiring study is the question of whether jhum cultivation as a cause of deforestation is being over-emphasised, while the timber industry is lost sight of. The latter is much more destructive and, moreover, its benefits are reaped only by a few and not by the masses.

Regarding jhum cultivation, it is said that the pressure in terms of increasing population has led to a shortened jhum-cycle thereby leading to further deforestation. However, it is to be noted that much of the pressure on food supplies caused by increased population is met by food imports. The North East is not as self-sufficient in food now as it once was.

Of course, non-optional practices like mono-cropping, etc. are also a constraint in the agricultural field. When talking of improved agricultural practices, we have to keep in mind the fact that these involve such unwanted side effects as those caused by most fertilisers and pesticides. In this context, it is perhaps a good sign that most tribals resist the idea; so that the North-East does not have to suffer later what other parts of the country are suffering now, namely the unwanted and unexpected ill-effects of the so-called green revolution. Industrial pollution has also begun to make its presence felt slowly, both as a result of manufacturing and mining.

Another factor hampering the development process is the increase of consumerism and the new socio-economic stratification. This is inextricably linked up with the imposition of an alien form of government and the corruption and moral decline of the people. This manifests itself in the 'easy money' culture prevalent among the newly emerged elite of all the North-Eastern states.

This new culture is often misunderstood and attacked as the 'Westernisation' of the North-East, an attack on the symptoms but not on the disease. Serious problems, it is admitted, have been caused by the 'new cultures' of drug addiction, alcoholism and moral laxity. Another vicious circle exists here: the government's concern for easy sources of revenue, through granting of liquor licences for example, ultimately takes its toll on the state.

A further development constraint (and a new one) is the state government's inability to absorb any more employees, as it is already bloated and top-heavy. It cannot absorb fresh entrants at different levels as was done up to the mid-1970s in a lavish manner after having emerged as separate political entities.

Also connected to this phenomenon is the new aversion to manual work or entrepreneurial ventures among our youth, who now only desire white-colour jobs.

Both these aspects have serious repercussions on the areas of education and employment. In the long run, this can lead to dissatisfaction that encourages extreme forms of disagreement, for e.g. in the form of the Valley insurgency in Manipur.

The lack of a developed media in the North-East is yet another factor. This leads to paucity of information, both inter-state and intra-state as well as about government schemes and processes, methodology and ideology of development.

A major constraint is the lack of credit and investment in the North-East. The deposit : credit ratio of the banks in the region is perhaps the poorest in the country. Due to lack of foresight, we see such situations as a tribal in Manipur who cannot get a loan from a bank because he has no collateral security to offer. At the same time he cannot mortgage his land because, first, he has no deed to it and second, by law it cannot be alienated. If the method adopted by the village development boards in Nagaland were adopted here it would prove a boon. Instead, we merely complain and then suffer.

All inputs in this region cost more, whether it is human power, capital or material.

The local trained or skilled human resources pool being poor or non-existent, personnel have to be imported from outside. This is at an extra cost, for instance the special North-East allowance paid to central employees. Venture capital does not exist here to the extent that it does elsewhere. There are no native industrialists or entrepreneurs who can afford to lay out large sums. Even the state corporations, etc., are functioning on a smaller scale than their counterparts elsewhere. Despite tax exemptions and lower local duties, everything costs more in the region - from newspapers to cement. One major factor, of course is the high cost of transportation.

There is also the sense among the people of the North-East that their resources are being drained away and that the region is being treated like the colony of an imperialistic and exploitative power. This feeling is prevalent as a result of the fact that no matter what the surplus generated by the resources here it tends to flow out.

An area of development that we may tend to overlook is the place of women in society and their role in the development process. While we in the North-East take pride in the fact that we treat our women better than the rest of the country does, the truth is that we do not.

It is true that dowry deaths and the like is alien to our way of life. However, what has happened is that while we may put our women on a pedestal, we do not give them actual rights. These rights have always been in the hands of man even in matrilineal societies as that of the Khasis in Meghalaya.

Women are still not paid equal wages in many sectors; they still do not have inheritance rights; they are discriminated against even on church bodies; daughters are always given second preference after sons when it comes to education, and so on. Decisions still rest in male hands. Having dealt with some of the many constraints that are hampering development in the North-East, it would perhaps be opportune to suggest tentative solutions. What are the prospects ahead of us? What are the alternatives that we can choose from? What sort of development is it that we want? More important, what sort of development is it that we need? A few aspects of an alternative vision of development are noted below:

So far, development has simply meant the approach of Oliver Twist - "Please, Sir, may I have some more?" Instead of thinking and then asking, we simply desired more of the economic and purely material benefits that went by the name of development.

The first priority, therefore, would be to attempt a more holistic approach to the concept of development. The kind of development we envisage should embrace not just the material aspects of our life. It should also embrace the culture and heritage of our people, the ecology and environment, the spirituality in our lives, the enhanced role of women, the regeneration of our traditional authorities - all these and many more. In sum, we need an alternative to the modernisation ideology that is currently fashionable.

Among the things we need to do is to energise the role played by voluntary organisations or Non-governmental Organisations (NGOs) in the field of development. The government itself has admitted as much and accordingly made the requisite provisions in the Five Year Plans.

Regarding ecological and environmental issues, we need to formulate proper measures. For example, in the name of afforestation, a lot of harm has been done by indiscriminately planting eucalyptus trees everywhere. These are the kind of mistakes we need to avoid. Why can we not plant indigenous species that provide fruit, fuel and fodder instead?

While improving our efforts in the field of agriculture, animal husbandry and horticulture, we need to keep in mind the traditional practices. At the same time, we need to look for viable alternative avenues of employment, as farming alone will not sustain future generations. In the field of healthcare, we need to move away from the doctor-centred and hospital base health culture and opt for a community-based healthcare system instead. At the same time, we need to utilise our traditional and indigenous methods of medicine and their practitioners, e.g. the '*maibas*' and '*maibis*' of Manipur need to be thought of as "medicine men" and not as "witch doctors".

The entire education system needs to be overhauled and streamlined and the present system that produces unemployable graduates needs to be recast. Non-formal and adult education have to be given emphasis and vocationalisation has to be undertaken from around the +2 levels, all the while keeping in mind our actual needs and our resources.

A major component of this alternative vision of development would be the participation of the people and not in just the planning, but in the entire process of development. To achieve this, we require a concurrent renewal and regeneration and (where required) a transformation of the traditional village-based authorities. This would remove a number of constraints.

I have already stated that the lack of awareness among our people is a major handicap to effective development. Therefore, we need to chalk out awareness programmes at all levels and for different sections (e.g. the women), so that our people are able to achieve what is rightfully theirs.

Once we are able to bring back the community and the human being towards the centre of things, we shall be able to achieve a lot. Many of the difficulties so far have arisen because instead of the people being at the helm of things it was the scheme or the project that was the focal point.

If we are able to do all these, we shall have succeeded in removing some of the major constraints that stand in the path of development of the North-East. We will have succeeded improving the prospects of achieving a more rounded and more worthwhile, as well as far more equitable, development of our people.

7

Why Tribal Poverty: Some Tentative Remedies

- Dr. Asok Kumar Ray

It is an irony that wealth and poverty are the two irreconcilable phenomena in history. Since poverty is a structural precondition for wealth, the latter can exist only by throwing the masses to the dismay of poverty.

When we undertake a study of tribal poverty we must guard against the methodological mistake of studying it in isolation. The causal factors of tribal poverty cannot be established unless we link up this phenomenon with the general situation of the poverty of society at large. In other words, we will have to unveil the macro-level (broad social level) causatives of poverty within the framework of which and in relation to which the micro-level (tribal level) causes operate.

Before we approach the issue of tribal poverty, it is necessary to look into the essentials of tribal economy in retrospect. In its ideal condition, tribal economy is basically subsistent in nature. It was meant to be an undifferentiated economy. By virtue of this, there was no room for wealth accumulation in a tribal economy. Unlike the agricultural economy, the former was a non-surplus-yielding economy. In contrast to the agricultural economy, in which peasantisation is a force to reckon with the emergence of a stratified society, tribal economy, though drawing heavily on land-base (which also includes forest) and partly on hunting as the subsidiary mode of livelihood, nevertheless carried a message of equality. But since tribal economy was a land-based one, the ownership of such land is often subject to certain critical questions. Broadly speaking; there are three kinds of land titles. These are land owned by the community; land owned by the chief and land owned by the individual. But the formal status of communal ownership did not rule out the use-right of the individuals nor did the individual's or chiefs' ownership block the use-right of the community at large. While the communal ownership is as such one of the archaic forms of tribal economy; individual ownership or chieftains' ownership has developed in certain specific historical situations and was never aimed at the appropriation of surplus in any case.

While the archaic characteristics of the tribal economy are real, it would be very difficult to find such an ideal in actuality. The present situation, in fact, deserves consideration in the light of state formation because the latter has severely affected the essentials of the archaic characteristics of tribal economy. In our context, we find that if tribal societies were not based on the division of classes there was logically no question of state as such. In this sense, tribal society was a non-state society. It was only by revolutionising the means of production, by the rapid growth of wealth in commerce and industry which led to the concentration of wealth in the hands of a few at the cost of making the masses paupers, that the state came into existence. The rise of the state among the Athenians[1] (which presents a very typical case of state-building in general) is an example in point. But the typical example for Athens apart, state formation in the primitive communal group has followed other alternative courses as well which did not essentially rest upon the conception of a change in the mode of production and the consequent inequality of property. To give it a broad outline, we can designate the Asiatic, the ancient, the feudal and the modern bourgeois mode of production.[2]

In European societies there are four stages in the division of labour and the forms of property. From tribal property to the communal and state property of antiquity, on to the feudal or state property and finally to the modern capitalist property.[3] But in non-European countries, the pre-capitalist social formation (including the Asiatic mode of production) did not follow the linear theory that was applicable in the western context. The pre-capitalist social formation (including the AMP) in fact "stood in contraposition to capitalism".[4] Within the context of the Asiatic mode of production we have seen that the hegemonic role of the state could extract the social surplus at the village-level (tribal level) community, though from a distance. The factors that mediated the appropriation of social surplus by the hegemonic state from the direct producers at the grass-root level are cultural diffusion, conquest and domination. Nevertheless, it was still not feudalism. Unlike the West, the Asian economy did not reach the landed property of feudalism. As R.P. Dutt said, "The conditions of cultivation were not comparable with private property in land and so arose the typical Asian economy of the remains of primitive communism in the village system below and the despotic central government above in charge of irrigation and public works; alongside waste and plunder".[5] It is interesting to note that in the Asiatic states, the structure of the economic elements of society remained unchanged even when there was no change in dynasty. It is this immutability of the Asiatic mode of production that did nothing but reproduce itself.

Commenting on the nature of land system in India, R.P. Dutt, quoting from R. Mukherjee's *Land Problem in India* (1933) opines that "before the British rule, the soil of India belonged to the tribe or its subdivisions - the village community, the clan or the brotherhood settled in the village and never was considered as property of the king."[6] During the Mughal period, the *zamindars* were tax farmers or officials appointed for the sole purpose of collecting land revenue. But the permanent settlement of 1793 brought about a sharp decline of the hitherto communal ownership of land. The old *Zamindars* "were turned into private landlords, possessing some but not all, of the rights of private property in land. For one, the bulk of the rent they derived from the tenants was to be handed over to the government. At the same time, they were made complete masters of the village communities. The present cultivators were transformed into tenants-at-will."[7]

The alternative to the *zamindari* system was the *ryotwari* system under which the government would collect revenue directly from the individual cultivators who were recognised by law as the owners of land they cultivated. This system was introduced to avoid the "disadvantages of the permanent settlement, securing the entire spoils itself without needing to share them with intermediaries."[8] But their right to ownership too was limited by the temporary nature of the land revenue settlements and by the high rate of revenue demanded which they often could not pay.[9] As a result of the high rate of revenue, land therefore actually went to the moneylenders. Thus as R.P. Dutt put it, "landlordism has spread extensively and at an increasing pace in the *ryotwari* areas."[10]

The impact of British rule is said to have "led to the evolution of a new structure of agrarian relations that was extensively repressive ... There arose landlords, intermediaries and moneylenders at the top and tenants-at-will, share croppers and agricultural labourers at the bottom. The new pattern was neither capitalistic nor feudalistic nor was it a combination of the old Mughal arrangement. It was a new structure that colonialism evolved - "it was semi-feudal and semi-colonial in character."[11]

The sword of the *zamindari* system did not spare the equalitarian tribal masses. We have the examples of the tribes of Bihar, Bengal, Orissa, and parts of Madhya Pradesh who were subject to the purges of *zamindars*, moneylenders and *mahajans*. Assam came under the *ryotwari* system after the British annexation and in the permanently settled estates, the plain tribals particularly were subject to exploitation by the *jotdars, dar-jotdars, jaradars* and so on. The influence of *zamindars* and moneylenders was increased thanks to British patronage. With the connivance of the British rulers, the moneylenders, traders and merchants who were mostly outsiders infiltrated into the land of the *adivasis* in Maharastra, notably the Worlis, and established themselves as landlords and gradually all the land possessed by the *adivasis* passed into the hands of such people.[12] In Andhra Pradesh, the British made an agreement with the local *mansabdar* (chief) and restored to him some villages which were leased out by him to the *muttadars* who in turn collected rent for the chief. After the death of *mansabdar*, his successors begun to exploit the tribals in various ways by leasing out the toddy trees (which yield an alcoholic beverage) to the non-tribals. The traders from the plains also started exploiting the tribals by crediting the poor. As against this, the Koya tribe of Andhra Pradesh revolted. After this, the *mansabdar* was deposed and the British government made an agreement with the *muttadars* directly who became powerful people in due course. The Bengal Renaissance leaders tried to commend the foundation of the notorious permanent settlement of 1793 by providing an ideological trench around the new arrangement, which deprived the thousands of the downtrodden and *Harijans*. (This ideological trenching did prove counter-productive though and the famous Santhal rebellion made headway).

The Tenancy Act, 1859 was a step further in the course of exploitation of the farmers. "In Mymensingh the medieval age evils like those of Tonk, Nanker, Bhawali, Khamar, etc. had ploughed the land system and the tribal villages of North Mymansingh were severely affected by this system."[14]

Therefore, it can be profitably concluded that tribal economy under the colonial state has undergone a very serious transition. The peasantisation-force became as real in tribal economy as in the general economy of the country. From here we can lead our discussion to the specific problems of tribal poverty.

1. *Alienation*

In any tribal society, we come across two kinds of alienation - (a) alienation from the land and (b) alienation from the product. Both are in fact inter-related phenomena. Alienation from land is regarded as a very common reason leading to tribal poverty. Whenever there is alienation, there is a simultaneous concentration of land in the hands of someone or the other. In effect, there has been alienation of land (i) from tribal to non-tribal and (ii) from tribal to tribal. Logically therefore, the tribal societies could no longer remain unstratified any more. Land concentration in the hands of the non-tribals (here by non tribals, we mean the rich people like moneylenders, businessmen, etc.) apart, concentration of land even in the hands of the tribals (i.e. rich tribals) is reaching alarming proportions and opening the way for affluence hitherto unknown on the one hand and mass pauperisation on the other.

Alienation from the product is a far more serious problem. The tribal peasants are to produce much gross subsistence value, which is more than what he consumes. Extraction of the surplus labour sometime becomes the core of alienation from the product.

2. **Indebtedness**

Indebtedness is a related phenomenon causing tribal poverty. Because the necessary labour could hardly provide them with subsistence, they would often compel the poor tribals to fall victim to moneylenders and *mahajans*.

At the operational level of production relation therefore, we may examine tribal poverty in terms of the rent, tenancy and credit triangle.

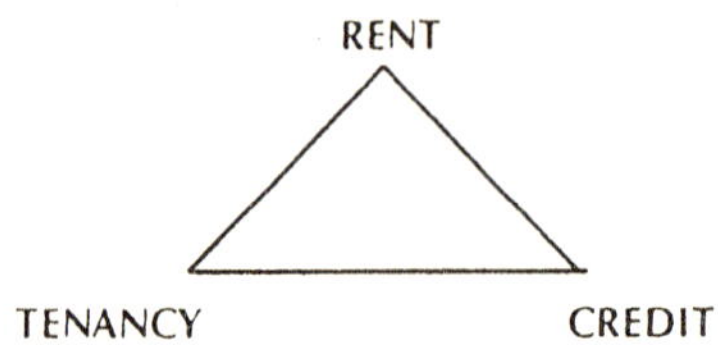

Remedial Suggestions: It will be very difficult to mention in a few words the remedial suggestions to tribal poverty. Objective conditions in which the tribals are to survive are not exactly the same nor are the ecological settings of the different tribals similar. Again, there is a difference in the ideological orientation, organisational level and leadership pattern. Taking all these limitations into consideration, the remedies we can suggest are likely to be highly experimental and tentative in nature.

At the experimental level, we can suggest a healthy land-reform programme as an institutional arrangement. It is unfortunate that even so many years after Independence, the aspect of land reforms has received no serious attention as such.

Immediate steps should be taken to see that land reform measures are judiciously undertaken and that alienation from both land and the product of the land is arrested so that the poor tribal masses can get some sort of relief.

Taking into consideration the fact that tribal farmers have less accessibility to capital inputs and some of the indivisible inputs like irrigation and land improvement measures are beyond the accessibility of small firms, land may controlled by cooperatives instead as a remedial measure. But cooperatives being a workable alternative cannot suit every ecological setting. In the latter case care should be taken so that:

1) Tenancy is defined;
2) There is no intermediary;
3) Alienation from the product is checked;
4) Domination of the small farm is brought under control and
5) The product of the land may have connection with local consumption and local marketing. From the subsistence point of view, commercial production may be discouraged for the time being so that farmers may at least feel inclined to produce that crop which has a connection with their own intake.

Stringent measures should be taken in order to check the moneylender's business by private agencies. Banks and public financial institutions should come forward to help the poor tribal farmers with credit liberalisation schemes. On the other hand, some of unproductive habits of the tribals should be cleaned up so that they can utilise whatever resources they have for productive purposes.

Apart from these institutional remedies, we should not forget that nothing would be fruitful unless the dependency of the tribal poor is reduced. The degree of dependency is too high among the tribals; hence there is all likelihood of the perpetuation of the poverty situation. But in organised relation, the dependency rate is reduced and at some level there can be a stage of no-dependency. And only when the dependency is reduced and/ or the stage of no-dependency is achieved, the poor tribals can effectively negotiate the wealth-poverty dichotomy.

References

1. Marx and Engels, *Selected Works*, Vol-3, Origin of Family private property and State, p. 284
2. Tom Bottomore, *Political Sociology*, B.I. publication, New Delhi, 1983 (Reprint) p. 61.
3. Ibid. p. 61.
4. Review Article by Diptendre Banerjee, *'Lawrence Krader and the Asiatic Mode of Production'* in Society and Change - Quarterly Journal of the Association for Studies in Society and Social Change, Calcutta, Vol. 2, No.1, 1980.
5. R.P. Dutt, India Today, Manishu Granthalaya (P) Ltd., Calcutta, 1985 (Reprint), p. 85.
6. Ibid, p. 222.
7. Bipin Chandra, Amales Tripathy and Barun De, *Freedom Struggle*, National Book Trust, New Delhi. 7th Edn., 1985, p. 17-18.
8. R.P. Dutt, op.cit., p. 234.
9. *Freedom Struggle*, op.cit., p. 18.
10. R.P. Dutt., op.cit., p. 236.
11. *Freedom Struggle*, op.cit., p. 19.
12. Godabari Parulekar, *Adivasis Revolt, The Story of the World Peasants in Struggle*, N.B.A. Calcutta, 1975, p. 42.
13. A.R.N. Srivastava, *Tribal Freedom Fighters of India*, Publication Division, Ministry of Information and Broadcasting, Govt. of India, 1986, p.42.
14. P. Gupta, *Tribal People on Liberation Struggle*, Puthipatra, Calcutta, p. 32.

8

An Aspect of Tribal Poverty and Its Remedy

- Dr. H. Kamkhenthang

In Manipur, we have only 3,87,977 persons belonging to Scheduled Tribes living in 9/10th of the total area of the state. This indicates that the tribal areas are scarcely populated, with a density of 64 people only per sq. km. The density in the valley is 414 people per sq. km. It goes without saying that the hill districts surrounding the valley of Manipur are not economically productive. The development of the state as a whole cannot take place unless the hill areas and its inhabitants are developed as well. The hill areas on their own are not self-supportive and exist only at the subsistence level. The valley on its too cannot be self-sufficient for its various needs without the hill areas. At present, however, the hill areas are more backward in various respects whereas the valley is comparatively better off. Essentially though, the poverty of the tribes of Manipur is poverty within poverty.

The tribesmen inhabit the inhospitable hill areas where the topography itself is a hindrance to socio-economic development in the area. In such a situation, it is absolutely imperative that man should face the environment and conquer it in order to not only survive but develop as well. If properly tapped though, this very inclement nature can yield bountiful blessings. The signs of poverty loom large as one enters a village in the hill areas. What poverty actually is can be explained in the context of the hill areas of Manipur. A seminar with the theme "Who are the poor?" was organised at Madras with the financial support of the Indian Council of Social Science Research. The participating social scientists accepted the definition of the poor as those "who lack the minimum requirements of food, clothing, shelter, medical and educational facilities." (B.K. Roy Burman 1984: VIII).

This definition, however, was found to be narrow by some scholars for certain operational purposes. But I think it is applicable in the case of the tribes living in the hill areas of Manipur where they are lacking these very facilities because of the absence of infrastructure. The environment with which they interact moulds the tribal way of life in these hills. B.K.R. Burman, remarking about the tribes of Manipur and Nagaland, points out that it is difficult to say the tribes perceive themselves as poor. In actuality, even at the tribal level of economy, a great majority of them see themselves as poor, needy and helpless, particularly in times of crisis. They also feel that there is a possibility of partial famine in case of any slight shift in the usual course of nature. We need not prove they are in the throes of poverty as we well know that what they really lack is the minimum requirement of food, clothing and medical and educational facilities.

In this paper, I would like to focus on the Chin-Kuki tribes, who are jhuming cultivators wherever they are in the hill districts of Manipur. They are also found in Churachandpur District. Some tribes found in other districts also practice jhuming cultivation. A few Naga tribes like Tangkhul and Mao are better off than the rest of the jhuming tribes with respect to food as nature blesses them with a more suitable topography and a never-ending supply of water for the purpose of permanent terrace cultivation. Any tribe that depends solely on shifting cultivation is in a far more deplorable economic condition than those that depend on settled cultivation.

The land ownership system among these tribes ought to be examined in this light. There are two kinds of land ownership systems among the tribes of Manipur. These systems give rise to two different kinds of economy and prospects for the betterment of the future of the tribes.

A peculiar tribal characteristic is persistently observable among the tribes of Manipur. A tribe is self-contained, self-sufficient and marked by the absence of specialisation as opposed to conditions prevalent in society today. A family is an economic unit in a village. Each family or household tries to procure what it requires without depending on others. No single person or family specialises in any of the economic activities. A family is supposed to produce the bare necessities at the subsistence level. It is expected to have paddy, millet, corn, bean, chilly, rice, etc. from its own jhum field. Since no one else has a surplus, it is more difficult to supplement one's deficit quantity of food grain. This is a situation in which there is no economic interdependence and specialisation in any trade, which retards the pattern of economic growth in one way or the other.

Due to the customs of jhuming tribes, they are no longer in a position to satisfy their biological needs of food without modification of the traditional means of eking out their livelihood. Deforestation, thanks to the short jhuming cycle, reduces the fertility of the soil. The land ownership system among the Chin-Kuki-Mizo tribes is not effective in itself to boost economic productivity as a result of the innumerable changes in the socio-political system of the tribes.

It may be observed that there is a difference between the various tribes practising shifting cultivation. The experience of the tribes that depend on shifting cultivation is annual, partial and regular famine year after year, whereas the tribes that depend on settled cultivation experience differently. They do not face famine or a scarcity of food. Among the jhum cultivators there are stories relating to famines and reflections of abject poverty whereas in the case of settled cultivators such a situation does not arise.

There are two types of chieftainships with their own accompanying systems of land ownership among the tribes in the hills of Manipur. The Naga kind of land ownership and the Chin-Kuki-Mizo type of land ownership are also responsible for economic development. We will look into the land ownership system among the Chin-Kuki-Mizo tribes. The traditional land management had been a primitive type. The village chief looked after the village and the village land and he allowed any household to farm on the village land on payment of an annual fee of paddy. The village chief welcomed any person who farmed on the village land, as he was to get paddy from each household that cultivated the land. The Naga type of land ownership is a more evolved type while the latter is purely primitive. In the Naga system, there is private ownership of land as well as community ownership. In the Chin-Kuki-Mizo group, ownership of land is vested with the village chief alone.

The scenario has changed since India's Independence. The villagers are no longer willing to pay the annual payment of paddy called *busun* and offer the animal's foreleg. The village chief is no longer interested in overseeing the management of the village forestland. The earlier concern to protect the forestland from wild fires is a thing of the past. Today, the village chief will even sell forest trees to anyone where he sees a chance of marketability in order to get a benefit that will compensate him for the loss of his annual payment of paddy. This raises objections among the villagers. In some villages it has been reported that the village chief even permits households of the next village to cultivate within the village land as long as they make him an annual payment of paddy. We have noted earlier that because of the present system of jhuming the villagers fail to make both ends meet. They are bound to become even poorer unless the traditional economic system is modified to suit the changing situation.

The wealth of the forests is like a diamond on the ocean bed. The resources of the forests have to be utilised to ameliorate the tribals' deplorable economic condition. Changes have to be weaved into the fabric of tribal society in respect of the position of village chieftainship and the land ownership system among the Chin- Kuki group of tribals. The village land has to be made the main source of income for the villagers.

The new system proposed is that first of all there should be private ownership of land. The piece of land that is farmed by a particular household should be retained by it. Since the hill areas are not productive, villagers would be permitted to divide the land among themselves in fragments without ceiling. The land should also be protected so that it does not go to outsiders. Individual rights of ownership should be statutorily recognised and no tribal exploitation by non-tribals should be permitted in any form in respect of land and its produce.

This system is bound to bring about discontent among the village chiefs. Accordingly, they should be compensated for the loss of control over the village land, as was the case in Mizoram.

A tribal villager is landless even though he has an annual lease for jhuming purposes. This condition forces a nomadic way of life. Since the tribal has no permanent ownership of land in a village, he has no sense of belonging. He cannot develop a particular piece of land for permanent cultivation purposes, as he cannot claim permanent ownership. A number of benefits will accrue to the tribal masses if the village land is distributed to the villagers for permanent and individual ownership. If translated into reality, this scheme will prove advantageous and will be the nucleus of tribal economic development.

If given permanent ownership of their own land, the tribals will individually and collectively prevent and resist any possible outbreak of wild fire. They will automatically be more protective of the forest and its resources. This arrangement will make for permanent settlement and put a stop to the nomadic and landless way of life. It will give them the incentive to work and produce more when they all have a piece of land they can call their own.

9

Rural Energy Scarcity and Undernutrition: A New Approach

- *M.R. Chakravarti and Rama Chakravarti*

So far, researchers have enumerated three major strategies to improve nutritional status, viz; (1) agricultural productivity; (2) income generation and (3) supplementary feeding of vulnerable groups. These are well-established approaches that are theoretically sound though there are areas of debate within each one.

The links between nutrition and the economy, such as agriculture, employment, income levels and so on, have been analysed. The effects of culture, geography, education and the social pattern have also been studied in relation to nutrition. However, energy expenditure patterns (human, commercial and traditional) and nutrition levels in terms of calorie intake and output have been neglected. In this paper, we use the term energy in a wider sense, signifying not only calorie energy for the body, but all the sources of fuel or power required for day to day activities - kerosene for lighting purposes, firewood for cooking purposes, animals for ploughing purposes and transport, or human beings for sowing, harvesting, fetching water and a host of other activities.

It is our contention that the scarcity of energy in rural areas, and the resultant dependence on human energy, has an impact on the nutritional status. This needs to be explored in detail.

Until recently, there was a lack of reliable data on energy utilisation patterns in villages, particularly in our country. ASTRA (Application of Science & Technology to Rural Areas), a cell of the Indian Institute of Science, Bangalore, has filled the gap to some extent by undertaking a detailed survey of 6 villages at their rural extension centre in Karnataka.

The survey shows that human beings contribute a significant share of the village's energy requirement through their labour. Men contribute 38%, women 43% and children 19% of the human energy. The point is some of this human energy could be conserved if more appropriate forms of energy were generated.

For example, in one village over 45,000 hours were spent in gathering firewood for cooking for which firewood-gathering families spent 2.6 hours each day per family and travelled 5 kms per day on an average. 82% of the firewood so gathered was used for cooking. If, instead of this, cooking fuel could be generated through bio-gas or adjacent wood lots, it would conserve a significant amount of human energy, especially that of women and children.

Again, agricultural implements have undergone many changes, which can improve energy usage and render many tasks less laborious without being expensive. There is alternative inexpensive appropriate technology to prevent one having to walk distances to fetch water. The appropriate technology is only beginning to explore the possibilities.

But what are the implications of such energy generation and technological innovations on health and nutrition status? Quite simply, that the energy outflow from humans, from women and children in particular, can be reduced. The energy thus conserved could conceivably decrease the 'calorie-gap' and permit the body to utilise a greater part of its input for growth, maintenance and resistance.

This is not all. The human hours thus saved could be utilised in several ways; as, for instance, non-energy-intensive home industries which generate additional income and therefore increase food intake; or education which may improve the usage of available foods and receptivity to new dietary concepts. May we stress that we mention here only the nutritional implications of such energy programmes; obviously there will be many others.

What is the cost effectiveness and cost-benefits of this strategy? More important, is it more cost-effective than other strategies?

There are no immediate answers to these questions in the absence of further data; but the questions must be posed. However, we may postulate that even if the cost of energy generation through the use of alternative technology is not less than other programmes, they may be easier to implement. Since energy scarcity is keenly felt in the rural areas, the energy programmes in particular may have more rapid acceptance than other strategies that involve changes in traditional methods, social relations and/or larger capital investment.

We may also point out that since the poorest sections expend the greatest human energy (labour being their only resource), energy programmes may tend to benefit them more than they would the affluent.

It is clear that the energy scarcity-nutrition nexus is an unexplored area of enquiry that requires further in-depth examination and exploration.

PART - II

ISSUES ON CONSTITUTIONAL AND ADMINISTRATIVE PROBLEM

10

Indian Constitution: Autonomy in Tribal Areas

- *Prof. M. Horam*

According to the English dictionary, autonomy means independence or a self-governing community. In order to appreciate as to how the Indian Constitution deals with autonomy in tribal areas, let me briefly mention the nature and the actual working of the Constitution.

The Indian Constitution is the lengthiest and bulkiest in the world: it contains 395 Articles and Eleven Schedules. It is also said that the Indian Constitution lacks originality; it is a borrowed constitution. The people who framed the constitution borrowed from the Government of India Act, 1935 (i.e. federal scheme, parliamentary form of government, office of the governor, emergency powers, bicameral legislatures and the structure and powers of federal judiciary); borrowed from the constitution of Ireland (i.e. the idea of directive principles of state policy, method of presidential election, etc.); borrowed from the constitution of Canada (i.e. giving residuary powers to the Union and the concept of "India is a Union of States"); borrowed from the constitution of Japan (i.e. Articles 21 dealing with right to life, etc.) and also borrowed from the constitution of Australia (i.e. the idea of concurrent lists).

Critics also argue that the Indian Constitution is neither federal nor quasi-federal; it is more appropriately a unitary with federal features. Commenting on this aspect, Dr. Rajendra Prasad once said; "Personally I do not attach any importance to the label which may be attached to it whether you call it a federal constitution, or, a unitary constitution or by any other name. It makes no difference so long as the Constitution serves our purpose."

Critics also maintain that the Indian Constitution is over centralised and the units have been reduced to the level of local bodies. It seems that the Central Government has been deliberately made strong with the sole object of maintaining the integrity and security of India.

It is also argued that the fundamental rights embodied in the Constitution are illusory and unreal. They have been hedged in on all sides by so many limitations that the people are unable to understand exactly, the content of the fundamental rights. From the democratic point of view, fundamental rights could be viewed from three angles:

a) To what extent they enable a man to take part in political life,

b) To what extent they enable him to express and develop his personality, and

c) Lastly, to what extent they enable him to lead group or cultural life. The theoretical implications of fundamental rights are that, authority is federal and limited and that the government should not be trusted too much. Take for example, the clause that all citizens are entitled to "freedom of speech and expression", but at the same time the government can impose a restriction in the name of libel, slander, defamation, contempt of court or any other which offends decency and morality or, more important, which threatens to undermine the security of the state or tends to overthrow it.

Critics also maintain that the directive principles of state policy serve no practical purpose. As the directive principles are not justifiable, they are ineffective. Every government can afford to ignore them.

Let us again examine as to what extent the Constitution of India contains the federal principle; there are strong differences of opinion among scholars and commentators on this issue. Some call it unitary, others say that it is more unitary than federal.

Even the framers of the constitution have such differences of opinion. Apparently, the essential federal principle, namely that the existence of two sets of governments is easily satisfied in a constitution; there is written constitution and there is the supremacy of the Constitution as well as an independent judiciary to enforce it; and even in an emergency, it may be noted, the very personality of the state is not wiped out. But strictly speaking and applying the tests more closely, we see that neither the historical antecedents nor the socio-economic conditions nor even the essential federal principle in reality exists in the Indian Constitution. Thus, we cannot call it a federal constitution in the strictest sense at all.

While the provisions in the Constitution providing for an independent supreme court and high courts are to be praised, it is contended that there is nothing to ensure the independence of the subordinate judiciary. Likewise, government servants are not content with their status under the Constitution. It rests with the concerned empowered authority to dismiss or remove a public servant, to decide whether it is reasonable to give him an opportunity to prove his innocence or not.

The institution of ordinance is condemnable. The issuing of ordinances in a democratic country is not justified at all. With the present means of communication and transport, it is always possible for the Government to summon to legislature at a moment's notice and the members can be expected to attend.

A special part of the Constitution, part XVIII, Article 352, out of 22 into which the Constitution is divided, is called "emergency provisions". This part contains only nine articles. No other set of articles is so unfortunately grouped together and so badly named, and no other set of articles carries so much constitutional weight and possibilities for good use as well as mischief.

The emergency powers of the president are criticised both by Indian critics and political analysts as well as friends outside India. Etymologically speaking, its use is unfortunate. Emergency means "sudden juncture demanding immediate action", and in popular usage is always associated with danger requiring quick action. Yet, there is always the inherent danger of its abuse. The only justification is that the abnormal conditions prevailing in our country and the state of affairs that have not changed for the better. Sri Jayprakash Narayan is stated to have observed as follows on 26 January, 1950, "Lastly, let us not forget that the Constitution that comes into force today and brings republic into being is itself a source of greatest danger, to both individual freedom and social justice. Therefore, at the earliest opportunity, as really representative constituent assembly must be convened to frame a new constitution that may become a fit instrument of social democracy"

Sri Narayan's words became prophetic as far as practice and interpretation of the Indian Constitution is concerned. For example, as soon as an Emergency proclamation is issued, Article 358 will have the automatic effect of suspending all the seven freedoms conferred by Article 19. The provisions are a means to guard the Constitution against possible danger in an emergency. To the critics they look equally as a means of subverting the constitution "not merely by agitation ... but also by those in office, or, in power", to establish dictatorship. History teaches us that dictatorship is established in three ways:

(1) By a military coup;

(2) By a party in power amending the constitution to suit its purposes;

(3) By a party in power otherwise misusing the power vested in it in order to creating favourable circumstances to establish itself.

The Indian Constitution has, therefore, greatest autonomy of the greatest number. It can be shaped, twisted and amended to suit the interests of the party in power. Let us take a few examples to prove our contention.

Talking of emergency provisions, to us these powers appear to be un-federal, undemocratic, impolitic, unwise and absolutely impracticable to be used with any success. The makers of the

Indian Constitution were emphatic on the point that they were creating a federal constitution of some sorts. If that is so, then Article 356 is a non-federal feature, and Dr. Ambedkar had termed it a "flexible federation". If a federation is what the framers of the Indian Constitution wanted, Article 356 should not have been there in the first place.

The use of the said article is undemocratic because of two reasons; one, it makes the Centre finally responsible for the good government of the state. Democracy means self-rule and in a democracy if for any reason the government is going wrong, it is for the people to apply the corrective themselves (like the USA). It is claimed that one of the virtues of democracy is the capacity for self-correction. But the practice now is, when there is a 'crisis' in the state all that the electors will have to do is simply to sit back and watch and allow people at the Centre to solve their problems. Certainly, this is not the democratic way in a democratic institution.

The Emergency provision is also "impolitic" on two grounds, first by placing the responsibility for the government on the Centre; it tends to make the state ministry feel 'irresponsible'. Secondly, the position of the services is made precarious; and it tends to impair their sense of loyalty and impartiality.

In normal times, they are under ministers and suddenly under Article 356 they are put directly under the governor. This access to the governor once again is out as soon as normal conditions are supposedly restored. This becomes more ridiculous when we remember that, in all probability, the Centre suspending the state ministry means one party suspending another party. Besides, the services would be involved in party quarrels and could even be used as political pawns and scapegoats in this tug of war fro power.

This "emergency provision" is also unwise. It is unwise because it is liable to be abused. Speaker after speaker in the Constituent Assembly cited examples of possible abuse for political purposes. It may be used, for instance, in order to suppress regional parties. Dr. Ambedkar himself admitted that there was a possibility of these articles being abused or employed for political purposes.

The Indian Constitution is autonomous in nature because it is independent and self-governing. In fact, as someone remarked, the Indian Constitution could make or unmake any issue by amending the Constitution, except that it cannot make a man a woman and a woman a man.

It is also often said that the Indian Constitution is, in the language of Dr. Jennings, the 'lawyer's paradise'. Criticising the Constitution, critics point out that the Indian Constitution can make people more litigious, more inclined to go to law courts, less truthful and less likely to follow the tenets of truth and non-violence. It opens up vast venues of litigation and will give our able and ingenious lawyers plenty of work to do. Indeed, the Indian Constitution is a paradise for lawyers.

The Fifth and Sixth Schedules of the Constitution of India, 1950, deal with the areas previously known as "Excluded Areas". During the British period, backward and tribal areas, especially those in Assam were called "excluded areas". But when the constitution was introduced in 1950, all excluded areas were to be known as "Schedule Areas" and their inhabitants "Schedule Tribes". But an exception was made in the case of the hill districts of Assam, which were to be called "Tribal Areas" and not "Schedule Areas". This is specified in the Sixth Schedule. The reason for this special arrangement was that all the tribal groups of Assam were more or less homogenous; most of them are decidedly richer and more educated than their tribal counterparts in the rest of India. The Sixth Schedule was extended to Khasi and Jaintia Hills, Garo Hills, Mizo Hills and other Tribal Areas of Assam. This arrangement, however, was refused and not accepted by the Nagas. Long before 1950, the Nagas had declared themselves as independent. A plebiscite, therefore, was held in 1951 and 99.9% widespread support for independence was registered. In 1952 the central election was boycotted by the Nagas, which was soon followed by civil disobedience, non-payment of taxes and boycotting of official and other Indian

National celebrations. While discussing the Indian Constitution, therefore, the Naga issue shall have to be discussed separately at different forums and at appropriate level.

The Indian Constitution, which wants to wipe out the problem of minorities by abolishing communal electorates, etc., could not help retaining part XVI which deals with certain safeguards for Scheduled Castes and Scheduled Tribes, and this is because of the peculiar problem presented by them. They are not only in a minority in India and, in every unit, formed by the Constitution but they are also educationally and economically backward and socially and culturally different from the rest of India.

The problems of the tribes can be viewed from two angles: first, the areas where tribal people are prominent can be demarcated into a separate unit, and this is the basis of the agitation started by Jaipal Singh called the "Jharkhand movement". The second one is the problem of treating them as an unfortunate minority long neglected, and giving them certain safeguards both to preserve their culture and social autonomy and also to bring them up to the level others are at. But the tribal leader, Jaipal Singh, for instance, never considered the tribals a minority at all. He said, "Our attitude has not been on being a numerical minority at all. Our position has nothing whatever to do with whether we are less than the Hindus or Muslims or more than the Parsis. Our stand is that there is a tremendous disparity in our social, economic and educational standards... we have our prescriptive rights, which no one can deny. We are not, however, asking for those prescriptive rights. We want to be treated like anybody else ... we have been isolated and kept, as it were, in a zoo. That has been the attitude of the people in the past. Our point now is that you have got to mix with us. We are willing to mix with you."

So, what the tribals wanted in essence were a few safeguards in order to protect themselves against exploitation. The tribal areas were theirs and within those areas they wanted to preserve their economy and culture. Fundamental rights given equally to all might be used against their interests, especially the right to free movement and acquisition of property throughout India, so they fought against this, and hence a safeguard in their favour (Article 19(5)).

There are also some inimical provisions, especially in the case of tribes. By far the most inimical are the provisions contained in Article 44 and 1 and 2 and of the current list in the VII schedule regarding a uniform civil and criminal code. Culture and law cannot easily be separated in the case of the tribes; and it will take a long time before these people can be educated in the so-called civilised law of majority groups.

It is to remove this hardship that the Constitution makes a special provision for them (the tribes) in the Fifth and Sixth Schedules. In fact, the Constitution divides these tribes into three classes, into those living in the plains, those living in compact areas within the administrative jurisdiction of the states, and those living in the hill districts of Assam. The first kind get no special safeguards except a tacit recognition that the "*adivasi* carries his law with him where he goes". The ones in the second category are treated on the same footing as those of the "partially excluded" and "excluded areas" of the 1935 Act, and their problem is tackled by Schedule V which gives them exemption from the operation of certain laws made by the Parliament and state legislatures. The problem of the Assam hill tribes is a special one, at least on paper, and they are given the greatest autonomy possible both in the social and administrative spheres by the Sixth schedule. But this schedule becomes ineffective because of the following reasons:

a) Absence of financial independence, and

b) Insertion of the Ninth Schedule (31.B) in the Constitution.

A word may be said that this VI schedule is never extended to Manipur tribal areas till date despite several demands made by different tribal organisations. Manipur tribals are conveniently left out for reasons best known to the central leaders.

The Constitution safeguards have been extended to certain communities of the North-East based on religious and linguistic considerations: e.g. Assamese were given Assamese language as their official language and Manipuri was the official language of Manipuri speaking people. But we have seen that the Constitution does not place the importance of preserving these tribal languages or scripts on the state, and so the tribals alone will have to look after them. And what is the use of preserving the script and language of the tribes in the face of the Eighth Schedule that recognises only a few select languages. So, the Constitution implies that they relegate, if not forget, their languages, while giving them a right to preserve them, and become Tamils, Oriyas, Assamese, Manipuri and Andhraites and so on ... (as the Schedule Castes became long ago). But this is not what the tribal leaders meant by "mixing with you". We may add here that due to the politics of language, Maharastra was divided into two states and Assam was cut to size by granting statehood to certain areas and these are now separate states called Meghalaya, Arunachal Pradesh, Mizoram, Nagaland and, of late, Bodoland.

Again, there was an act of 1873 that was extended to the tribal areas of the North-East (then Assam) in order to prevent the British Indians from encroaching upon the land of the tribals thereby prohibiting any non-tribal going beyond a certain line without a pass or licence. In his visit to the North-East, the Home Minister of India Sri Chavan said that this act would be lifted. His utterances are fraught with danger.

Again, there is a tremendous influx of foreigners in the North-East, migrants and refugees coming from Bangladesh, Myanmar (Burma), Bhutan and Nepal. There is a fear in the minds of all the tribals and non-tribals of this region that if the large-scale influx of foreigners continues at the present rate, very shortly the region's indigenous people will become a minority in their own land.

The Sixth Schedule of the Constitution intends to protect the fundamental rights pertaining to land and forests: but the insertion of the Ninth Schedule (31.B) silences the court, and the tribal society is systematically watered down. The addition of the Ninth Schedule in the Constitution is a very important development and is in fact a severe blow to the rule of law on the one hand, and has laid the foundation of authoritarianism on the other.

Though in the first instance, only 13 Acts were mentioned in the schedule in order to save them from a judicial challenge, and most of them pertained to the abolition of *zamindari*, later on the Ninth Schedule was used for violating many of the fundamental rights without amending the Constitution by merely placing a particular legislation in this schedule (for e.g. Central Act 33 of 1960).

Yet again, in the name of the 'law and order problem', the central government can declare any area as disturbed, taking advantage of the Disturbed Area Act of 1981. In these so-called "disturbed areas", the armed forces (Assam and Manipur) Special Power Act, 1958 is enforced in all Manipur, Nagaland and Assam areas. This act confers special powers to any commissioned officer, warrant officer, non-commissioned officer, or any other person of equivalent rank in the armed forces in a disturbed area, who may:

a) Fire upon or otherwise use force, even to the causing of death;

b) Arrest without warrant, any person, and

c) Enter and search without warrant any premises, etc.

This act is dangerous, to say the least. It can be misused on whims and fancies if any officer wishes to do so or it can be used to serve certain vested interests. In short, this act is undemocratic, against the fundamental rights the Constitution exonerates and, above all, it is against human rights.

In conclusion, it may be pointed out that a flexible constitution and the rights of minorities cannot go together. Once we uphold these rights of minorities as inviolable, what follows naturally is a rigid constitution guaranteeing that the rule of the game cannot be changed without the consent of all, or almost all. However, rigid as it appears to be, the Indian Constitution is not rigid enough to serve the purpose for which it is intended. Take for instance the fundamental rights, especially those guaranteeing freedom of speech and religious worship. Is the one-third to suffer and lose these freedoms if the two-thirds (because they are a majority) decide otherwise? Or, are the tribals to lose their cultural and educational rights if the majority (say Hindus) decide thus? Are the minorities perpetually to live at the mercy of the majorities? If this is so, a written constitution is as good as any worthless piece of paper.

We have said earlier that the fundamental rights have "political significance", especially in an Emergency. Emergencies could just as well be 'created' to provide an opportunity for those with vested interests to suspend fundamental rights and to suppress opposition parties. Such determined political parties in power might also misuse their power of amending the Constitution, especially of amending the chapter on fundamental rights. It would have been better if the Constitution had provided for greater protection to the minorities: political, social, religious and others by making some other provisions for the alternation of fundamental rights than the one by 'brute majority'. This is especially true of those who are elected for one purpose but propose to do another, elected to function according to the Constitution but propose to alter it while "We, the people of India", the so-called "sovereign people", will be left to gaze in utter helplessness all the while.

11

The Constitution 73rd Amendment Act, 1992 Vis-a-Vis The Hill Areas of Manipur

- Prof. Lal Dena

The 73rd Amendment Act, 1992 of the Indian Constitution is perhaps the most revolutionary legislation, which has as its objective to further democratise district administration in the shape of district governments by vesting more powers and responsibilities in the self-governing bodies and involving the people in the making of their own destinies. The main objective of this essay is to highlight the basic features of the act and then indicate what they mean in the context of the traditional self-governing institutions in the hill areas of Manipur.

I Basic Features of the 73rd Amendment Act:

1. In the context of Manipur, the 73rd Amendment has provided for the constitution of a two-tier *panchayati raj* - the *gram panchayat* at the village level and the *zilla parishad* at the district level.
2. The *gram sabha*, the most important body and source of power is to be established. Its size is fixed at a population of not less than 3,000 but not more than 6,000. Its functions are to give assistance to the implementation of development schemes, mobilisation of voluntary labour, contribution in kind, promotion of adult education and family welfare, promotion of unity and harmony among all sections of the society in the village.

3. The act has provided for the reservation of (a) seats for Scheduled Castes, Scheduled Tribes and women in the *gram panchayats* and *zilla parishad*; (b) 30% seats in the *gram panchayats* and *zilla parishads* for women and (c) 30% offices of the *pradhan* and *upa-pradhan* in the *gram panchayats*, and *adhyakshas* and *upa-adjyakshas* in the *zilla parishad* for Scheduled Castes, Scheduled Tribes and women.

4. A wide range of functions is meant to be carried out by the *panchayats* covering the 29 subjects listed in the 11th Schedule of the Constitution. The *panchayats* are also authorised by the legislature of a state to levy, collect and appropriate taxes, duties, tolls and fees.

5. Another novel feature of the act is the provision for the constitution of the District Planning Committee, which is to coordinate and consolidate the plans prepared by the *zilla parishads, gram panchayats, nagar panchayats* and municipal councils in the district.

6. The provision for the constitution of finance commission is also very significant. The commission is to ensure regular and sound finance for the *panchayat* bodies. The flow of funds both from the state and central government to the *panchayat* bodies is well ensured under the act.

7 Under the act, there is a provision for the constitution of a State Election Commission for every five years to carry out the superintendence, direction and control over elections to the *gram panchayats* and *zilla parishads*. This is to ensure that the *panchayat* bodies are not kept in a cold storage for more than six months from their dissolution.

These are indeed far-reaching changes towards the realisation of the dream of giving power to the people. But the states of Nagaland, Mizoram and Meghalaya remain out of the orbit of the 73rd Amendment; and the hill areas of Manipur, where the district councils minus the Sixth Schedule provision were once there, also do not come under the purview of the 73rd Amendment. Because of article 371(A), 371(C) and 371(G), the states of Nagaland, the hill areas of Manipur and Mizoram enjoy a special position with respect to the extension of laws made by the Parliament, without the necessary initiative and concurrence by those state legislative assemblies.

One emerging opinion is, however, that the 73rd Amendment regarding the *panchayati raj* institutions should be extended to every part of the country, including the areas covered under the Fifth and Sixth Schedules of the Constitution. Before we proceed further to examine the applicability of the new act to the hill areas of the state, let us first see the evolution of the self-governing institutions in the hill areas from the historical perspective.

II Evolution of Self-Governing Institutions in the Hills:

1. Self-government was much more pronounced in the hill areas of Manipur. At some point of time in their historical evolution, the hill people evolved traditional socio-political structures, institutions of chieftainship and village councils. The specific character and composition of the council varied from tribe to tribe and sometimes even from village to village. The council combined within itself executive, legislative and judicial powers and there is no case that the council cannot decide according to traditional practices and customary laws. The colonial system of indirect rule formally recognised the institution of chieftainship and village councils and used them as instruments of colonial establishment.

2. After colonial rule, the Manipur state council placed the responsibility for the administration of the hill people in the Maharaja in council as provided under the Manipur State Hill People (Administration) Regulation, 1974. According to the regulation, the hill territory was divided into circles and sub-divisions. In each village of 20 tax-paying houses or above, there was a village authority that replaced the traditional village council. It consisted of the chief and elders nominated in accordance with the customs

of the concerned village. Another notable feature was the constitution of circle authority above the village authority. The circle authority comprised one circle officer and a council of five members elected by the village authorities falling within the circle.

The circle authorities could exercise executive power over law and order, levy assessment or collection of taxes on houses, produce of land, lower and upper primary education, construction and maintenance of bridle-paths, public health, personal hygiene, clean water supply, maintenance of land records, etc. Criminal justice was administered by the court of the village authority, the court of the circle authority, the hill bench at Imphal and the chief court of the Manipur state as constituted for the trial of hill cases under the Manipur State Courts Act, 1947. The court of a village authority settled cases relating to theft, cattle theft, the illegal slaughter of animals, simple hurt and assault. The circle bench (court) exercised the powers of a magistrate of the first class and comprised the circle officer and any two members of the circle council. The hill bench of Imphal exercised the powers of a Sessions Court and comprised a judge of the chief court with two hill men as judges.

3. To initiate people's representation at the grass-root level, the state government enacted the Manipur (Village Authority in Hill Areas) Act, 1956, which, for the first time introduced the election of the members of the village authority on the basis of adult franchise by repealing the hill people's regulation of 1947. The composition of the village authority was fixed as follows: (a) five members where the number of tax-paying house in the village was not less than 20 but not more than 60; (b) seven members where the number of tax-paying houses was more than 60 but less than 100; (c) ten members where the number of tax-paying houses was more than 100 but not more than 150; (d) twelve members where the number of tax-paying houses was more than 150.

According to the act, the chief was the ex-officio chairman of the village authority and the term for the members so elected was fixed at three years from the date appointed for its first meeting. The village court had jurisdiction both in criminal and civil cases as specified in the Code of Criminal Procedure of 1898 and the Code of Civil Procedure, 1908. The main function of the village authority was to maintain law and order and for this purpose, it could exercise the power and duties generally vested in the police as provided in the Police Act of 1861. On certain specified offences, within the limits of its jurisdiction, the village authority could also order the arrest of persons without any order from a magistrate and without a warrant.

4. The state legislature passed the Manipur Hill Areas (Acquisition of Chief's Rights) Act, 1967 on 14th June 1967, which authorised the government to acquire the rights, title and interest of chiefs in and over land in the hill areas of Manipur. The chiefs were, however, to be compensated by taking the following points into consideration: (a) the amount of land under the chiefs; (b) the total number of households within the chiefdom; and (c) whether compensation was to be given in instalments or as a lumpsum. The act, though passed, could not be implemented because of objections raised by some of the chiefs.

5. When Manipur attained statehood in 1972 and subsequently divided the state into districts, the state government introduced the Manipur (Hill Areas) District Council Act, 1972. According to the act, each district council consists of eighteen members elected directly on the basis of adult suffrage. There are also two nominated non-official members in the council. There are a chairman and a vice-chairman elected from among the members of the council. The term of their office is five years.

   As regards their powers and functions, the district councils have control over some moveable and immovable property, construction and maintenance of roads, bridges, channels and buildings, establishment and management of dispensaries and primary schools, markets, animal ponds, allotment of land for the purpose of agriculture, grazing or residential purposes, regulation of the practice of jhum and shifting cultivation, etc. The district councils also have the power to collect taxes on professional, trades, animals, vehicles, beats, ferries and entry of goods into a market for sale. It should be noted that no Sixth Schedule provision has been extended to the district councils. Therefore, pending the granting of the Sixth Schedule to the hill areas of Manipur, the said district councils have been kept in abeyance for the last six years.

6. In the meantime, the state legislature had amended the Manipur (Village Authorities in Hill Areas) Act, 1956 in 1983. One of the most significant features of the act is the constitution of a Circle Village Court (CVC) for a village or a group of villages comprising a population of 1,000 to 3,000 and a maximum number of five members who were appointed by the government on the recommendation of the deputy commissioner of the concerned area. The act also laid down that every rule made either in the VAs or CVCs was to be laid before the hill standing committee and thence to the legislative assembly, which had the final authority to modify or annul the rule so made or recommended. The act also specifically mentioned that no transfer or allotment of land be made to the non-tribal without the prior permission in writing of the deputy commissioner of the concerned district. Under the existing rules of the district autonomous councils, the deputy commissioner had to secure the consent of the council for the purpose.

III Comparative Appraisal of the two Systems:

Given the basic features of the 73rd Amendment and also the historical evolution of the self-governing institutions in the hills, let us now make a comparative appraisal of the two systems. The position of *gram sabhas* and the *gram panchayats* are like that of the villages and the village authorities. Both the members of the *gram panchayats* and the village authorities are elected directly by the people. The *gram panchayats* are headed by elected *pradhans* and *upa-pradhans,* and the village authorities are headed by chiefs wherever they are as ex-officio chairmen. Above the *gram panchayats,* there shall be *zilla parishads* to be headed by *adhyakshas* and *upa-adhyakshas* at the following districts: Imphal, Bishnupur and Thoubal.

In terms of powers and functions, the 73rd Amendment has added, as mentioned earlier, the 11th Schedule, which lists 29 subjects as under the jurisdiction of the *panchayat* bodies. It has also provided for the establishment of a separate finance commission, election commission, district planning committee and the state consolidated fund, etc. for the *panchayat* bodies. This is to say that the *panchayat* bodies have much higher developmental functions than the district councils under the 6th Schedule. The *panchayat* bodies are expanded to exercise superintendence and control over secondary schools, hospitals and primary health centres, whereas the district councils can have control over primary schools and dispensaries. On the whole, the organisational structure of the *panchayat* bodies is more or less similar to those of the village authorities and the district councils in the hill areas of the state. Prima facie, there appears to be no conflict between the spirit, essence and purpose of the traditional self-governing institutions of the tribal people and the *panchayat* bodies in the valley. But on close scrutiny of the two systems, a number of social scientists and administrators have expressed the view that the modern statutory P.R. system under the By-Amendment has not been found entirely suitable for the tribal areas of the country. To quote Bhupinder Singh,

> "The traditional tribal societies were accustomed to regulation of their domestic, social, religious, economic,

> political and even judicial affairs through the combined wisdom of village and regional leaders through consensus. Introduction of the statutory *gram panchayat* has sent eddies into the placid tribal waters."

Bhupinder Singh has expressed his fear that conflicts are likely to surface particularly in mixed *panchayats*, that is, those that have both a tribal and non-tribal membership. Therefore, before one thinks of the extension of the 73rd Amendment to the hill areas, there are some important issues which need serious examination: (a) whether the tribal customary laws need modification; (b) whether uniform or separate land laws be formed for the whole of Manipur or only the hill areas of Manipur; and (c) whether such administrative arrangements are to be made which will enable the tribal community to manage their own affairs in conformity with the traditional practices of tribal life and history.

Conclusion

In the context of the mushrooming of tribal movements for separate homelands in different parts of North-East India, the principle of internal self-determination and the strategy of sustainable self-development or ethno-development would better ensure the beginning of the process of emancipation of the tribal people. Internal self-determination for autonomy over their economies, territories, culture and future would be a powerful tool for genuine democracy and federalism. Therefore, the Sixth Schedule as the basis for working out the principle of self-determination and ethno-development might just be the answer.

12

Administrative Changes in the Hill Areas of Manipur

- *Prof. Ksh. Bimola Devi*

Every society, be it large or small, has its own administrative model. Some may have a simple administrative system while others a very complex system of developed administration. There is also a third category of administrative system that contains the elements of both the simple and complex developed system of administration. The level of development in a society always corresponds to the nature of the administrative system that changes from time to time. No administrative system can remain static. It always responds to the changing character of society at large.

In the given context, an attempt has been made to study the administrative changes that have taken place in the hill areas of Manipur since the pre-British days.

Traditional Administrative System

The two major tribes, i.e. the Kukis and the Nagas, inhabit the hill areas, which forms one tenth of the whole territorial area of Manipur. There are some minor tribes as well. These tribes have their own traditional political systems. The traditional political systems of these tribes in the hill areas of Manipur may roughly be classified in three categories - authoritarian, republican and semi-democratic. The third political system falls in between the authoritarian and republican systems. The authoritarian administrative system mainly exists among the Kukis. Hereditary chiefs head the majority of the Kuki villages. The chief is assisted by a village council that consists of people appointed or nominated by the chief. Though hierarchical in nature, the chief possessed supreme power in the administration of the village. The chief, in most cases, exercised the power of veto i.e., rejecting the decision of his council. He decided both civil and criminal cases according to the customary laws of the village. He also acted as a police officer, and could arrest a person who had committed a crime and punish him. In short, the chief exercised supreme power in the administration of his village.

The villages in a Naga-inhabited area are generally ruled by chieftains. The chiefs are either elected or selected for a definite period or for lifetime. In some cases the post is hereditary. In cases of election or selection, the chief usually possessed certain qualities such as a good physique, an impressive personality, and the gift of speech, courage, kindness and leadership.

The chief was assisted by a council that consisted of the most senior male heads of the clans of the village. The chief was responsible for the promotion of the general happiness of the people, for all social and religious gatherings and festivals of the village. He was the administrative head of a village. Inefficiency in the discharge of his administrative duties could result in his dismissal from chieftainship. In times of war, the chief also played the role of commander-in-chief.

The powers and functions of the chief varied from tribe to tribe in the Naga villages. But he did not exercise unlimited powers. The village council was responsible for the implementation of the decisions taken by the chief-in-council. The chief and the village council strictly followed the customary laws of the village.

The administration of the villages in the hill areas of Manipur enjoyed a great deal of autonomy under the rule of the king of Manipur. He did not interfere in the day-to-day administration of the village. The chiefs of the villages in the hill areas of Manipur had only to pay an annual tribute to the king.[1] The Meitei king assumed the role of an emperor. His *gaddi* (throne) was decorated on all sides by nine *sekpin mathol* (decorated umbrellas). One *sekpin mathol* or one *thakan* meant that he was the lord of the hill areas, another signified that he was lord of the land of the *chakpas* and the remaining seven illustrated that he was the emperor of the seven kingdoms.[2]

The British Period

When Manipur came under British control after the 1891 war, the hill areas of Manipur also came under British control on behalf of the maharaja. The *sanad* issued by the British authority to Raja Churachand Singh clearly stated that the final authoritative control rested with the British.[3] "Further, you are informed that the permanence of the grant conveyed by the *sanad* will depend upon the ready fulfilment by you and your successors of orders given by the British government with regard to the administration of your territories, the control of the hill tribes dependent upon Manipur"[4].

When Raja Churachand Singh came of age, he was entrusted with the power to rule on 16th May 1907. Certain conditions were laid down and conveyed through a letter from Lord Minto on 21st January 1908. That there would be the formation of a *durbar* with the raja as the head of Manipur and an officer especially selected by the government of East Bengal and Assam would be vice-president was one of the conditions. The vice-president was allotted the portfolios of finance and revenue. Another important condition mentioned in the letter was that the administration and control of the hill tribes would be in the hands of the vice-president. The administration and control of the hill tribes should be in accordance with the rules that were approved by the government of Assam. In the administration and control, the raja was to be consulted. 'The political agent in consultation with the vice-president shall try to give effect to the wishes of the raja, so far consistent with the orders of the government.' If the political agent was unable to give effect to the wishes of His Highness, the matter was referred to the government of Assam. Thus the real administrator of the hill tribes of Manipur was the *durbar's* vice-president.

The *durbar* was also the highest criminal court in the state and tried all criminal cases not covered by the jurisdiction of the *cheirap* court. However, cases relating to the hill tribes were tried independently by the political agent.

Thus, since the coming of British rule to Manipur, the maharaja of Manipur was divested of all his powers over the hill areas. He was the president of the *durbar* according to the *sanad.* Later on, however, by an amendment of the rules, the maharaja was removed from the post of president. An officer especially selected by the government of Assam was appointed president and the administration of the hill areas was taken over by him.

The president of the *durbar*, a British officer, administered the hill areas on behalf of the maharaja of Manipur. As the hill areas are vast, it was not possible for the president to carry out the administration directly. In 1892, the British authority in Manipur introduced the system of the *lambus*. Altogether, there were 42 *lambus*. The hill areas were divided into five charges. Each was placed under a *sardar*. Each *sardar* was assisted by a number of *lambus*. The main duty of these *lambus* was to act as interpreters. But in actual practice, the *lambus* performed multifarious functions. They also investigated all cases within their respective areas. They were supposed to hold a position of trust and dignity in the administration of the hill areas. But they were at first not paid any salary for the services they rendered. As a result, the *lambus* plundered and pillaged the common villagers.

Besides the *lambus*, there were the *lam subedar* and four head interpreters. The *lambus* periodically sent a report through the *lam subedar* on the state of affairs in their area to the government of Manipur.

The introduction of the *lambus* system did not improve hill administration. There was no personal interaction between the officers of the state government and the villagers. This gap was partly responsible for the Kuki rebellion of 1917-1919. The president and the *durbar* had no time to look into the details of the administration of the hill areas. There was rampant discontent and suffering among the people. To express their grievances, the tribals had to undertake long and expensive journeys to Imphal.

In 1919, the *durbar* introduced certain reforms. The hill areas were divided into three sub-divisions. Each sub-division was placed under a sub-divisional officer. The sub-divisional officers were all European officers. Churachandpur, Tamenglong and Ukhrul were the headquarters of these sub-divisions. But the working of the hill administration on the sub-divisional basis was not satisfactory. So, in December 1929, the sub-divisions were abolished on an experimental basis for three years. Imphal, the capital of Manipur, was made headquarters of the hill administration. The whole hill area was divided into two - north and south. Each was placed under one assistant.

In 1934-35, the hill areas were again divided into three sub-divisions - Sadar, Ukhrul and Tamenglong. Each sub-division was placed under one officer.

The Post-Independence Period

With the passing of the Indian Independence Act in 1947, Manipur, along with other princely states of India, became independent. When British supremacy lapsed, the administration of the hill areas was in the hands of the maharaja of Manipur. In response to the demands for the introduction of a democratic responsible government in Manipur, the Maharaja of Manipur framed the Manipur "State Constitution Act, 1947". Another act for the administration of hill areas, called the Manipur State Hill Peoples (Administration) Regulation Act, 1947, was also framed.

The Manipur State Hill Peoples (Administration) Regulation Act, 1947:

The Act provided for the establishment and regulation of village authorities in the hill areas. One village authority was formed in each village that had 20 tax-paying houses or more. The village authority consisted of a *khullakpa,* one representative from each clan and the village elders. The primary function of the village authority was to maintain law and order. It was authorised to arrest certain criminal offenders without any order from a magistrate and without a warrant. It had to immediately inform the sub-divisional magistrate of every unnatural, suspicious or sudden death and any case of a heinous crime in the village.

In case there was any dispute in the village, the village authority informed the sub-divisional magistrate. It also had to furnish any information required by any officer of the state government.

The village authority was responsible for the administration of justice. It had jurisdiction over civil as well as criminal cases. It had the power to try those cases the value of which did not exceed Rs 500. Appeals against the decisions of the village authority could be taken to the circle bench. The village authority was guided by customary laws of the village in the discharge of its judicial functions. The village authority could impose a fine not exceeding Rs 200 and could also award payment of compensation. Pleaders were not allowed to appear in any case before the village authority.

Circle Authority

The Hill Peoples Regulation Act 1947 also envisaged a higher authority called the circle authority. They could hear appeals against the decisions of the village authority. All the villages inhabited by the hill people were grouped into nine circles. There was one circle authority for each circle. A circle authority consisted of a circle officer and a council of five members elected by the village authorities in the circle. Thus the democratic system of elections was introduced for the first time in the hills to elect the members of the circle authority.

Elections to the circle authority were held every three years. A village with less than 20 tax-paying houses was not entitled to vote. The rest were allotted votes on the basis of the number of tax-paying houses.

Sl. No.	*Number of tax-paying houses*	*Number of votes* [5]
01.	20 to 50 tax-paying houses	One
02.	51 to 100 tax-paying houses	Two
03.	101 to 200 tax-paying houses	Three
04.	201 to 300 tax-paying houses	Four
05.	301 to 400 tax-paying houses	Five

The circle authority was responsible for the administration of lower and upper primary education, the construction of bridle paths and bridges, the supply of drinking water, the improvement of terrace cultivation, to reduce or eliminate jhum cultivation, the maintenance of land records, collection of taxes, the preservation of forests - both ordinary and reserve, etc.[6]

The circle authority had the power to try both civil and criminal cases whose value did not exceed Rs 1,000. It also heard appeals against the decisions of the village courts. On the criminal front, the circle authority exercised the powers of a first class magistrate.

Appeals against the decisions of the circle authority were taken to the hill bench and then to the chief court. The decision of the chief court was final. The chief court could set aside the decisions of the hill bench and of the circle authority.

This administrative system in the hills continued till Manipur was merged into the Indian Union in 1949. Even after the merger, the administrative system under the Hill Peoples Regulation Act, 1947, continued to remain in force though the hill bench and hill courts were abolished in 1950. The circle bench was abolished in 1955.

The Manipur Village Authorities (in Hill Areas) Act, 1956:

The Parliament passed the Manipur Villages Authority (in hill areas) Act, 1956, for the administration of the hill areas of Manipur. It was implemented in 1957. This act determined the number of members of a village authority on the basis of the number of tax-paying houses.

Sl. No.	*Number of tax-paying houses*	*Number of members in a village authority*[7]
01.	20 to 60 tax-paying houses	5
02.	61 to 100 tax-paying houses	7
03.	101 to 150 tax-paying houses	10

This act, for the first time, introduced the elective element in village authority. Members of the village authorities were elected on the basis of adult franchise. Earlier, the chief of the village used to nominate members of the village authorities.

There were 725 village authorities constituted under the Manipur Villages Authority (in the hill areas) Act, 1956, in seven areas of the hills.

Sl. No.	*Name of Sub-division /Circles*	*No. of village Authorities*	*No. of Elected Members*
01.	Sadar Hills	68	263
02.	Tengnoupal Sub-Division	105	568
03.	Tengnoupal Circle	82	371
04.	Ukhrul	121	702
05.	Mao	121	76
06.	Jiribam	16	89
07.	Churachandpur	112	571
TOTAL		725	2640

This act also put certain limitations on the position and powers of the chief. Before the introduction of the act, the chief along with the village authority functioned as the village court. But, under the act, the head of the state was authorised to appoint two or more members of the village authority to act as the village court. If the chief were not a member of the court, he could not preside over it. The court selected one of its members as the chairman of the court.

This act may be regarded as one of the first important steps towards the democratisation of hill administration in Manipur. By placing certain restrictions on the powers of the chief and by introducing adult franchise at the lowest level of administration, i.e. the village authority, the common villagers became aware of democratic values and practices.

The Manipur Hill Areas Acquisition of Chief's Rights Act, 1967:

Through this act, an attempt was made to abolish chieftainship in the hill areas of Manipur by paying compensation. There was a difference of opinion between the Hill Areas Committee and the Legislative Assembly regarding the passing of the bill. While the former did not agree with several provisions of the bill, the latter passed the bill and with the assent of the governor, the bill became an act. But the act has not been implemented properly. Chieftainship continues to exist with all its rights and privileges in the hill areas of Manipur.

The Manipur (Hill Areas) District Council Act, 1971:

On the eve of Manipur's attainment of statehood, in 1971 the Parliament passed the Manipur (hill areas) District Council Act of 1971, to establish autonomous district councils in the hill areas of Manipur. According to the act, all the hill areas of Manipur were to be divided into six autonomous districts each with a district council of its own. Each district council was to consist of 18 elected members and two nominated members. These autonomous districts are:

Sl. No.	*Name of the District*	*Headquarters*	*Population*[8]
01.	Manipur South	Churachandpur	98,114
02.	Manipur North	Senapati	38,424
03.	Manipur East	Ukhrul	62,229
04.	Manipur West	Tamenglong	44,775
05.	Manipur Sadar Hills	Kangpokpi	68,751
06.	Tengnoupal	Chandel	38,723

The act was finally implemented in August 1973. The members of the district councils are elected on the basis of adult franchise. The chairman and the deputy chairman are elected by members of the district council. The council has the power to remove a chairman by a two-thirds majority of the total strength of the council. But if a resolution is passed by less than a 2/3 majority but by an absolute majority, it is left to the discretion of the government to remove the chairman. Such a resolution shall not be brought before the district council within one year from the date of chairman's election. The chairman may nominate from amongst members of the council a panel consisting of not more than two deputy chairman.

Each district council has a fund called the *"council fund"*. All money received by or on behalf of the council under the provisions of the act is credited to this fund. The council fund is mainly utilised for the construction and maintenance of public buildings and public roads, maintenance of all land and other property transferred to the district council by the administrator by way of gift or otherwise for public purposes[9]

Functions of the District Council:

The district council has a number of functions as prescribed by the Manipur (hill areas) District Council Act. These are as follows:

Executive Powers: [10]

As many as seventeen functions are given to the district council by the act.[10] These are the maintenance and management of such property, movable and immovable and institutions as may be transferred to the council by the administrator, the construction, repair and maintenance of such roads, bridges, channels and buildings, the establishment, maintenance and management of primary schools, dispensaries, cattle, ponds, markets and fairs, the construction, repair and maintenance of all buildings, embankments, the supply, storage and prevention from pollution of water for drinking, cooking and bathing purposes, the supply, storage and control of water for agricultural purposes, the preservation and reclamation of soil, the preservation, protection and improvement of livestock and prevention of animal diseases, public health and sanitation, the management of such ferries as may be entrusted to the charge of the council by the administrator, the initiation, inspection and control of relief works, the allotment, occupation or use or the setting apart of land, other than land acquired for any public purpose or land which is a reserved forest, for the purpose of agriculture or grazing or for residential or other non-agricultural purposes or for any other purposes likely to promote the interests of the inhabitants of any village or town situated within the autonomous district, the management of any forest not being a reserved forest, the regulation of the practice of jhum or other forms of shifting cultivation, and any other matter which the administrator may, in consultation with the hill areas committee, entrust to the district council in the field of agriculture, animal husbandry, community development, social and tribal welfare village planning, etc.

The functions of the district council are executive in nature. It is supposed to look after the welfare of the villagers by exercising and implementing the various functions entrusted to it.

Legislative Powers

The Manipur District Council Act, 1971 did not give the district council any legislative power. But it can recommend legislation on certain matters concerning the Scheduled Tribes. These are the appointment or succession of chiefs, inheritance of property, marriage and divorce and social customs.

The district council may make rules and regulations or bye-laws in relation to maintenance and management of schools, stipends and scholarship of students, construction, repair, control and management of dispensaries including supply of medicines and protection from pollution of water for tanks, springs, wells, parts of rivers, streams, channels and water sources for drinking purposes.

Financial Powers

The district council has been given financial powers under the act.[11] These are to levy taxes on items such as taxes on profession, trades and employments; on animals, vehicles and boats, on the entry of goods into the market for sale therein and tolls on passengers and goods carried in ferries, on the maintenance of schools, dispensaries or roads and any other tax falling under list II of the Seventh Schedule to the Constitution which the Manipur legislature may, by law, empower the district council to levy. The district council may fix and levy school fees and fees for the use of or benefits derived from any of the works done or service rendered under this section of the act. With the prior approval of the administrator, the district council also has the power to remit or reduce any fee or exempt any person or class of persons from liability.

Judicial Powers

Unlike the district councils established under the Sixth Schedule of the Constitution of India, the district councils in Manipur do not hold any judicial powers. The judicial power for the administration of the district lies solely in the hands of the state government. All cases are decided by the district court. The council exercises only nominal powers in judicial matters.

Relationship between the District Council and State Government:

The district councils are supposed to function independently of the state government. The main objective for the framing of the Manipur District Council Act, 1971, was to grant autonomy to the district councils. The only relation between the district council and the state government is grant. The state government has to grant money for the working of district council. The district council administration is a mini-government concerning the welfare of the people of the district. But from the working of the district council in Manipur, we know that the deputy commissioner of the district controls these councils. The controlling officer is the Deputy Commissioner who is empowered to suspend or prohibit any action of the council if he thinks it works against the interests of the public. The administrator, on receipt of a report from the deputy commissioner, can supersede any council, not exceeding one year. During this period, all the powers and functions of the district council are exercised and performed by any authority appointed by the administrator. The deputy commissioner of the district is usually given this responsibility. In actual practice we find that the district council is subordinate to the district administration.[12]

The district administration exercises supreme control over the district council in executive, legislative and judicial matters. The proposals for the making of rules, regulations, by-laws, developmental works, and executive and judicial matters are submitted to the district administration after passing them in the district council. The district administration has to approve of these proposals. Generally, the important executive, legislative and judicial activities are carried out by the district administration. As regards the annual budget, though the district council prepares and passes it, the council has to submit the budget to the district administration for approval. The district administration usually approves the budget within the limit of funds granted by the hill commissioner. Therefore, the deputy commissioner has the power to change or modify the budget prepared by the district council. The resolutions passed by the district council in legislative, executive, judicial and financial matters are usually sent to the deputy commissioner of the district for approval. The amount of funds granted by the hill commissioner, government of Manipur, depends on the funds available in his department. On the other hand, it is upto the legislative assembly of Manipur to allot funds for the development and administration of the hill districts. If the legislative assembly provides sufficient funds in the budget as proposed by the hill commissioner after discussions with the Hill Areas Committee, district councils usually get the amount as proposed in the budget. It is also reported that the taxes collected by the district council from paan shops, octroi and others go to the district administration.[13] Even professional taxes collected from employees of the district council are submitted to the administration of the district council.[14]

The main problem faced by the district councils seems to be the lack of funds from the government of Manipur. The complaints from the Ukhrul district council are that teaching aids and furniture have not been supplied for the past five years, no construction work could be taken up due to the non-availability of funds, and no medicines have been distributed to the civil dispensaries.[15]

In addition to the financial problems, the district council also suffers on other fronts. First, it cannot work smoothly due to frequent political interference. No chairman or vice-chairman of the district council can remain in office without the support of the ruling political party. Second, the nature of decentralisation to the district council is debatable. The district council does not possess the qualities of real local self-government. Third, though Rule No. 98 of the Manipur (hill areas) District Councils Rules, 1972, envisages a relationship between the village authority and district council, it is more an administrative rather than a democratic one. Lastly, the basic foundation of autonomy and local self-government is lacking for the successful working of these district councils. Though elected, certain members of these councils lack a workable degree of political consciousness and awareness. Most of them are mere followers and supporters of politicians at the state level. They do not even have their own political ideas and principles.

Thus the autonomy granted to the district councils under the act is only in name. The survival and working of the district councils greatly depends on the government of Manipur via district administration.

References

1. It is similar to the kind of relationship that exists in a confederation in the form of loose political unity. The chiefs of the hills could assert their independence on the basis of their strength.
2. Sharma, Nandalal, Meitrabak, Imphal, O.K. Store, 1960, pp.1-2.
3. Churachand was granted the title of Rajah of Manipur by the Governor General-in-Council.4.
4. Clause 4 of the Sanad issued to Raja Churachand Singh.
5. Clauses 9(i), 9(ii), The Manipur State Hill Peoples' (Administration) Regulation, 1947.
6. Clause 12, Ibid.

7. Clause 3, The Manipur, (Village Authorities in Hill Areas) Act, 1956.
8. Census of India, Manipur, 1981.
9. Govt. of Manipur (Planning & Development Deptt.), The District Council Act, 1971, pp.10-13.
10. Ibid.
11. Section 33, The Manipur District Council Act, 1971.
12. The findings are based on the research works conducted in the Political Science Department, Manipur University regarding the working of the Churachandpur District Council, 1992-93, Churachandpur and Ukhrul District Council 1993-94, Ukhrul, Manipur.
13. Some of the District Councils e.g. Ukhrul District Council has not levied any kind of fees or taxes upto 1993-94.
14. The writer could gather this information from the research study of the Churachandpur District Council. Churachandpur, Manipur.
15. The information has been collected from the Ukhrul District Council, 1993-94, Ukhrul, Manipur.
16. The principle of adult franchise was introduced in the hills of Manipur for the first time by the Manipur Village Authorities Act, 1956.

PART - III

ISSUES ON EDUCATION

13

Education in North East India: Problems of Democratization

- *Prof. Gangmumei Kamei*

Emerging Regional Identity

India's North-East, with her cultural and social pluralism, has emerged as a distinctive entity in the national life of the country. This regional identity is the legacy of a long history and a rich cultural heritage; the ancient Hindu kingdom of Kamarupa, the Ahom kingdom of Assam, the kingdom of Manipur, Tripura and small tribal principalities and of the emerging identity that is found in the multi-ethnic, multi-lingual, multi-religious and multi-cultural characteristics of the various social groups in this region. The democratic and socialist goals of the Indian Republic, with its policy of secularism that provides the opportunity of ethnic identity, self-assertion coupled with comparative geographical isolation and social insularity, have given a new dimension and meaning to this identity. However, this region appears to be different from the rest of this country; at the same time, there are intra-regional differences in the form of ethnicity, social and economic situations and political aspirations which are being resolved, thanks to the dynamism of Indian democracy, by the formation of the seven states. Nation building on a democratic basis is an on-going process in North-East India, Therefore, educational development and its concomitant problems assumes a regional character though universal and national in essence.

Pre-Colonial Education System

Education in the pre-colonial period had a feudal character. The traditional educational system was exclusively for the production of a priestly class that was utilised by the rulers to perpetuate their rule. The Ahom rulers, the Meitei kings, the Kachari and Tripuri rajas patronised learning and learned people. Royal patronage to education, religion and literature was not open to everybody as education was restricted to the priestly classes: the Hindu Brahmins, the Ahom deodhais and bailungs, the maichous of Manipur. This royal patronage succeeded in building up a rich tradition of scholarship in the fields of religion, literature and history. The services of these priest-scholars were put to use by the state for religious, literary and administrative works. The ultimate objective of the royal patronage was to strengthen the monarchy and the perpetuation of ruling dynasties. The members of royalty and the feudal nobility were imparted education by the priestly-scholars but there was no regular educational institution as such. This restricted educational opportunity naturally deprived the masses of access to knowledge and learning. The Vaishnavite Satras of Assam established by Sankara Deva, the great Vaishavite reformer and teacher, however, became great centres of learning, religious and social activities that included the common people. The Satras may be regarded as the first step to the imparting of education to the masses. The mosques provided informal education to the Muslims. The Hinduised Ahoms introduced some "Gurukuls" for Brahmin students. In Manipur, the Maichous who were priestly-scholars imparted learning to the royal princes, sons of nobility and certain select commoners. Among the tribal people who inhabit the hilly tracts of the eastern Himalayas, traditional education was imparted through their dormitories in the form of training in martial arts and warfare, handicrafts, creative arts, custom, tradition, morality and discipline. The objective of traditional tribal education was to make an individual an all-rounder - tribal warrior, committed member of the village community with full knowledge of the creative arts, dance and music, well versed in the tradition and folklore of his tribe, clan and village. Thus in traditional society, despite the absence of literacy in the strictest sense, the social and moral fibre of the people helped sustain society.

Education during the Colonial Period

The introduction of western education during the early colonial period was a result of the acceptance and adoption of "welfare" as a responsibility of the state by the colonial government under the influence of the utilitarian philosophy. The British conquest of North-East India coincided with the formulation of an educational policy and decision taken by the government of the East India Company to introduce English education in India. Administrators were sent to manage the affairs of the eastern frontier where people who were wedded to this ideology had adopted paternalism as the guiding principle of their administration. In the nineteenth century, education had become the 'social right' of subject peoples; and the government of India both at the Centre and provinces created departments of education. Greatly influenced by European ideas of civilising the Asians as one of the goals of imperialism, Christian evangelism went hand-in-hand with British colonial rule. Both the government and the Christian missionaries, whose aim was to civilise natives by converting them to Christianity, took up the onerous task of spreading education among the subject people in the North-East and elsewhere. English education was designed to inculcate within the people European liberal ideas, literature and science, and at the same time to produce educated people who could be conveniently employed to play a role in the efficient running of colonial administration. On the other hand, the Christian missionaries wanted to train Christian workers from amongst the indigenous people to spread Christianity among the non-believers and to spread the minimum literary knowledge so that the people could read and understand the Bible and related literature.

Western education was a gift and instrument of British colonial rule, the original objectives of which were to maintain law and order, collect revenue and adjudicate disputes among the subject people. In the whole of the North-East, education was spread by three agencies: Christian missionaries, the provincial government and the private social service bodies. The American Baptist missionaries worked in Upper Assam, especially in Sibsagar and among the Nagas while the Welsh mission worked among the Khasis, Garos, Darang and Nowgong. Later on the missionary work spread to Manipur and Mizoram as well. The government of Assam, under the inspiring leadership of dedicated administrators like David Scott, the first commissioner of Assam, Francis Jenkin and others, opened up educational institutions consisting mostly of primary schools. But it was after the famous Wood's despatch of 1854 that the government started grant-in-aids to the schools with the initiative of the people. Since 1845, new private venture schools came up and sought grants from the government. Successive chief commissioners of Assam took special care to promote education and Gauhati became the centre of western education in the region.

Education was theoretically made open to everybody in the colonial period. However, the progress of education was slow, as the sponsoring agencies did not have enough resources at their command to run the schools. But in the second half of the nineteenth century and early part of the twentieth century, enlightened leaders of the Brahmaputra valley gradually started influencing the government in quickening the pace of educational development in Assam, starting with the Gauhati seminary to Cotton College (1901). In Manipur, western education was introduced at the initiative of the British political agents, starting with Nathall (1872) who began a school to Johnstone (1985). Later on the American Baptist missionary Rev. William Pettigrew who worked in Manipur (1892-1903) started founding schools. He was the pioneer of western education in Manipur. Watkin Roberts, with his Indo-Burma Thado Kuki Pioneer Mission worked in the south Manipur hills. Rev. Clarke was the pioneer educationist among the Nagas. Savidge and Lorrian were the pioneers in Mizoram. One should remember the royal patronage to education in the princely states of Manipur and Tripura in the North-East and the role of nationalist leaders of the region in spreading education among the masses.

During this period, the failure or irrelevance of the traditional education system to meet the requirements of the new regime was noticeable. Yet the traditional system particularly Sanskrit education, though incorporated in the new curricula, continued to exist for the propagation of Hinduism. At the end of colonial rule, the North-East region made some progress in western education. A new class of the English educated elite had emerged; the middle class emerged in Assam and Manipur. The importance of western education was well accepted as the key to modernisation. S.I. Rudolph and L.I. Rudolph, thus observe, "Education became a key determinant of wealth, status and power." It was accepted as an instrument to enable economic growth, as a means to improve the quality of life, to enhance human resources, and to create new knowledge, new technology and new ways of managing resources.

Educational Problems of the Region

There has been tremendous expansion of education since India's Independence in 1947 at all levels - primary, secondary, higher and professional education - due to the boost it was given by the national government. With the quantitative expansion of education came the problems of quality, standard of education, management, resources availability and contents of education. The government of India appointed several educational commissions to examine the problem and suggest remedies. This expansion of education was possible because of the universalisation of education as a national goal. Education is a state subject in the Indian Constitution; the responsibility of educational administration is vested in the state governments. Therefore, it was really difficult to evolve a uniform national education policy and common education system. At the same time, the cultural and linguistic character of the Indian states (mostly on the basis of language) made things difficult. Later on ethnic and historical considerations influenced the state governments to evolve the education system in such a manner so as to suit the ethos of the area, especially taking linguistic aspirations into consideration. During the post-Independence period, along with the attempts to evolve a national system of education, Indian education assumed a regional character that was accentuated by regional interests and requirements. Therefore, "Indian education has become a series of educational systems with varying capabilities, policies and output."

In the North-East, education assumed different patterns; and language or the medium of instruction was an important criteria in the fashioning of this pattern: in Assam, Assamese is the medium of instruction as it is the official language: Bengali is the medium in the predominantly Bengali inhabited state of Tripura and Cachar district of Assam whereas English continues to be the medium in the hill states and it is Hindi in Arunachal Pradesh and Manipuri in Manipur.

The expansion of education in the region during the fifty years after Independence is symbolised by the establishment of the Gauhati University in 1946 and the Tripura University in 1987. And Guwahati, Shillong and Imphal have become the three main centres of higher education. Guwahati is the greatest centre of learning. Shillong has been described as the "Mecca" of western education. Imphal, with its rich cultural background and the establishment of the university, is becoming an important centre of higher education as well in the North-East..

The central government, after the inclusion of education in the concurrent list of the Constitution, has moved into the educational field. During this period, education was imparted by the state governments, central government in the union territories (now the states of Manipur, Tripura, Mizoram and Arunachal Pradesh), private organisations, mostly the mission schools and colleges and schools run by private parties. The efforts of the R.K. Mission in the field of education cannot be expanded. Along with maximum growth, many problems have surfaced as well. These include:

i) The non-availability of adequate financial resources for education is the biggest problem. At the same time, there are disparities in resource availability between different sectors. While the central government, through the North-East Council, has given funds to centrally sponsored institutions other state-sponsored institutions are not adequately financed though they perform similar tasks.

ii) The lack of a uniform and socially relevant curricular in schools, colleges and universities has been the main weakness of education in this region. The recent vigorous implementation of the NCERT course and UGC guidelines on higher education, especially in the introduction of the three-year degree course and rationalisation of syllabi in the university, provides the silver lining to this not-so-happy situation. The role of the state boards of secondary education has to be commended in this aspect.

iii) The teaching profession has not been able to attract competent and qualified talent. This non-availability of qualified teachers at the higher levels of education has been the major drawback of education in all the states of this region. The incentives to higher and additional degrees have given some encouragement to in-service teachers. At the same time, the more qualified teachers are drawn to metropolitan universities and institutions.

iv) The extraordinary expansion of education has led to increasing enrolment in colleges and universities. But the graduates produced by the universities face difficulties in securing employment in the region. Thus, there is no correlation between the manpower requirement and the production of graduates in the region.

v) Facilities for scientific and technical studies are limited. The medical, engineering and agricultural colleges and universities have not been able to meet the great rush for admission to their courses.

vi) The examination system in this region is not uniform and has been the subject matter of much criticism.

vii) The issue of medium of instruction in schools, colleges and universities also pose a problem. While at the primary level, the mother tongue is the best medium of instruction; at the secondary level, it is the regional languages. There is no problem with respect to Assamese, Bengali, Manipuri and Hindi and some developed tribal languages like Khasi, Mizo and Garo. But there are many tribal communities that have to adopt either a regional language or Hindi or English. Naturally, they are at a disadvantage. English would probably be the best bet for them. In the universities too, English should continue to be the medium of instruction, as it cannot be easily replaced in the hill areas of this region.

viii) There are wide variations in the level of literacy in different parts of this region. Mizoram has the highest literacy level and is above the national average whereas Arunachal Pradesh and some hill districts of Nagaland, Assam and Manipur have a very low average of literates.

ix) The tribal population of this region continues to suffer from economic, social and educational disabilities despite the large-scale incentives given to the Scheduled Tribes students and tribal areas.

Problems of Democratisation of Education in the North-East:

India as a democratic, secular and socialist country guarantees freedom and equality to her citizens. As education is the key to the success of a democracy, there is a movement to democratise education, which has been a populist slogan and used in common parlance. Though not well defined, it has come to mean the process of providing equal educational opportunities to all sections of society in a democratic state, and the democratic management of a socially relevant and equalitarian education system for promoting among other things, a democratic way of life. This has two implications, the preparation of the people to inculcate and practise social democracy in all aspects of life, and the application of institutions ranging from the primary level to the universities. However, it must be admitted that translation of this ideal into reality in the Indian context is a difficult and extremely slow process.

Despite the lack of conceptual clarity on the part of the policy planners and decision makers, one can discern that the process of democratisation has been initiated in the region through several educational legislations adopted by the state legislatures and implemented through different agencies of the government. Democratisation is reflected in the several attempts to implement the universalisation of education for the masses. Primary education has become free in the whole region. Secondary education is highly subsidised and for the tribes in the hill states, education is free from primary to secondary school except in colleges and professional colleges where fees are reimbursed by the state government by way of scholarships. With the massive expansion of secondary education, there is always a great rush for entry into colleges and universities, which have introduced diverse courses in the liberal arts and science, technical and scientific education and professional studies. Special facilities are provided for the Scheduled Castes, Scheduled Tribes and other backward classes in the form of reservation of seats for admission and scholarships. Supervision of secondary education has been carried out; the universities in this region academically administer the state boards of secondary education and higher education. School curriculum and university syllabi have been rationalised and updated according to the guidelines provided by the NCERT and the UGC. Attempts were made to provide infrastructure in the schools and colleges to improve the social and economic status of the teachers by giving incentives in the form of revised pay scales, fellowship and advanced increments for more qualified teachers. Provisions for hostel facilities for colleges and, to some extent, for schools, have been made. The medium of instruction has been either the mother tongue or Hindi or English. Education has developed both quantitatively and to some extent qualitatively in professional colleges and universities. Adult and continuing education programmes have been taken up to erase illiteracy and provide non-formal education to the masses. Education for women and the weaker sections including the physically handicapped and the blind has been provided. Inner democracy or at least a semblance of it has been introduced in the management of the aided schools and colleges. Universities have been granted statutory autonomy.

This rosy picture of the democratisation of education, however, is one-sided and mostly on paper or in the well written programmes of the governments of the region. The ground realities are quite different. There are several gaps in this process of democratisation.

i) Democratisation is associated with the politicisation of education. As the state governments provide funds for the establishment and maintenance of educational institutions, both government and private aided, and appoint teachers; the political leaders, mostly the members of legislatures control the allocation of resources, implementation of educational programmes with an eye to retaining their influence and strengthening their political base. As the ruling party always tries to promote its own vested interests, this high level of politicisation in the administration of education has led to highly partisan politics.

ii) The extreme poverty of the people, both in the plains of Assam and hill areas has been the major cause of a slowdown in the progress of education. Poor parents can ill afford to send their children to schools and they end up being employed as child labour. On the other hand, educational opportunities have been taken advantage of by the children of rich parents. The rich send their children to English medium schools and privately managed mission schools while the poor children have to be content with schools run by the government. There is also a great imbalance between the urban areas, including the hills, with respect to educational opportunities and facilities. This disparity would favour the rich children with better education. Those who have had a better education man the state bureaucracy and industrial establishments. For real democratisation of education to take place, this wide gap between the two classes has to be bridged. But it would be difficult since the Indian social situation actually enforces a social hierarchy based on caste and economic status. Thus, democratic education in the true sense of the term would be a difficult concept.

iii) The state has financially and administratively controlled the schools and colleges established by the government or by private agencies. In the government schools and colleges that are administered by the state bureaucracy there is no question of democracy in management. The aided institutions have to function in accordance to the whims and fancies of the state educational bureaucracy and those who wield political power.

iv) In institutions managed by Christian missions and private agencies, there is no internal democracy as the management is controlled by the church or by the private body. Though they do impart good education, the commercialisation of education is not conducive to the democratic concept. There is no security of service for either teachers or employees.

v) Because of the financial dependence on the government, the autonomy of the university is in theory only. It all depends on the policy of the state education department or the political managers of education. Luckily for the universities of the region there has been some respect for the autonomy of the university. It is due to the reluctance of the state government rather than their lack of power to actually control the universities. There is a great disparity between the funding of the central universities and that of the state universities. This disparity has to be removed if a uniform healthy university education is to flourish in this region.

vi) The Scheduled Tribes have benefited from the facilities provided by the government, and a tribal elite consisting of bureaucrats, technocrats, contractors, businessmen and politicians has emerged. This elite group has taken the lion's share of government facilities in education and the poorer sections of the tribals have been deprived of access to good education. While the kinship base of

> tribal society is still strong, the stratificat ons of tribal society based on economic status have created an incipient class distinction between the different sections of tribal population. And so, education has gradually encroached upon the egalitarianism of tribal society. This misguided democratisation of education has now threatened the social democracy of the tribal people.

Despite these gaps, education is extremely important for the survival of democracy. The new education policy, despite its deficiencies, which should be rectified in due course, will go a long way in strengthening the educational base and in promoting a democratic ethos in our society.

14

Universalisation of Elementary Education in the North East

- Dr. L. Ibotombi Singh

Introduction

The North Eastern states are not only similar in their racial, climatic and demographic features but also share their backwardness in the field of education, particularly at the lower levels. Since Independence, both the central and state governments have done a lot to provide more opportunities for the primary education of children below the age of 14. Apart from this, a number of NGOs and Christian missionaries rendered their valuable services for the cause of education in the region. However, 35% of the child population between the ages of 6 years to 14 years is still not covered by the UEE (Universalisation of Elementary Education) scheme.

According to the 1991 census, there has been an increase in the literacy level of the region. The literacy rate in this part of the country is 45.47, out of which 64.53 are males and 49.76 are females. However, this figure is still 6.47% below the national average. Mizoram retained its highest position by being on top with an 82.27 literacy rate in the region. Arunachal Pradesh was at the bottom with a literacy rate of 41.59. In addition to this, the literacy rate among women in the state is far behind the rest of the states with a record of 29.37. Except for Meghalaya, the literacy rate in other states is above the national average.

Status of UEE in the Region

During the 50 years of Independence there has been a gradual expansion of primary and upper primary school facilities in the region. According to the information available, there are about 40,000 primary and 10+ thousand upper primary schools, showing a ratio of 4.13:1, which is above the national ratio of 3.47:1. The ratio of Assam, Manipur and Tripura are found above the national ratio. However, Mizoram and Sikkim are behind the national ratio. This clearly indicates that the first three states had one upper primary school for every four primary schools, whereas Sikkim and Mizoram had 2.88:1 and 1.68:1 respectively.

According to the Assam Elementary Education (Prov) Rules 1977, every inhabited village should have at least one primary school at a distance of 1 km, provided there is a population of more than 200 in the village. In the case of upper primary schools, the minimum distance should be 3 kms provided the population of the village is above 500. As per the Sixth All India Education Survey Report, there are 12.748 revenue villages without a primary school in this region. States like Assam, Meghalaya and Tripura had the highest number of villages without a primary school. Exceptionally, every village in Mizoram had one primary school. Still, in most of the states, there are no inhabited areas that do not have at least one school.

On the other hand, the enrolment of students in primary and upper primary schools in the five states is 66.07 lakhs and 19.94 lakhs respectively. This may increase to above 70 lakhs and 20 lakhs when the data for the remaining three states is added. The ratio of enrolment at both the levels are found to be 1:175 and 1:250. However, the proportion of female enrolment is rather discouraging in all the states except in Manipur where enrolment is above 81% at the primary and 64% at the upper primary level.

During the Eighth Plan, on an average 6.7% of the state's budget was spent on elementary education. Per capita expenditure on elementary education is Rs 514. However, priorities differ among states in so far as budget allocation for elementary education is concerned. In some states, the above figure is even higher. For instance, in the case of Assam, the percentage of expenditure on education has been well over 26 % (Revenue) and 5.8 (SDP) during 1992-93.

There is at present no legislation for free and compulsory education in the eight sister states. However, no tuition fee is levied for primary and upper primary classes in government and aided schools. But as regards the payment of scholarships to students, all the states adopted different policies. The governments of Assam, Arunachal Pradesh and Sikkim provided free textbooks to all students. Children belonging to the two districts of Nagaland, which are educationally and economically backward, are given free textbooks whereas in Tripura, only SC and ST students are given such facilities. Further, in Assam, attendance scholarships are given to SC/ST students at the rate of Rs 60 per student plus special scholarship for SC/ST female students at the rate of Rs 240 for a year. The government of Manipur on the other hand provides special scholarships to every disabled child in the form of Rs 400 per annum for books and stationary, Rs 200 per annum for uniforms, Rs 50 per month as transport allowance and Rs 2,000 or actual cost of equipment. Likewise, the government of Nagaland has been funding a scheme of a special stipend at the rate of Rs 50 per month for select girl students, which has encouraged the enrolment of girls in schools over the years. Similarly, in Sikkim, a special stipend at the rate of Rs 100 per month is provided for select students. Mid-day meals and free uniforms are provided to all the children at the primary stage including female SC/ST students. Further, cash incentives are also provided to SC/ST students. In Tripura, SC/ST students are given book grants. Such facilities are extended to meritorious students whose parents' income is below Rs 750 per month. Other incentives include mid-day meals, free uniforms for SC/ST girls and attendance scholarships for SC/ST girls. Unfortunately, the children of Mizoram and Meghalaya could not be given similar facilities, as both the states have not been able to meet the cost of education due to a financial crunch.

Issues

Before Independence, the extent of formal education in this region was pathetic. During the pre-Independence period, the people of Arunachal Pradesh did not have a single school. This is almost true in the case of other states except for Assam. There are many factors that affect the growth and development of education in this region. All the states are economically backward, fully dependent on central assistance and have not been able to open schools and provide facilities for all the inhabited areas. Above all, the region consists predominantly of hill states with a considerably large area that has an inaccessible terrain. A fair number of inhabited areas have a very low population that is below the norm that facilitates the opening of a school.

At present, there are thousands of single-teacher primary schools. Meghalaya alone had 600 single-teacher primary schools, 239 schools with four classrooms, 545 with three classrooms, 2,160 with two classrooms and 760 with a single room. Other states are in a similar condition. During the past two decades, the rapid expansion of the population in the region has resulted in the increased demand for further expansion of infrastructural facilities, which the state governments are often not able to meet in totality. All the state governments face problems in transporting material to the interior hill areas for the construction of schools and teachers' quarters.

Above all, attracting well-qualified and dedicated teachers is a problem in all the states. Over the years, the education, training, calibre, social status, idealism and social sensitivity in teachers has deteriorated because of the unattractive service conditions, corruption, nepotism, ad hoc appointments and insurgency in some states. Apart from this, none of these states' communities are involved in the monitoring of school activities. At the same time, the supervisory machinery is totally redundant. The failure to retain children in school once they have enrolled causes a delay in achieving the desired goal. The need of the hour is for a continuous effort in order to remove these deficiencies phase by phase.

Concrete Measures to Achieve the Goal

These are as follows:

1. The statistical machinery for collection of educational data should be strengthened to monitor the progress of UEE and also to evaluate annually the gross enrolment ratio, net enrolment ratio and drop out rates.
2. The state governments should make provisions to give adequate aid to local bodies, which should keep in touch with the community and seek the cooperation of citizens in achieving these goals.
3. The state's education budget on elementary education should be increased.
4. The problems being faced by the school should be brought to the notice of the educational authorities and ways and means to improve them ought to be suggested.
5. In order to induct tribals to modern education it is proposed to establish ashram schools in all the tribal districts where there are less inhabited areas.
6. It is highly recommended that state departments of education adopt a common policy for providing scholarships so that a particular section of community is not exploited or left out.
7. Incentives like free textbooks, uniforms, stationery, mid-day meals and school bags are proposed to be provided at the primary and upper primary levels and these should be linked with the economic status of families and be provided only to those families that live below the poverty line irrespective of caste and creed.
8. Existing schools should be renovated and equipped with modern infrastructural facilities.
9. The object should be to create awareness and mobilisation of the community in order to increase enrolment.

10. The implementation of special programmes for the benefit of disabled children must be carried out.

11. To establish single teacher schools where ashram schools cannot be set up should be the goal.

References

1. Report of the Committee of State Education Ministers on Implications of the proposal to make Elementary Education a Fundamental Right, Government of India, MHRD, Department of Education, No. 1997.
2. Submission of the Solicitor General of India to the Hon'ble Supreme Court of India in the matter of Satyapal Anand vs. Union of India and others. WP (c) No.81/94, Government of India, MHRD, Department of Education, No. February 1997.
3. Towards A New Education Order Report - II: State Education Commission, Government of Manipur.
4. S.K. Sachadeva: Competition Success Review: Year Book 1997, New Delhi.

15

Universalisation of Elementary Education in the Hill Areas of Manipur

- Dr. L. Leiren Singh

The national policy on education 1986 gives unqualified priority to the Universalisation of Elementary Education (UEE) in India laying specific emphasis on the three thrust areas of elementary education viz - (i) universal access and enrolment; (ii) universal retention of children upto 14 years of age; and (iii) a substantial improvement in the quality of education to enable all children to achieve essential levels of learning. The government of India had already decided to provide education for all (EFA) by 2000 A.D. Within such a context, the government of Manipur is making a concerted effort to achieve the target for universalisation of elementary education in line with the constitutional provisions of Article No. 45 of the Indian Constitution. This gives emphasis to the state in general and five hill districts of Manipur in particular, as the hill areas of Manipur are educationally backward in comparison with the valley areas of Manipur. For the sake of convenience, elementary education may be divided into two sub-stages - (i) universal primary education for children in the age group of 6 - 11 years, which was to be tentatively achieved by 1995; and (ii) universal elementary education for children in the age group of 11 - 14 years, which was to be achieved by 2000 A.D. It may be pointed out that there are inter-district disparities in the 5 hill districts of Manipur in matters of enrolment and provision of facilities so far as elementary education is concerned.

Management of Primary Schools

There is a difference in the management and control of primary schools between the valley areas and hill areas of Manipur. Primary schools in the 4 valley districts of Manipur Imphal West, Imphal East, Thoubal and Bishenpur are under the direct control of the Department of Education, government of Manipur. But the primary schools - government, aided and unaided, in the hill areas of Manipur are under the indirect control of the state government as these educational institutions are under the control of the hill district councils under the Manipur (hill areas) District Council Act, 1971 that has been amended from time to time.

District Council Schools

There are 804 primary schools in the state under the hill district councils as per the 1990-1991 census - in the break-up of 130 in Tamenglong, 162 in Churachandpur, 156 in Ukhrul 226 in Senapati (70 Senapati and 156 Kangpokpi) and 130 in Chandel. But the total number of this category of primary schools in the hill areas of Manipur has been decreased to 779 in 1996-97. The break-up of the district council schools is - 130 in Tamenglong, 162 in Churachandpur, 157 in Ukhrul, 220 in Senapati (70 Senapati and 150 Kangpokpi) and130 in Chandel Hence, the total number of district council primary schools has been decreased in 1997 instead of increasing the total number of primary schools under the control of district councils. There is an increase of only 1 primary school in the Ukhrul district and the decrease of 5 primary schools in Senapati district. It is also a fact that many of the district council schools are lacking in essential facilities to provide quality education like school buildings, classrooms, furniture, etc.

Government, Aided and Recognised Schools

In addition to the district council primary schools in the hill areas of Manipur, there are also a number of educational institutions imparting primary education. They are - 46 L.P. school under the education department (S) that come into the category of villages without schools, 28 aided primary and 9 recognised primary schools in Tamenglong District, 273 primary schools under the education department (S), 11 aided primary schools and 2 recognised primary schools in Churachandpur district, 27 primary schools under the education department (S), 36 aided primary schools and 4 recognised primary schools in Ukhrul district, 67 primary schools under education department (S), 71 aided primary schools and 3 recognised primary schools in Senapati district and 42 primary schools under the education department, 42 aided and 2 recognised primary schools in Chandel district.

Literacy Rates of the Hill Districts

The main objective for the universalisation of elementary education by means of establishing a number of educational institutions under different management in the hill areas of Manipur, among other things, is to increase the percentage of literacy among the people. But it is very disappointing to note the literacy percentages of hill districts of Manipur as per the 1991 census shown in the following table:-

TABLE - I

District-wise Literacy Rates of Hill Districts of Manipur according to the 1991 census

District	*Percentage of literate persons*	*Male*	*Female*
Tamenglong	50.16	59.92	39.68
Churachandpur	58.17	66.38	49.30
Ukhrul	62.54	72.11	51.57
Senapati	46.04	55.26	36.13
Chandel	46.68	57.39	34.40

From the above table, it is very clear that the percentage of literates in the Ukhrul district is the highest from amongst the five hill districts of Manipur. Churachandpur district ranks second and Senapati and Chandel districts have the lowest literacy rates.

Hence, special attention should be paid on the universalisation of elementary education in the Senapati and Chandel districts of Manipur. The progress of universalisation of elementary education has been hampered, to a great extent, because of the crucial problem of school dropouts. The problem is acute in the rural and hill areas.

School Dropout Rates

Despite the concerted efforts made by the government of Manipur to increase the enrolment of children every year at the primary school stage, the whole purpose has been defeated by the high rate of dropouts. This is especially true in the hill areas of Manipur. The dropout rate is higher in Class I, and that too amongst the girls and it gradually decreases at the higher stages of education. There are various reasons for increasing school dropout rates. Some of the important reasons attributing to this at the elementary stage of education in the present study are: financial problems, family troubles, social problems, lack of support, household duties, lack of interest, etc. The extent of school dropouts at the primary stage in the hill areas of Manipur will be evident from the following table of the different benchmark surveys conducted by the government of Manipur in 1983-84.

TABLE - 2

District-wise number of School Dropouts in the Hill Districts of Manipur

District	*No. of students in primary schools*	*No. of drop out school*	*Total no. drop-outs*
Tamenglong	5858	1400	4503
Churachandpur	4038	362	1888
Ukhrul	6303	217	1714
Senapati	4147	140	812
Chandel	3510	80	492

In the district council schools, the rate of dropouts is very high. For example, in Tamenglong, Senapati and Chandel districts, out of 100 pupils admitted in class IA/IB in 1986, only 3-5 pupils remained upto class V as per the Singhal Committee Report of 1991. Hence, special attention will have to be given to reduce the incidence of dropouts at the primary stage of education in the hill districts of Manipur.

General Measures of Reforms

To achieve the target for the universalisation of elementary education within the stipulated period, certain general measures of reforms should be taken up on a priority basis in the hill areas of Manipur. For this purpose, special emphasis should be given to the removal of disparities and the equalisation of educational opportunities for the deprived sections of the society. Education should also be used as an agent of basic change in the status of women. The eradication of illiteracy among women and the obstacles inhibiting their access to and retention in elementary education should receive top priority. Hence, the following measures should be taken to bring the Scheduled Tribes inhabiting the hill areas of Manipur on par with other developed sections of Manipur:

(a) Priority should be given to establishing schools in the hill areas. The construction of school buildings may be undertaken in these areas on a priority basis through normal funds for education meant for the hill areas, as well as under the Jawahar Rozgar Yojna, tribal welfare schemes, etc.

(b) The socio-cultural milieu of the tribal people of Manipur has its distinctive characteristics. The 29 recognised tribes of the state speak 29 dialects. Hence, there is a need to develop instructional materials in most of the tribal dialects in addition to the 5 major dialects, namely, Hmar, Paite, Tangkhul, Lushai, Thadou (Kuki), which are used as the medium of instruction in primary schools in the hill areas of Manipur.

(c) Educated and promising Scheduled Tribe youths in the hill districts of Manipur should be encouraged to take to the teaching profession with a sense of dedication.

(d) Residential schools including ashram schools would be established in those areas where such facilities are not available and schools already established should be qualitatively improved.

(e) Incentive schemes would be formulated for the tribal students keeping in mind their special needs and lifestyles. Scholarships, special remedial courses and other programmes to remove socio-psychological impediments will be provided to improve their performance in various courses.

(f) Angalwadis, non-formal and adult education centres will be opened on a priority basis in the hill areas of Manipur to pave the way for the proper development of elementary education.

(g) The curriculum should be designed in such manner so as to create an awareness of the rich cultural identity of the tribal people of Manipur and their cordial relationship with the major ethnic groups that have co-existed from time immemorial.

Specific Measures of Reforms

In addition to the above general measures of reforms, the following specific measures should also be taken up for the early universalisation of elementary education in the hill areas of Manipur:

a) To achieve universal primary education for children in the age group of 6-11 years, special attention should be paid to the enrolment drive in certain hill districts. Enrolment at the primary stage of education has been decreasing in Tamenglong and Senapati district and it is almost stagnant in the Ukhrul and Chandel districts.

b) Efforts should be made to increase the retention of pupils in primary schools in hill areas and the high rate of school dropouts should be reduced to the minimum by means of opening non-formal education centres at suitable places that will provide condensed kinds of courses so that they can be brought to appropriate stages of formal education.

c) Urgent steps have to be taken to provide basic physical facilities essential for providing quality education in the Ninth Five-Year Plan to the primary schools in the hill areas of Manipur.

d) There should be a cordial relationship between the state education authorities and district council authorities for the effective implementation of various schemes under the decentralised management of the district councils.

e) All the single-teacher schools in the hill areas of Manipur may be upgraded gradually to two-teacher schools subject to having a prescribed minimum number of pupils. Proper training should be imparted to the teachers at regular intervals. For this purpose, SCERT should discharge its functions as the model agency to give training to primary school teachers, adult and non-formal education. Hence, DIETS should be made functional in all the hill districts of Manipur.

f) Adequate arrangements should be made for the construction of teachers' quarters in the remote hill areas of Manipur so that they may be in a position to take up their assignments with a missionary zeal by means of regularly associating with the parents of the pupils and securing their cooperation and coordination in all developmental plans of the school for the benefit of the local community.

g) The District Primary Education Programme (DPEP) launched in 1994 in India with hopes for the universalisation of elementary education can be taken up in some of the hill districts of Manipur on an experimental basis. The programme had been taken up in 64 districts in 14 states of India as a centrally sponsored programme with external funding support from various international agencies.

h) Adequate provisions should be made in the state budget for the qualitative improvement of primary education in the hill areas of Manipur. The earmarked funds should also be made available to the district councils in time so that financial constraints do not stand in the way of the proper implementation of any developmental plans for primary education. For this purpose, effective utilisation of funds is also an essential requirement.

In concluding our present discussion, it may not be out of place to point out that political will is essentially required to achieve the target for the proper development of hill areas as education is the key to all developmental programmes.

This gigantic task can be successfully executed by adopting the mission mode approach to get the full benefits of the minimum levels of learning after achieving the target for the universalisation of elementary education.

References

1. Bose, M.L.: *Historical and Constitutional Documents of North Eastern* Indian (1824-1973), Concept Publishing Co., Delhi, 1979.
2. Govt. of Manipur: *Tribal Benchmark Surveys of Manipur West District, South District, East District, Senapati District and Tengnoupal District,* Directorate of Economics and Statistics, Imphal, 1983-84.
3. Govt. of Manipur: *Education in Manipur Towards a New Education Order,* Report I & III, Imphal, 1991-92.
4. Govt. of Manipur: *Statistical Handbook of Manipur 1992,* Directorate of Economics and Statistics, Imphal, 1993.
5. Govt. of Manipur: *List of Institutions for Schools (General Education 1996-97),* Directorate of Education (S), Planning & Statistics Section, Imphal, 1997.
6. Govt. of India: *National Policy on Education 1986 (with modifications undertaken in 1992)* MHRD, New Delhi, 1992.
7. Govt. of India: *Programme of Action 1992,* MHRD, Department of Education, New Delhi, 1992.

PART - IV

ISSUES ON FOREST AND ENTREPRENEURSHIP

16

Entrepreneurship Development in Hill Areas of Manipur: Problems and Prospects

- Dr. G.P. Prassain

Introduction

The word "entrepreneurship" has been derived from a French root, which means to "undertake". According to Higgins, "Entrepreneurship is the function of seeking investment and production opportunity, organising an enterprise to undertake a new production process, raising capital, hiring labour, arranging the supply of raw materials, finding site, introducing a new technique and commodities, discovering new sources of raw materials and selecting top managers for day-to-day operations of the entreprise".[1] Thus, "entrepreneurship is the purposeful activity of an individual or a group of associated individuals undertaken to initiate, maintain and aggrandise profit by production or distribution of economic goods and service".[2]

Joseph A. Schumpeter sees the entrepreneur as an integral part of the economic growth process. He has emphasised on changes that may take place through innovations. One who introduces these changes may be called an entrepreneur. Since then various schools of thought have propounded the concepts of entrepreneurship by linking the variables like social, ecconomical, cultural and psychological. Marx, however, perceived the entrepreneur to be a social parasite. All these interpretations naturally corroborate the view that an entrepreneur is one who takes initiative for a creative venture. According to this view, entrepreneurship also signifies activity.

In the Indian context of economic development, the term entrepreneurship connotes a restricted sphere of enterprising endeavour. It refers to the existing practice of establishing new enterprises. Entrepreneurship development would therefore signify development of entrepreneurs to entrepreneurial rank.

The Dynamics of Entrepreneurship Development

Entrepreneurship is normally considered as a dependent variable because certain forces are likely to influence it. For instance, social, cultural, economic, environmental and support systems always influence entrepreneurship. Thus individuals take initiative and establish enterprises to generate entrepreneurship in a society. Similarly, environmental forces consisting of political, social, cultural, economic and many other forces directly influence entrepreneurship. The third influencing force is the support systems. The support systems influence entrepreneurship development in various ways. Such support systems include financial, commercial, industrial, institutional, research and training support.

Entrepreneurship is also assumed to be an independent variable because an individual is capable of influencing many factors, especially the socio-psychological factors. An individual is likely to motivate himself and acquire the necessary skills for the purpose. Of the various motivational factors, the motivation to achieve, personal efficacy and coping capacity are by far the most important. The achievement motivation techniques are widely followed in developing entrepreneurship. Various research findings also speak in favour of this technique. Personal efficacy, on the other hand, is required to develop the sense of being effective and to exercise control over others. The coping capability however, enables one to cope with the situation by adopting certain strategies. Thus, an entrepreneur is to create himself through self-development and enhancement. This is perhaps the criterion of entrepreneurship development. This being the entire process of entrepreneurship development, the dynamics of such development always speaks of the individual's effort, the environmental impact and support systems. In this context, it may be said that the opportunity envelope for setting up a productive activity can be possible only when certain factors like education, training, professional experience, financial help, government support etc., in different combinations are considered to be of some help to prospective entrepreneurs. It appears, therefore, that the primary task of entrepreneurship development is to seek out potential entrepreneurs through implementation of appropriate schemes. But in most of the cases, human and financial constraints generally block those possibilities.[3]

Manipur - Its Industrial Scenario

Manipur is a land-locked state situated in the extreme corner of North Eastern India. The state is rectangular in shape with a mountainous terrain. The highest mountain is 3,000 metres above sea level. It lies within the latitude of 23.83°N and 25.68°N and longitude of 93.03°E and 94.74°E. The total geographical area of Manipur is 22,327 sq. kms. It has two distinct areas of hills and plains. The area of plains or valley, which is located in the centre of Manipur, is only 1,862 sq. kms. There are 8 districts in Manipur out of which 3 districts are situated in the sprawling hills. Manipur occupies 0.68% and 8.75% of the area of the whole country and the entire North-East region respectively.

Manipur is still industrially very backward in the context of the backward N.E. region of India with a per capita income far below the all-India average, viz., Rs 3,502/- at current prices at the end of the Seventh Plan Period in 1989-90 as against the all India average of Rs 4,252/-[4]. As many as 45.06% of the people of the state live below the poverty line in 1992-93[5] as against the all-India average of 25% by the end of Seventh Plan. There are not enough industries to keep pace with the rapid growth of population and to deal with the growing problems of unemployment, poverty, lack of housing, medical care, etc.[6] Added to this, there is the problem of comparative neglect of industrialisation in the State Planning. For instance, the 6th Plan allocation for the industrial sector in Manipur was 8.33% as against the all-India average of 12.28.[7]

There are hardly any major or medium industrial units in the state worth mentioning and the few that have already been established are now suffering from varying degrees of industrial sickness. The development of large-scale industries has to follow its own logic and such major industrial units cannot be established anywhere. But this is not so in the case of small-scale and household industries. Given the proper policies and programmes and reasonably adequate infrastructural support, there are no small-scale and household industries, either demand based or resource based, which cannot be successfully established in Manipur.[8]

The Hill Region of Manipur

Out of the total geographical area of 22.327 sq. kms. of Manipur, nearly 20,000 sq. kms. consist of hill areas. Again, out of the total population of 18.36 lakhs, 6.5 lakhs are found in the five hill districts of Manipur. Table No.1 and Table No. 2 show the population of five hill districts and three valley districts and also the percentage of Scheduled Tribe residing in all the eight districts of Manipur.

TABLE - 1

Districts	*Population in lakhs according to year-wise census*			
	1961	*1971*	*1981*	*1991*
Senapati	9.72	1.04	1.55	2.08
Tamenglong	0.37	0.45	0.62	0.86
Churachandpur	0.62	0.98	1.35	1.76
Chandel	0.28	0.39	0.56	0.71
Ukhrul	0.49	0.62	0.83	1.09
Imphal	3.19	4.34	5.56	7.11
Bishnupur	0.79	1.08	1.41	1.81
Thoubal	1.35	1.82	2.23	2.94
TOTAL	7.81	10.72	14.20	18.36

TABLE - 2

DISTRICT	1971		1981		1991	
	ST Population in 000	*% to District Total*	*ST Population in 000*	*% to District Total*	*ST Population in 000*	*% to District Total*
Senapati	83	79	106	68	175	84
Tamenglong	44	98	29	47	83	96
Churachandpur	92	94	116	86	165	94
Chandel	34	89	38	68	61	86
Imphal						
Bishnupur	21	3	24	3	47	4
Thoubal						

Out of the five districts situated in the hill areas of Manipur, Senapati District has the highest population of 2.08 lakhs followed by Churachandpur, Ukhrul, Tamenglong and Chandel, according to the 1991 census. The percentage of Scheduled Tribes to the district population is 96 in Tamenglong, 94 in Ukhrul, 94 in Churachandpur, 86 in Chandel and 84 in Senapati. This shows that more than 90% people living in the five hills district of Manipur are from the Scheduled Tribes.

There are two kinds of small industrial units in Manipur, viz; SIDO (Small Industrial Development Organisation) and non-SIDO. In the SIDO group, there are Small Service Establishment (SSE) units such as colour photography, X-ray, Xeroxing, Automobile Workshop, etc. In the Manipur Small Industries (MSI) units there are those not in the reserved items such as knitting, embroidery, blacksmith work, carpentry and handicraft items etc.[9] The total number of SIDO and non-SIDO units, employment, investment and production in all the eight districts of Manipur upto 1994-95 are shown in Table No. 3.

TABLE - 3

S.No	*District*	*Sido*	*Non-Sido*	*Total*	*Empl-oyment*	*Investt (Rs. in crores)*	*Prodn. (Rs. in crores)*
1	*2*	*3*	*4*	*5*	*6*	*7*	*8*
01.	Imphal	1774	2161	4935	25357	16.17	12.12
02.	Bishnupur	420	160	580	2516	1.90	8.35
03.	Thoubal	305	96	401	2121	1.32	5.77
04.	Churachandpur	429	104	533	2781	1.76	8.68
05.	Senapati	251	49	300	1616	0.99	4.38
06.	Ukhrul	715	88	803	4134	2.62	12.56
07.	Tamenglong	248	203	451	2371	1.49	6.49
08.	Chandel	209	129	338	1805	1.12	4.87
TOTAL		**5351**	**2990**	**8341**	**42720**	**27.37**	**123.84**

Sources: Nucleus Cell, Department of Commerce and Industries, Government of Manipur.

The table reveals that till the year 1994-95, the total number of permanently registered units in the SIDO group were 5,351 and 2,990 in the non-SIDO group. The total number of permanently registered units in both SIDO and non-SIDO groups were 8,341 with total investment, production and employment of Rs 27.37 crores, Rs 123.16 crores and 4,27,720 persons respectively.

Out of the eight districts mentioned in Table No.3, five districts are situated in the hill region of Manipur. Out of the 5,351 SIDO and 2,990 non-SIDO enterprises, 1,852 SIDO and 573 non-SIDO enterprises are found in the hill region. 29.61% employment, 29.61% investment and 30% production are the figures for the hill region of Manipur.

Entrepreneurship Development Programme

The District Industries Centre (DIC) is established in all the five hill districts of Manipur. It is an institution at the district level that provides all services and facilities to entrepreneurs at one place so that they may set up small and village industries. These services and facilities include identification of a suitable scheme, the preparation of feasibility reports, arrangement for the supply of machinery and equipment, provision of raw materials, credit facilities and input for marketing and extension services, quality control, research and entrepreneurial training. The district Industries Centre would also ensure that these small industries continue to be viable. For this purpose, it provides all facilities to the entrepreneurs under one roof at the district as well as at the sub-divisional level.

All the DICs give various kinds of training programmes to the entrepreneurs without which industries that are bound to play an active role in the growth process of the hill economy would not flourish. Entrepreneurial motivation and training are the most important factors that help accelerate the pace of industrial development by inducing people to undertake risk-bearing activities. The main objective of conducting this Entrepreneurship Development Programme (EDP) is to motivate young and promising entrepreneurs for self-employment after the successful completion of their training. The first batch of the EDP in Manipur was taken up in the year 1983-84 under the sponsorship of the State Bank of India, which trained 24 persons including 2 women. Since then, several batches of EDP have been conducted from time to time by the state directorate of commerce and industries under the auspices of different organisations such as NISIET (National Institute of Small Scale Industries Extension and Training), NEITCO (North Eastern Industrial Training Consultancy Organisation), SISI (Small Industries Service Institute), etc. By 1991-92, 997 people altogether were given training under the EDP.[11]

EDP training courses and other entrepreneurial activities conducted by all the five DICs of hill districts and the three DICs of valley districts with the help of different consultancy agencies cover EDP training courses, EDP on science and technology, EDP for backward classes, rural EDP, EDP training on food processing, entrepreneurs and enterprise building programme, industrial management, institutional meets, financial management, district level seminars, etc.

The EDP training courses conducted by the eight DICs of Manipur from the year 1985-86 to the year 1995-96 are shown in Table No. 4.

The trained entrepreneurs are provided with different incentives/facilities by the state government to assist them in the developmental process. In terms of the industrial policy, the incentives include:[12]

1. Allotment of land except to the village and household industries;
2. Allotment of sheds to SSI units;
3. Manpower development;
4. State capital investment subsidy to the priority sector;
5. State transport subsidy for transportation of raw materials and finished products;
6. Interest subsidy;
7. Power subsidy;
8. Subsidy on draw of power line;
9. Subsidy for feasibility study and project report preparation;
10. Subsidy for technical know-how;
11. Price preference;
12. Reimbursement and exemption of local sales tax;
13. Reimbursement of stamp duty and registration fee;
14. Quality control subsidy; and
15. Rehabilitation of viable sick industrial units.

Problems

The efforts to promote and develop entrepreneurship depend on the performance of a number of activities - stimulatory, support and sustaining activities. These are to be performed in a balanced and coordinated manner to have the desired impact on entrepreneurship development. But all these activities are not performed in a balanced manner in the hill areas. Support activities are over-emphasised while stimulatory and sustaining activities are neglected.[13]

TABLE NO. 4

EDP TRAINING COURSES CONDUCTED SINCE 1985-86 TO 1995-96

(Below each column that states the year during which the EDP programmes were conducted are shown the number of programmes and then the number of participants for the various districts)

Sl. No.	Base of DICs	1985-86		1986-87		1987-88		1988-89		1989-90		1990-91		1991-92		1992-93		1993-94		1994-95		1995-96	
		No. of prog.	No. of particip-ants	No. of prog.	No. of particip-ants	No. of prog.	No. of particip-ants	No. of prog.	No. of particip-ants	No. of prog.	No. of particip-ants	No. of prog.	No. of particip-ants	No. of prog.	No. of particip-ants	No. of prog.	No. of particip-ants	No. of prog.	No. of particip-ants	No. of prog.	No. of particip-ants	No. of prog.	No. of particip-ants
01	DIC Imphal	1	25	3	60	3	74	1	25	-	-	2	55	2	49	6	185	7	233	4	76	a.EDP(Y) 1 b.EDP(G) 1	25 26
02	DIC Thoubal	-	-	-	-	2	50	1	25	-	-	-	-	1	35	1	25	-	-	1	25	EDP(G) 1	25
03	DIC Bishenpur	-		-	-	1	25	1	25	1	24	-	-	-	-	-	-	1	26	1	25	-	-
04	DIC C.C. Pur	-	-	-	-	-	-	1	25	-	-	-	-	-	-	-	-	-	-	1	25	-	-
05	DIC Senapati	-	-	-	-	1	20	1	30	1	25	1	25	-	-	-	-	-		-	-	EDP (Y) 1	25
06	DIC Ukhrul	-	-	-	-	1	25	-	-	-	-	-		-	-	-	-	1	28	-	-	-	-
07	DIC Tamenglong	-	-	-	-	1	18	-	-	-	-	-	-	-	-	-	-	-	-	-	-	-	-
08	DIC Chandel	-	-	-	-	1	25	1	25	1	25	1	30	-	-	-	-	-	-	1	25	-	-
TOTAL		**1**	**25**	**3**	**60**	**10**	**237**	**6**	**155**	**3**	**74**	**4**	**110**	**3**	**84**	**7**	**210**	**9**	**287**	**8**	**176**	**4**	**101**

Source: Directorate of Commerce and Industries, Government of Manipur.

There are a number of factors hindering the development of entrepreneurship in the hill region. These include:-

(i) Lack of a comprehensive programme for the development of entrepreneurship.

(ii) Absence of information relating to industrial potentiality, marketing, raw materials, etc.

(iii) Lack of collaborative efforts by organisations.

(iv) Lack of adequate infrastructural facilities - particularly transport, power, communication, storage, etc.

(v) Ethnic crisis.

(vi) Deteriorating law and order problem.

(vii) Lack of appreciation of potential industries based on skills.

(viii) Unwelcome/uncooperative attitude towards outside entrepreneurs who may be willing to invest and set up industries in Manipur.

(ix) Unwillingness of banks to finance small entrepreneurs.

(x) Unwillingness of the entrepreneurs to go and settle in the hill areas.

(xi) Migration of educated people from the hill to valley areas of Manipur as necessary amenities is not available in the hill areas.

(xii) Problems of finance.

(xiii) Shortage of raw materials.

In the industrial policy announced by the government of Manipur, there are proposals to provide infrastructural facilities in the form of industrial sheds, developed land, power, etc. to the small entrepreneurs. However, these are seldom made available on time. There is no permanent land ownership/patta system in the hill region of Manipur due to which there is inevitably a delay in the allotment of sheds, land, etc. to the entrepreneurs. Project implementation naturally gets delayed and consequently there is an increase in project cost. Of all the problems, finances remain a major constraint for entrepreneurs in the hill areas of Manipur. In order to grant loans, banks want a land certificate/patta, which are not issued in the hill areas due to non-implementation of the Manipur Land Revenue Act. There are also problems relating to the delay in the issuing of loan applications, in sanctions and disbursements of loan, etc. While entrepreneurs state that banks are reluctant to sanction loans to small entrepreneurs, the banks contend that they do not get viable proposals for financing.[14]

Prospects

Despite these problems, prospects for development of entrepreneurship in the hill areas of Manipur are quite good. The hills of Manipur are endowed with forest and mineral resources and various agricultural products. There is a vast reserve of virgin land for the development of extensive agriculture and plantation of various commercial crops. If only 5% of this surface area could be brought under cultivation instead of the existing 3%, the state could become self-sufficient in food grains and become an exporter of fruits and other plantation crops as well. This is all the more necessary since there is not much scope for extensive cultivation in the valley. The existing cultivation is also affected by the non-availability of essential inputs like irrigation water, seeds, fertilisers, etc, on time.

There are many mass consumption goods that are being brought to the region from the rest of the country. Most of these can be produced locally to meet the local demand. Particularly there is scope for tea industry, forest-based industry, coffee industry, sericulture industry and horticulture in the hill regions. Pineapple, Orange, Lemon, Ginger, etc. are grown in plenty in the hill districts especially in Tamenglong and Churachandpur district of Manipur where squash manufacturing industries can be set up. There is an urgent necessity to identify the potential industries based on available resources of the hill region and match them with prospective entrepreneurs.

Many of the resources are in the form of raw materials alone without any value addition. It is imperative that these resources are identified and their exports made after value addition is made inside the region. All the hill districts of Manipur have got manpower skills in specific area, particularly in handloom and handicrafts. The commercialisation of the handloom sector itself will lead to an emergence of entrepreneurship among women, most of who are expert in making handloom clothes.

Conclusion

About 35% of the total population of the state of Manipur live in the hills which constitutes about 90% of the total geographical area that is industrially and economically backward due to the lack of training as regards entrepreneurship. The promotion and development of industries will enhance entrepreneurship prospects. Needless to say, industrial development cannot be achieved without entrepreneurial development. The entrepreneur, therefore, is one of the most important inputs in the economic development of a country. He is the key person who envisages new opportunity, new techniques, lines of production, new products and coordinates all other activities. Thus the entrepreneur who is the propeller of progress should be trained and developed in a systematic manner.

There is also a lack of awareness among the educated youth about entrepreneurship opportunities. The socio-psychological attitude towards industrialisation has also been a hindrance to entrepreneurial development. What is actually needed is the effective coordination among all organisations and institutions - District Industries Centres, industrial consultants, Small Industries Service Institutes, National Small Industries Corporations, All-Manipur Entrepreneurs Association, All-Manipur Trained Entrepreneurs Union, banks and financial institutions which are involved in entrepreneurship development in the region - to ensure a better impact of programmes.

The Prime Minister Rozgar Yojana (PMRY) that has already been implemented in the state may be linked with EDP to achieve greater success in promoting first-generation entrepreneurs in the hill region as well. It has been observed that the projects taken up by the most of the new entrepreneurs are generally within the limit of small enterprises, so many of them will qualify to be micro enterprises. As such, if the EDP is linked with the PMRY, success can be assured in the promoting of entrepreneurship.

Marketing strategies should also be taken into account, as the whole exercise will depend on the how the product is received by consumers. The organisation dealing with EDPs and loan assistance should also formulate a marketing mix for their entrepreneurs. Institutions involved should take feedback and the utmost attention is to be directed towards the selection of such entrepreneurs who can mobilise available raw materials, local manpower and capital in the right proportion, thereby attaining economic-independence and efficiency. Along with these, industrial and educational policies must be coordinated at various levels for a harmonious and balanced growth to tap the power of human resources for the successful development of the hill economy of Manipur.

References

1. Higgins, B.: *The Economic Development*, p. 219.
2. Cole, Arthur H.: *Business Enterprise in its Social Setting*, Harvard University Press, 1959, p. 44.
3. Bhattacharjee, M.K. and Lahiri, R.K.: *Making Entrepreneurship Development work - The challenges before us.* The Indian Journal of Commerce, Vol. L., No. 192, Part-III, Sept.1997, p.20.
4. Government of Manipur, Annual Plan, 1993-94, p.6.
5. Ibid., p. 6.
6. Singh, H.N.: *Review of Plans, Policies and Incentives of Government and their impact*, Paper presented in the Seminar on Dynamics of Entrepreneurship development in Manipur (unpublished), p.1.
7. Background Note for state planning board meeting, Manipur held on 17.11.89.
8. Singh, H.N.: op.cit., p.2.
9. Ibid.

10. Desai, Vasant: *Organisation and Management of Small Scale Industries*, Himalaya Publishing House, Bombay, 1982, p.110.

11. Government of Manipur, EDP Section.

12. Government of Manipur: Industrial policy, 1990 and 1995, Part-III.

13. Mali, D D.: Entrepreneurship Development in North-Eastern Region: Problems and prospects, ACTA Journal, p. 11.

14. Ibid.

PART - V

ISSUES ON LAND

17

Land-Use System of the Kukis of Manipur

- *P.T. Yamthang Haokip*

In a bygone era, the entire land of Manipur was the property of an individual such as the Maharaja of Manipur. This was till new administration came into being after India's Independence in 1947. However, the produce of the land was enjoyed by everyone. This was without any right to ownership of any specific part of the land one tilled. As kingship was hereditary, land ownership too was hereditary. Such hereditary kingship and land ownership is very much similar to the chieftainship of the Kukis in Manipur. In fact, to understand the land-use system of the Kukis, one has to study the institution of chieftainship of the Kukis.

Power Vested in a Kuki Chief

The chief of a Kuki village enjoys the right over the land within the specified jurisdiction bestowed upon him. He also enjoys the right over his subjects who would pay him tributes of paddy, whether big or small, out of their annual harvests. The chief, in turn, helps the villagers with paddy whenever famine breaks out in the village.

With India's Independence, the Maharaja of Manipur granted individual ownership of land to his subjects and collected land tax from every individual according to the size of his land. Such a land-holding system was regularised by the Manipur Land Revenue and Land Reforms Act 1960. But this act could not be extended to the hill areas of the state, unfortunately depriving the hill people from enjoying the benefits of the popular act.

Purchase of Land

By custom and tradition, the genealogical head of a chief's family is the right person to establish a new village. He can purchase a specific land for his own and establish a new village, inviting his near and dear ones to settle down in his village where he himself shall enjoy maximum power in every aspect. Here every villager has the liberty of tilling the soil within the boundary of the chief as long as he pleases the chief and wins his confidence. Whenever the chief finds insufficiency of land for the year's cultivation for the entire households of his village, he would divide the areas of land according to the size of the families by stretching out ropes across the land. The chief, however, would not give fertile land to any person of the village who did not sow seed or who did not harvest or who did not clear out the reeds of the green field in the last year's tenure of jhuming.

Chieftainship Politicised

Since India's Independence, there has been a move to convert the formerly autocratic villages into democratic villages by the Manipur Village Authority Act. But the move proved unsuccessful. In fact, chieftainship in the hills has been politicised. The electoral system of a village is controlled by the villagers with the advice of the chief in favour of a particular candidate.

In the 1989 Assembly election, certain families of the Aihang village in 41 A/C exercised their franchise individually in favour of a candidate whom the chief did not favour. As a result, the disloyal villagers were threatened that they would not be allowed to continue tilling the land. These villagers begged for forgiveness from the chief with a promise not to displease him in future. They were pardoned and permitted to continue tilling the soil.

The practices of a Kuki village are subject to changes from time to time however, in different forms with the changing times.

Checking of Economical Growth

As Kuki chiefs control the affairs of land and politics, the land-use system hinders the economical growth of the villagers.

They could debar the villagers from taking up permanent, semi-permanent and land development projects. As a result, producing cardamom, tea, rubber, mango, orange, pineapple and lemon is very rare on Kuki soil.

Land Use in the Sadar Hills

Land use in Sadar hills is not an exemption to other hill districts of Manipur. Its characteristics are more or less similar with that of the Kuki ethos.

However, there are certain areas in Sadar Hills where the MLR and LR Act 1960 is extended. For example, lands lying in the areas of Yaingangpokpi, Hangoipat and Saikul are surveyed and issued Jamabandis under the MLR & LR Act 1960. Landholders accepted the same without any objection though the larger areas of land on the up-hills are not surveyed but are left to the possession of chiefs.

Traditional land ownership in Sadar Hills is a controversial one as all the terrace fields had been brought under survey whereas the hill-slopes and other barren lands are ignored. Under the same administrative unit there prevail three land holding systems:

a) The terrace fields are owned by individuals under the patta system;

b) The areas of hill-slopes are left under traditional ownership;

c) Tribal lands are not transferable to non-tribals.

According to the special provision of Scheduled Tribes, the prohibition of sale of land by a tribal to a non-tribal is enshrined in the MLR & LR Act, 1960, Article 158, but in the Sadar Hills landholders are found selling their lands to non-tribals, without the prior permission of the concerned Deputy Commissioner.

As such a practice is very common in the Sadar hills, tribal settlers are more or less landless now. Almost the entire land of the Sadar hills is occupied by non-tribals and even foreigners.

Remedy

The government ought to take stern action against this illegal transfer of land that is so widely practised in the Sadar Hills with the view of safeguarding the tribals in these areas as has been enshrined in the Act.

Extension of MLR & LR Act, 1960

The extension of the MLR & LR Act 1960 in the hill areas in general and in the Sadar hills in particular is nothing but a sort of democratisation of land for public use in order to promote economic growth. This will help landholders to invest labour, energy and productivity of land, and also help arrest the migratory practice among the Kuki settlers of the hills.

Remedies

Looking deep into the matter as discussed, it would be preferable to switch to the MLR & LR Act 1960 to improve the lot of the hill people and protect their land holdings. Declaration of village avenues for permanent settlement for the villagers will certainly accelerate economic growth much faster than before when every villager could claim ownership of land and take up self-developmental steps. Further, with the extension of the Act of 1960, the chiefs of the Kuki villages could be paid land compensation in a lumpsum as a reward for the loss of their traditional privileges.

18

Land Use System of the Marams

- *Francis Ngajokpa*

The Marams are originally said to have migrated from Makhel and settled down at Sapakizang called Pungtainamai, presently known as Maram Khullen. The first man known as Tingfiingarapai had 8 sons, blessed them and assigned different responsibilities to all. Tamlhung, the eldest son was entrusted to look after the laws and rituals related to marriage and intermarriages; Machiipa was assigned to take care of land including tax and rituals, cultivation and forest land; Mapouba, a warrior, was responsible for defence, Mapongba was to ensure the demarcation of boundaries for all types of allocation of land. Hona was asked to be the engineer for roads. Houpa, a benevolent man, was to help the poor and needy and the youngest son Ngakiiba was made the king.

The British administration did not interfere with the customary land rights and the Indian Constitution continues to safeguard the same. The land-use system of the Marams can broadly be categorised into four groups with respect to ownership, namely, common village land, clan land, *morung* land and individual land. The common village land includes those areas which are too far for cultivation - forest land, cattle grazing land, places of worship, playground, public entertainment place and land reserved for public purposes. The village authority takes care of the management of these lands but any decision has to be approved of by the villagers. This common land/property is neither inheritable nor transferable nor can it be sold to another village or tribe. The clan lands generally belong to a particular clan and are passed on from one generation to the next. It has got a very specific significance as the clan always extends a helping hand to the needy.and provides a portion of it if one of its members is in desperate need of it to survive. The clan also gives land to immigrants on the condition that the immigrant agrees to become one of them. The clan also generously helps divorced women or widows if they decide to live with them and remain faithful. The *morung* (a common sleeping house for bachelors) land includes woodlands where firewood is gathered for their common use. They also possess forestland, jhumland and terrace/wet-rice cultivation land for common use which is not transferable to any of their members individually or to any outsider.

The individual land includes forestland, jhumland, wet-rice fields, grazing ground and large grasslands for hunting purposes. These kinds of lands are well demarcated by stones or natural boundaries for a particular family. This is normally inherited permanent property. All these lands are held individually, are inheritable and transferable but this is not recognised by customary laws. The right of an individual to cultivate jhum land is not attached to any fixed parcel of land. An individual cultivator has the permanent right over a field if that particular land has never been cultivated. However, he has to pay the customary tax to the owner of the land, be it in the form of paddy or millet (a basket-full or two according to the quantity of the harvest). The regulation of jhum (shifting cultivation) is carried out once in every five years so as to regain the fertility of the soil. The community/clan jhumland is not transferable to another community or individual except with the permission of the community.

No restriction is made nor is any tax imposed on the community by the landowner for keeping animals on a particular land meant for grazing purposes. The forest and grass lands which are too far to cultivate or are yet to be cultivated both for jhum or terrace cultivation are reserved for future cultivation. They are utilised for hunting and trapping animals. The chest and leg of any animal killed in those forests by trap are given to the landowner as tax. Nevertheless, no tax is levied on animals killed with a spear or gun, etc. in the case of individual hunting. Hunting in the large grassland reserved for the purpose of community hunting takes place in the month of February. The owner of the land, on the eve of community hunting, performs a sacred ritual by confining himself in his house without touching anyone and at dawn kills a cock and implores God to grant him good fortune. On finding the omen satisfactory, the community hunting takes place that day, however, he remains confined inside the house till the hunting fires burn out. The head of the animal killed on that day is given to the landowner and both the hunter and the owner will take only rice beer and abstain from sexual relations on that particular night as a mark of respect for the land.

To undertake any new permanent/wet-rice terrace cultivation, the person concerned has to request the entire community for help. The owner kills a bull for the community feast and the labour for the day is contributed without wages. As a mark of respect for the new land, the owner will abstain from sexual relations and implore God for a good harvest and protection from natural calamities. Every year on the eve of harvest, before bringing the fruit of the land, special rituals are performed by appointing an elderly person who constructs a tent and stays inside for seven days imploring the lord of the land for a good harvest. In case the person dies during this period, the dead body will be kept till the end of the seventh day.

The demarcation of boundaries is by means of ditches, stones, hill ranges and rivulets according to customary laws. Every village has a main gate/entrance and roads leading to the village are given a degree of importance according to the sacrifice made to the land. A dog is sacrificed and its head and legs are fixed to a post on the roadside signifying the importance of the road and is an appeal to the powers that be that no misfortune may occur in the village. As years go by, with the increase of population, new settlements increase and a person can go in for a new plot of land for the construction of a house and will only have to pay a shawl as compensation to the landowner.

Marams being a patriarchal society, the succession of landed property goes to the male sons of the owner after his death. If he doesn't have a son, the inheritance rights are that of his nearest male kinsman. The property is not evenly distributed among the sons. However, the custom of primogeniture is not prevalent. The eldest son gets the lion's share although all the sons inherit the father's landed property almost equally. The house and the best wet-rice fields inherited from the forefathers will automatically go to the eldest son and the rest are distributed among the other sons. Daughters are debarred from inheriting paternal land or landed property of the father. Nevertheless, on the day of their wedding, they are given a necklace depending upon the capacity of the parents. The ancestral immovable properties distinguished from self-acquired property cannot be alienated. The only provision for a daughter to inherit the property of the parents is that acquired during her married life.

According to the customary law or convention, the owner of wet-rice or permanent cultivation has to pay a land tax in the form of a basketful of paddy once in a generation. However, in the case of jhuming, land tax is paid once and for all. No community land can be transferred or sold to another village or other communities or tribe. In case any person(s) sell(s) the community land, a heavy fine is imposed on the person concerned and the community returns the land and is not bound to refund the amount to the buyer. In case of any dispute that cannot be settled amicably over boundaries between individuals, groups or communities, the promise of killing a dog or a cat in the presence of the village council is made. Another method of deciding the matter on the spot is by summoning both parties who will dive into a deep pond; the guilty party who may be a good swimmer will float and the innocent person remains under water. Practices such as these exist even today, as the Marams normally do not go to court to seek justice due to the absence of written documents that clearly define boundaries.

19

MLR & LR Act, 1960 and Sixth Schedule in Relation to Hill Areas

- *K.C. Guite*

The Manipur Land Revenue and Land Reforms Act, 1960 (MLR & LR Act) is enacted by the Parliament to consolidate and amend the law relating to land revenue in the state of Manipur and to provide for certain measures of land reforms. The state legislature make rules, i.e. MLR & LR Rules 1961 (under the act), to carry out the purposes of the act.

During the British period, the administration of the entire hill areas of Manipur was under the responsibility of the president of the Manipur state *darbar* who was a British I.C.S. officer and later on became the chief minister (the 1st chief minister) of Manipur under the Manipur Constitution Act, 1947. Administration of the hill areas was carried out as per the act known as the Hill Peoples Regulation Act. Before the application of any land laws in Manipur, the raja of Manipur claimed absolute ownership of all lands within his territory in the valley from the earliest times and collected land revenue.

House Tax in the Hill Areas

There was no land revenue in the hill areas. During the British period after 1892, the Chin hill regulation was applied to the hills of Manipur and a house-tax was imposed at the rate of Rs 3/- per year per household. At present the amount is fixed at Rs 6/- though there is a proposal to increase it to Rs 10/-.

Application of Assam Land & Revenue Regulation 1886

The Assam Land and Revenue Regulation 1886 and the rules framed therein were applied to Manipur by the state *darbar* resolution No. 5 of 23.5.47. Subsequently, it was again applied by the Manipur Government Notification, 15 May 1952, and survey operations were started. In this operation, lands were classified according to productivity and location and different rates were proposed for different classes.

The Assam Land and Revenue Regulation, 1886, was replaced by the Manipur Land Revenue and Land Reforms Act, 1960 (MLR & LR Act).

The MLR & LR Act, 1960, is modelled on the pattern of the Tripura Land Revenue and Land Reforms Act, 1960, but the MLR & LR Act was amended several times enacting new provisions which further widened the gulf between the legislations of Manipur and Tripura.

Brief Summary of the Provisions

The state is the absolute owner of the property. The first eight chapters of the act are concerned with revenue administrations, preparation of record-of-rights, mode of recovery of revenue arrears, mutation and partition of estates and the like. The only basic thing dealt with in these chapters is the declaration that all lands including forests, mines and minerals therein are not the property of any person but are the property of the state (S.II). This is in conformity with the Manipuri tradition that the king was the absolute proprietor of all the lands within his territory in the valley.

Every person who, at the commencement of the act, holds any land from the government for agricultural purposes, whether as a settlement holder or as a pattadar, his successor-in-interest, shall, subject to the provisions of sub-section (2) of Section 99, become the owner thereof as and from such commencement.

Ceiling on Landholdings

The ceiling provision of the MLR & LR Act fixes two limits - one for irrigated land and the other for non-irrigated land.

The ceiling for a five-member family is 5 hectares of irrigated land. Where the number of family members exceeds five, the limit may be increased by one hectare for the additional member and 10 hectares in case of non-irrigated land. Besides this, if there is an adult son (who is excluded from the definition of family) then the limit shall further be increased by one-half of the area, which the adult son would otherwise have been entitled to hold.

Exemption from Ceiling

The provision of this chapter shall not apply to land owned by the government or the central government or a local authority. The state government has the power to exempt several categories of lands from the scope of the ceiling provisions (S.150). These are chiefly as follows:

i) Land held for plantation of tea, coffee, rubber, cardamom or cocoa and for purposes ancillary thereto or for their extension.

ii) Land held by a cooperative bank, commercial banks, agricultural universities, colleges or research centres.

iii) Sugarcane farm held by a sugarcane factory not exceeding 40 hectares.

iv) Land held by a cooperative farming society.

v) Land held by existing religious, charitable or educational trusts not exceeding 50 hectares.

There is also a provision on the prevention of fragmentation of holdings.

Restriction on Transfer of Land

(By a tribal special provision regarding STs)

For the protection of tribals, there is a special provision under Section 158 which prohibits the transfer of a tribal's land to a non-tribal without the prior permission of the deputy commissioner and the previous consent of the district-council, but unlike the Tripura act, the MLR & LR Act, 1960, has no provision for regulating transfer by a non-tribal of his land situated in the predominantly tribal inhabited villages.

Sec. 158: No transfer of land by a person who is a member of STs shall be valid unless -

a) The transfer is to another member of the Scheduled Tribes; or

b) Where the transfer is to a person who is not a member of any such tribe; it is made with the previous permission in writing of the deputy commissioner who shall not give such permission unless he has first secured the consent thereto of the district council within whose jurisdiction the land lies; or

c) The transfer is by way of mortgage to a cooperative society.

* The provision to clause (b) was inserted by the Manipur Act No.10 of 1976.

Many attempts have been made to remove the restriction of transfer to a member of non-ST by inserting the provision to clause (b) of the section (miscellaneous amendment) ordinance 1976.

The next attempt to remove this restriction on transfer is the MLR & LR Act 6th, amendment bill 1989, wherein the proposed amendment bill seeking insertion of new sections i.e. 158-A, 158-B, 158-C and 158-D, after section 158 of the principal act, namely:-

158-A. Restriction on Transfer of Land

No agricultural land shall be transferred to any persons except for his personal cultivation.

Provided that the deputy commissioner concerned may, subject to rules as may be prescribed, allow any non-tiller to purchase any land in the absence of any willing tiller to purchase the same land.

158-B. Restriction on transfer of land to non-residents

No land shall be transferred in favour of any person unless he has been ordinarily resident in the state: provided that the deputy commissioner may permit transfer of land in favour of a person who has not been ordinarily resident in the state if he has been a resident of the state for not less than 30 years.

Explanation: No person shall be deemed to have been ordinarily resident in the state unless he was born and brought up in the state.

Comment: This amendment, if it comes into effect, shall remove all the restrictions given by S. 158 of the principal act because the necessary consent to be obtained prior to the transfer is removed for members/persons who are residing within the state of Manipur and also to persons who obtain a certificate of 30 years residence from the concerned deputy commissioner.

158-C : Restriction on new settlement, etc

There shall be no new settlement or formation of any machet in the hill areas without the permission of the state government and no such permission for new settlement or formation of any machet in hill areas should be given unless the new settlement or formation of any machet has 50-75 families. This part of the amendment bill is contradictory to the District Council Act, and V.A. Act.

This amendment also proposed to repeal the Manipur Hill Areas (house tax) Act, 1966, by inserting under section 16-A, of the MLR & LR Act, making liable to payment of an annual tax in lieu of land revenue at the rate of such tax determined by the state government having regard to the rates of land revenue and the assessed tax be realised in such manner as may be prescribed.

This amendment further attempts to regulate and control jhum or migratory cultivation by making rules in the name of protection of environment.

There was much talk in this amendment bill about the proposed amendment in sub-section (2) of section 1 of the said act, where the term "except the hill areas thereof" and the provision thereto shall be omitted.

In order to understand the meaning better, the legal wording of the section of the act is reproduced below - Section 1 (of MLR & LR act 1960).

(1) This act may be called the Manipur Land Revenue and Land Reforms Act, 1960.

(2) It extends to the whole of the state of Manipur except the hill areas thereof - provided that the state government may by notification in the official gazette, extend the whole or any part of any section of this act to any of the hill areas of Manipur also as may be specified in such notification.

(3) It shall come into force on such date as the state government may, by notification in the official gazette, appoint, and different dates may be appointed for different areas and for different provisions for the act.

The new sixth amendment bill intends to remove the word except hill areas thereof: and the provision thereto, in sub-section (2) of section 1, above, which means that the extension of the act is to be made absolute or be made the statutory authority including the hill areas of Manipur.

At present the act provides in itself the provision for extension of the act to hill areas under the said provision, by notification in the official gazette to extend the whole or any part of any section of this act to any of the hill areas of Manipur also as may be specified in such notification.

And the same shall come into force on such date as the state government may, by notification in the official gazette, appoint.

But at the time of considering the bill, the said proposal of removing/deleting the word except hill areas thereof was dropped. But the provision for extension was already there since the 1975 amendment act.

The hill people, the students and other political parties vehemently opposed the proposed amendment bill, submitted memoranda and representations to the governor and other high dignitaries to withdraw and not to give assent to the bill. It is also said that during the consideration/discussion of the said bill some tribal MLAs walked out from the assembly in protest. Due to such opposition from the hill people the amendment bill has not been implemented. Various organisations opposed the amendment bill and among them ATSUM is one. While submitting a memorandum to His Excellency the governor of Manipur, ATSUM reiterated among other things: -

That, "the Manipur legislature assembly recently passed the MLR & LR (sixth amendment) bill 1989 amidst protest by the ATSUM in particular and the tribal people in general. In protest of this bill, the union had called for a 24-hour bandh of the hill districts on September 12th 1989, with satisfactory response from the public. Also, the ATSUM submitted a memorandum to the chief minister of Manipur to withdraw his spurious bill on the 11th September 1989, but all these demonstrations of the tribals drew no attention of the chief minister; instead he turned a deaf ear to the plea of the weaker sections of his state and created a new chapter of exploitation to the backward classes.

The bill came in the guise of bringing development for the tribals in the form of ecology balancing, bank loan facilities and landslide protection, etc. but, we have lived a harmonious life for centuries with nature and prospered by making the earth yield rich harvest season after season. Today the government destroys our forests with their greedy contractors. Unsatisfied with these, they try to encroach upon our forest so that they may run business with timber, natural resources and other forest by-products by enforcing this bill.

The Indian Constitution guaranteed to uphold the principles on which our society, economy and culture are based. It protects us from violations by exploitations. The protection guaranteed in the Constitution is threatened by greedy politicians and the bill cunningly mended is against the spirit of Indian Constitution.

The ATSUM approach Your Excellency to consider the matter so that this bill may not get your assent since this bill, if passed, shall provoke the peaceful living of the hill people and shall be forced to seek protection by any possible means from the encroachers and exploiters of our land by going for a separate administration".

That another bill, the 7th amendment bill 1992, was published in the gazette notification seeking new amendment insertion, introducing new sections to remove the restriction of land transfer from tribal to non-tribal, and control of jhum cultivation in the hills and making the revenue tribunal the highest revenue court for the purpose of determination of any question or dispute under the MLR & LR Act, retrospectively from the 1975 amendment and no further appeal shall lie from this court.

This means that one cannot go to appeal in the high court or the Supreme Court concerning revenue matters, as the tribunal is the highest court for this purpose as per the proposed amendment.

It may be recalled that the Parliament recently passed an amendment bill on the tenancy act, investing the tribunal with the power of the high court and the appeal from this tribunal to lie with the Supreme Court.

That despite the non-extension of the MLR & LR Act, SDO's issued notice under section 62 of the Act to realise hill house tax as if a revenue tax though the same has not been extended in the hill areas intentionally or knowingly permits complications in the administration.

As per the act, at the time of bringing it into force in 1961 in the valley of Manipur, the rights of the landowner, ceiling on land holdings and rights of tenancy were omitted which were the basic principles of land reforms. Their exclusion showed that the state was not ready for land-reform measures at that time.

Question of Extension of the Act to the Hill Areas

The MLR & LR Act, 1960, does not apply to the hill areas of the state but the state government may extend the whole or any part or any section of the act to any of the hill areas of Manipur under the said provision. The hill districts do not automatically become "hill areas", which term under the MLR & LR Act, 1960, has been assigned a specific meaning. According to section 2(1) of the MLR & LR Act "hill area" means such areas in the hill-tracts of the state of Manipur as the state government may by notification in the official gazette, declare to be hill areas. The state government has since notified that the following are the hill areas:

1. Jiribam sub-division (mainly plains). Hill areas and 24 villages, the MLR & LR Act, 1960, was extended under government notification No. 142/12/60-R, 22.2.62 and these 92 villages were included in the plains of Imphal district.
2. Tengnoupal sub-division 190 villages - hill areas.
3. Tamenglong district - 190 villages - hill areas.
4. Ukhrul district - 244 villages - hill areas.
5. Mao & Maram district - 312 villages - hill areas.
6. Churachandpur district - 225 villages - hill areas.

In the remaining 89 villages of Churachandpur, the act was extended in 1962 vide notification No. 142/12/60-M, 22.2.62 and Makhau tampak valley of Manipur. In the above named hill areas, the act did not apply (till 1985). In Bunglawn village, the act was extended recently (at Churachandpur). Due to non-extension of the act in the hill areas, survey work cannot be taken up since there is resistance from the public and village chiefs. The government however holds the view that extension should be carried out gradually in a planned manner and in selected pockets.

The act is also extended to 14 villages of the Senapati district, situated in the Sadar hills circle vide notification No. 138/4/64-M, 26.2.65. 809 hectares of land in Khoupum valley of Tamenglong district vide notification No.3/12/83/LRC, 14.11.1978.

To sum up then, the MLR & LR Act, 1960, applies to about 665 villages out of which 550 villages are situated in the three plain districts and the rest 105 in the plain areas of the hill districts. Most of the later villages lie in the Churachandpur district and some in Senapati district. The total number of villages in the state of Manipur being 2,109, the territorial jurisdiction of the MLR & LR Act, 1960, extends to about 31% of the total number of villages of the state. But as regards to population, it extends over about 71% of the total population of the state. Jiribam sub-division, though separated from the main valley by hills of the Tamenglong district, is included in the Imphal district for purposes of general and revenue administration, as it is almost wholly a plain area, with only 24 villages in the hills out of a total of 166 for the whole sub-division.

But a sizeable number of villages in the hill-districts are also situated in the more or less plain areas of the foothills. To these villages within the hill districts the MLR & LR Act has been extended as well by declaring such villages as plain areas by a notification in the official gazette. Under such a situation, inhabitants or annual patta holders were asked to convert themselves to landowners by paying premiums and those who did not do so within a specified date became stateless and were recorded only as occupants and encroachers on government khas land, which was a rather harsh and anomalous step. There are double taxes i.e. hill house tax and revenue tax.

Land Occupation in Plain Villages in the Hill Districts

Let us examine the position of some villages:

Saikot (A Hmar village)

The village was founded in 1920 (as per available material) by the great grandfather of the present chief. Before Independence, the villagers got settlement of land with the permission of the chief and used to pay him in the form of paddy and the front leg of an animal killed in the jungle. The forest inside the village land belonged to the chief. The village had fixed boundaries within which the chief exercised absolute power. After Independence, the powers and influence of the chief sharply declined. By and by, villagers began to stop the payment of a share of paddy or animal meat, but the chief carried on administrative functions as before. People were not required to pay any land tax to the government.

In 1960, the MLR & LR Act, 1960, was extended to this village (Saikot) along with 88 other villages of the district, as per the Manipur state government notification. No sooner had the act been enforced, peculiar problems began to crop up. All occupants, even those whose families had come at the time of establishment of the village, were regarded as possessors of vacant government land. Under Section 15 of the MLR & LR Act, 1960, they were in the eye of law, trespassers or encroachers and were advised to apply under Section 14 for the allotment of land they had possessed for generations without any hitch. Some did but many did not. Those who did get allotment only got it after they had paid a premium under rule 11 of the allotment rules, at the rate of 20 times the annual net income in case of cultivated lands and 30 times the annual land-revenue in case of other lands. Besides, the allotment holders had to pay land revenue every year - something they had not done before. The matter did not end there.

They had to continue to pay the house (hill house) tax, which they paid in lieu of land revenue. House tax everywhere is paid in lieu of land revenue, but here they had to pay it in addition to land revenue. They pointed out that the people of the valley did not pay house tax in addition to land revenue and asked they, the hill tribes, were made to pay both for the same piece of land - was not this tantamount to double taxation and discrimination?

The peculiar situation to which the hill-tribe cultivators have been pushed into by the extension of the MLR & LR Act, 1960, has given rise to grievances among those who have been brought within the ambit of the act as well as those who are proposed to be so brought within its ambit, by further extension of the MLR & LR Act. It appears curious that even the chief (Saikot) had to pay premium for obtaining allotment of the land which he had personally cultivated and also for his homestead land which he had possessed for decades. Had he not done so, he says, he would have been treated as an encroacher. In the case of those who did not pay premium nor applied for allotment of the land under his occupation nor paid any land revenue, their names do not appear as owners in the record of rights, only as occupants. The state is shown as the owner.

The annual patta granted under the Assam Land & Revenue Regulations 1886 are required to pay premium for obtaining allotment, as there is no provision for annual patta in the MLR & LR Act, 1960.

In the Saikot village, on the whole 15 plots which were previously occupied under the chief have now been covered by allotment order on payment of premium and 13 plots so occupied are still not covered by the allotment order and occupants are treated as unauthorised occupants of government land. This peculiar situation has come about as a result of the extension of the MLR & LR Act to villages in the hill districts.

Pearsonmun is yet another village where the same situation prevails. This is a village inhabited by the Paite tribe. It was established with the permission of Major Pearson, I.P.S. who was the then president of the Manipur state *darbar* who granted the entire area for establishing the village. Major Pearson's order runs as follows:

> "Mr. Thankhai has been given a village site by me in the Khuga valley area and has done well to get 20 houses in the first year. He has done well to break up new land; patta for his land should be issued as soon as the land can be surveyed".

Crux of the Problem

The crux of the whole problem is whether the land has automatically become government land wherever the MLR & LR Act has been applied. According to the Kuki customs regarding the rights of their chiefs, the Kuki chief is the owner of the lands within his jurisdiction. He realises premium at the time of settlement of land and also the annual crops rent regularly from the villagers. In times gone by, he could even turn out a villager from his village.

Today, of course, these privileges are honoured more in theory than in practice. Nevertheless, these customs clearly indicate that the chief's rights over the land do not lapse automatically on extension of the MLR & LR Act, 1960. Section 11 of the act, clearly provides that only those lands which are not the property of any person are the property of the government. The chief of the Kuki village has rights over the village land, and these rights constitute his property. In the case of villages like Pearsonmun and Molnom, Churachandpur, the government itself gave them the land and there was no condition that it could take it back on a whim. The chiefs, whether created by government or by custom, simply cannot be divested of their property in village land except by way of acquisition.

Under the Sixth Schedule of the Indian Constitution and the Manipur (hill areas) District Council Act, 1971, power to allot land is vested in the district council.

Under the Sixth Schedule, the district council is also empowered to assess and collect land revenue in respect of such lands in accordance with the principles that are being followed (by the government of the state in assessing lands for the purpose of land revenue).

The MLR & LR Act, 1960 and the Sixth Schedule and their Relation with Tribal Land:

In view of the above stated facts, the following suggestions have been made:

(i) That the power of allotment and others mentioned under the Sixth Schedule of the Indian Constitution be transferred to all district councils in Manipur.

(ii) Land records, including all relevant records of the land lying within the district, be handed over to the district councils from the state government settlement and revenue departments.

(iii) Land laws for the hill districts shall be enacted separately by the committee comprising of tribal members with an expert on the subject.

(iv) The state should not encroach upon the lands lying within the hill districts except in exceptional cases of acquisition as mentioned in the Sixth Schedule of the Indian Constitution.

(v) The district councils should be constituted and elections held as early as possible and the powers and functions as laid down in the Sixth Schedule should be transferred to the district councils in totality.

Such delegation of powers to the district councils will promote national integration and its denial will invite more problems. The land record, issue of patta and record of rights of land should be made and maintained by the district councils within whose area the land lies.

20

Land Use and Ownership System: Churachandpur District

- L. Chinzakham Ngaihte

Manipur is a small state divided into only 8 districts. Churachandpur district, formerly known as the Manipur south district, is one of them. It is situated in the south-western part of the state. It is the largest of all the districts covering an area of 4,570 sq. kms.[1] It comprises 20.47 % of the total geographical area of the state. This hill district has only a small portion, i.e. 0.32% area, of plains along the borderline with the Bishenpur district. In terms of population, it accounts for 9.48% of the total population of the state as per the 1981 census.[2]

Land Holding and Ownership System

The traditional land holding system was based on the principle of communal ownership with the assumption that the chief is the custodian of the village, customs and laws of the village community. It may be recalled that colonial administration had brought about far reaching change on the agrarian relations of the district. But such change was not in the nature of reform with a view to improving the economic condition of the cultivators but with a view to collecting more revenue. It, therefore, legitimised the right of the chief over the land by legalising the ownership of land of the chief for practical purposes.

In 1892 Maxwell,[3] the then political agent of Manipur, introduced a house tax of Re 1/- per homestead in the valley and Rs 3/- per house in the hill areas that was payable per annum. This was followed by another landmark. Col. J. Shakespeare (the political agent of Manipur from 1905-1908) demarcated the chief's land and 'pattas' were issued to all the village chiefs thereby strengthening and legalising the chief's right over the land. The direct result of such revenue administration was that each village land became the private property of the chief and, as a result, traditional communal ownership and freedom of the common people was minimised.

The agrarian system prevailing in the economy[5] is somewhat akin to the semi-feudal type of land ownership. The chief has, by way of convention, overriding power over the utilisation of the village land. Lands, however, are distributed and each villager is allowed to cultivate a plot of land every year. Besides, once the chief has accepted an outsider or new immigrant into his fold then the chief is duty-bound to provide him with land that he can cultivate. In other wards, cultivation of a plot of land is the entitlement of bona-fide villagers but such an entitlement does not, under any circumstances, constitute permanent individual ownership of the land. When the jhum 'season' is over, the land reverts to being the village chief's.[6] Soon after the jhum course is over, the land tenure of the cultivator over the land is also over. This is an 'oral lease system'. There is, therefore, no incentive for the cultivators to improve the land. The absence of this 'individual holding right' is conspicuous. The chief, who continues to be lord of the land, does not carry out any land improvement programme either. Only the chief enjoys 'right' over the land.

The institution of chieftainship occupies a special and important place in the structure of the economy - the economy of the district. It may be due to a peculiar ownership pattern of land in the economy. Ownership of land being preserved, the tribal chieftains had power, status and authority in the economy only till recently. It may be mentioned that there are some chiefs[7] who still hold powers and exercise authority like autocrats in certain parts.

The villagers or the tenants-at-will for that matter, as a rule, pay grain-rent or Buhsun or Tangseu to the 'absentee' landlord, i.e., to the chief. This subscription was a kind of agricultural tax or fee for cultivating the chief's land by the individual farming families. The chief has the right to exempt any villager from the purview of the tax. By virtue of being the 'owner of the village land' there are other customary entitlements that the chief enjoys. Levies collected by the chief include:

a) Front leg of any animal killed in his chiefdom;
b) Forced labour from the villagers. It is 4-day labour of the villager in a year;
c) Mithun levy;
d) Sale levy;
e) Death levy; and
f) A levy on a wild honey in the forest.

The chief is entitled to appropriate 4-day labour of his villager in a year. But the villagers receive nothing in return. It was their customary duty and, for the chief it was his customary right. He is the "sovereign" of his little realm.

A group of councillors assists the chief. They were known as "*hausa Upa*" or the chief's council. It was a highly coveted post. They were chosen by the chief. Their services were liable to be dismissed by the chief at any time. In return for their services, they were exempted from the rigour of grain-rent. Another privilege of the councillors is the right or chance to select a jhum site or plot before the other villagers.

However, commenting on the image of the chief, the law research institute, Gauhati High Court, Gauhati, noted:

> The chief is not like a traditional zamindar collecting rents from those persons cultivating his land and driving them out whenever he likes. He is more like a father of the whole village distributing land to the villagers for their maintenance ... All this shows an image of the benevolent father-figure. In actual fact, he looks like a holy man of the church. He has shorn himself of most traditional powers of a chief and allows the village authority (his councillors) set up under Manipur law to exercise them.[8]

All the same, the chief's court is the highest tribunal court in the village. He even has the power to hear murder trials and settle such cases.

The Manipur (Village Authority in Hill Areas) Act, 1956

The spread of democratic ideas and institutions has gradually led to the decline of absolute chieftainship. By introducing the element of an elective system in the composition of a village authority, the act may be said to have set in motion the declining process of the institution of chieftainship. It may be noted that before the introduction of the act, the chief had the overriding or unquestioned power of nominating any one of his villagers to be his councillors. Such hand picked councillors held office till decided otherwise by the chief. The above act designated him "ex-officio chairman" of the village authority thereby avoiding the use of the title 'chief'.

The Manipur Hill Areas (Acquisition of Chief's Rights) Act, 1967

The village authority act of 1956 was followed by the Manipur Hill Areas (acquisition of chief's rights) Act, 1967. The act, in fact, reduced the powers of the chiefs though it did not abolish chieftainship completely. Traditional subscriptions like grain-rent, forced labour and front leg of the animals killed etc., were gradually stopped in most parts of the economy. But there are chiefs[9] who still continue to enjoy *Buhsun* and *Saliang* almost as usual even today. However, such privileges have been slightly modified now.

By mutual understanding, i.e. between the chiefs and the villagers, the rate of grain-rent has now been reduced mostly from 5 to 3 tins or baskets per year per cultivating household. Thus, chieftainship remains more or less an accepted institution in the economy despite various legislative measures aiming at its abolition. In fact, the immediate effect of the passing of the act of 1967 has become a matter of controversy both for the chief and the villagers.

Despite the act, the village chief, as usual, has to provide local hospitality to visiting government officials without receiving traditional dues and subscriptions from his villagers. He does not receive any benefits from the government either. He becomes poorer despite his vast lands. Under the circumstances, he has no alternative other than to sell the product of his land so that he can maintain his status as the village chief. But the villagers object to his selling of the product of the land on the plea that the government has acquired their 'right' over the land. It is the argument of the chiefs, privately of course, that their 'rights' over land have been as intact as before, in that, they were not given any compensation to effect the acquisition. In the ultimate analysis, the economy is facing a sort of increasing antagonism between the chiefs on the one hand and the common people on the other.

It appears that the government is playing delaying tactics as regards this matter. Mention may be made in this connection with the chief's union,[10] Churachandpur district, that has submitted a memorandum to the chairman, Hill Areas Committee of the Manipur Legislative Assembly, requesting the government to take a clear-cut urgent decision on their 'existence' or 'abolition' and express their willingness or readiness either to accept abolition with honourable compensation or the restoration of their chieftainship as per the 1956 position. It appears that the chiefs themselves are unclear about their present position and status.

The Manipur Land Revenue and Land Reforms Act, 1960

The MLR & LR Act, 1960, is another significant legislative measure that has an important bearing on the land holding system of the tribals as a whole. The act, whenever and wherever extended in the hill areas, does away with the existing pattern of ownership especially in the Churachandpur district where chieftain holding is common and widespread. The act seeks to end communal holding and replace it with individual holding or ownership. But the implementation of the act left much to be desired not only in Churachandpur district but also in other hill districts of the state. Out of the 2,00,890 hectares of the five hill districts, only 0.33% could be surveyed, i.e. 6,712.22[11] hectares, and that too only by 1986-87. Less than 1% of the total area of the hill districts was recorded as surveyed. The figure is 0.17 % in the case of Churachandpur district.

Nine-tenths of the total area of the state is covered by hills. It is generally argued that the act does not apply to the hill areas, but the fact is that the government can extend the whole or any part or any section of the act to any hill areas of Manipur by calling upon section 2 (j) of the act. According to this section, the term "hill areas" means such areas in the hill-tracts of the state of Manipur as the state government may, by notification in the official gazette, declare to be hill areas. Therefore, according to the MLR & LR Act, 1960, a hill area does not simply constitute a "hill area" by virtue of its being located in the hill districts. It requires 'declaration' by notification in the official gazette.

On the strength of the above section of the act, 225 villages in the Churachandpur sub-division have been 'declared' to be hill areas and in the remaining 89 villages the act was extended in 1962 vide notification No. 142/12/60-M on 22.2.62.[12] The section enables the Government to extend the act in the hill areas in a calculated and surreptitious manner.

Section 158 of the act prohibited the transfer of land by a tribal-owner to a non-tribal, except with the permission of the deputy commissioner who, before giving such permission, has to secure the consent of the district council concerned. Section 158(c) admitted the mortgage or transfer of land to a cooperative society. This section, through skilful manipulation, offers a convenient and safe route for non-tribals to possess land and become patta-holders. It is understood that through the manoeuvrability of this latent lacunae, there are now more than 100[13] non-tribal patta-holders in the town of Churachandpur. Despite such protective measures, there is, it appears, a steady inflow of non-tribals into the hill areas virtually rendering the provision into a half-hearted measure.

The 'special provision' mentioned above has now been removed by the MLR & LR (6th amendment) bill 1989, amidst angry protests by some members of the community belonging to the Scheduled Tribes. The amendment bill has now been made ready to become an act pending the assent of the state governor. The amendment has sent shock waves and apprehension throughout the hills of the state. It was responded to with bandhs, processions and demonstrations, spearheaded by the All Tribal Student's Union of Manipur (ATSUM) and various community-based parties that forgot their petty differences for a common cause.

It is observed that the extension of the MLR & LR Act, 1960, to villages inhabited by tribals has created many complicated problems.[15] We have already noted that the above act was extended to 89 villages; mostly located at the fringe of Manipur valley, of the Churachandpur sub-division, in 1962. Relating to the topography of the land, these villages are similar to other villages of the Manipur valley, but the customs in relation to the land systems of these villages are different. According to the customs of the tribals living in these 'fringe villages', all land in the village belongs to the chief of the village. The villagers were practically his tenants and they used to subscribe regular rent in kind. But under the Assam Land Revenue and Regulation Act, 1886, these 'tenants' of the chief were brought into direct contact with the state government by issuing annual patta, etc. How could those 'tenants of the chief' be brought into direct contact with the government without first acquiring or abolishing the ownership rights of the chiefs? It is unfathomable why the state government was issuing pattas to the tenants and not to the chiefs who possessed sanads granted by the king or British officers recognising their right over the land. It appears that the existence of the chief's rights over the land was completely ignored at the time.

If the government is sincere and honest enough in attending to the interest of the tribal community as a whole, it has to 'reconsider' those sections that open their land to the access of non-tribals. Adequate compensation should also be given to the erstwhile village chiefs, as it has been given in Mizoram. Forced termination of the village chiefs, who are literally sovereign in their respective villages by customs and tradition, could not possibly be the right step.

Double Taxation

Another grievance of the people of the area where the act was extended is the payment of double-taxes in the form of land revenue plus hill house tax for the same piece of land. They are paying hill house tax because these villages are administratively located within the hill districts where it is imposed as a substitute for land revenue. Due to the change of possession every year, land revenue cannot be imposed on shifting cultivation and, therefore, a house tax is imposed on the cultivators of these areas (Cf., Maxwell 1892). At the same time, these villages are paying land revenue in addition to the hill house tax simply because of the extension of the application of the MLR & LR Act, 1960, to these villages. However, in these fringe villages, where cultivation is mostly fixed and boundaries of land permanent, assessment of land revenue after acquisition of the chief's rights, appears to be reasonable and justified provided the collection of hill house tax is discontinued. Because of this irregularity, they are made to suffer the anomaly of double-taxation on the same piece of land. This distortion is tantamount to discrimination and ill treatment. This blatant irregularity deserves the immediate attention of those in the corridors of power because hill house tax everywhere is essentially meant to be a substitute for land revenue.

Reference may also be made of the hill house tax rate. It appears quite high when compared with the prevailing rate in neighbouring states like Arunachal Pradesh where it is Rs 2/- per household, in Meghalaya Rs 3.95[16] and in Manipur itself it was Rs 3/- during the British period. It was raised to Rs 6/- in 1975 and there is a proposal to further raise it to Rs 10/- now. Such a rate would definitely weigh heavy on the poor hill-dweller.

The Land Reform Act, 1960, undertaken with the objective of providing better means of earning in the long run, thanks to all these distortions and discrepancies, is being looked at with misgiving in the hills. There is no gainsaying that the act would give 'land rights' to the cultivators. But the hill peoples' main concern is that such an open extension of the act, without adequate and effective protection and safeguards, would mean the opening up of the land to outsiders i.e., the plain people, who have more and better resources at their command. Without such an effective measure, the land would thus become a purchasable commodity open to one and all. Being economically weaker and less fortunate they would perhaps be hard pushed to sell their land for money. It is, therefore, apprehended that most of their land would finally pass into the hands of the plain people and they would be left with no land to live by. This is the perspective of the tribals as a whole.

The extension of the MLR & LR Act, 1960, in the hill areas of the state would perhaps be less contentious and quarrelsome when appropriate and adequate measures effectively protecting the interests of the tribals is part of the package of the land reform policy. Provided that there are adequate and effective safeguards for the tribals, this essay is arguing in favour of the extension of the act in the hill areas. The basic rationale behind this argument is the consideration of 'individual holding right or ownership'. Reference may be made in this connection of the report on development of tribal areas which, inter alias, states:

> "Sometimes progressive measures like those of land reforms, have adversely affected the tribal communities because those laws did not take into account the special situation in the tribal areas . . . All transfer of land from tribals to non-tribals should be prohibited and prohibited effectively. Where no such laws exist, a suitable law should be enacted immediately."[17]

Individual Ownership or Holding Right

The economy is characterised by the virtual absence of individual ownership or holding rights of land. Keeping the weak economic base and the fragile nature of the tribal subsistence in view, which is the result of the existing system of land-use and ownership pattern, there is, it is felt, a need for serious introspection and experimentation with the system of 'individual holding or ownership'. The National Committee on Development of Backward Areas has recommended 'individualisation' of communal ownership in the North-East for the sake of 'progress'.

The Committee argued that

> "From the point of view of development there are two important changes which are required. The widespread nature of the community rights in land has led to difficulties in individual development. The incentive to undertake improvements and increase productivity has been blunted, as the individual does not know how long the land will be in his possession. Permanent rights over settled land are increasingly being recognised and the movement from community to individual has begun. However, the individual needs to be given a legal right to land".[18]

Despite a cautious note[19] against the total individualisation of communal ownership, the system of individual holding or ownership has got currency and acceptance in the country as a whole. It is considered 'progressive'. It is assumed to be an equalising device. The present land-use system offers no incentives to cultivators. He cultivates the land but the land does not belong to him. He has no permanent rights over the land he cultivates. This type of holding basically kills the will of the farmer to improve the land. Credit facility and other financial assistance either from the government or from other financial institutions is hard to come by owing to the absence of 'right' over land. The economy can no longer thrive in isolation. It has got to adapt itself with the current system of private holding. On the merits of private holding, it is asserted that:

> *"Give a man a secure possession of a bleak rock and he will turn it into garden; give him a nine years' lease of garden, he will convert it into a desert."*[20]

Thus, the system of individual holding rights in land becomes imperative in view of the stagnation and disabilities the economy suffers. Holding right is stated to be a 'key' to growth and development. Perhaps, this is the main theme of land reform policies everywhere. Permanent holding right would possibly make the credit flow easier and, therefore, a productive investment may become a feasible proposition. . Incentive to work and investment may thus be seen in full circle.

References

1. Government of Manipur, Directorate of Economics and Statistics, Statistical Abstract of Manipur, 1989, Imphal, p.1.
2. District Statistical Office, Churachandpur, District Socio-Economic Survey, Churachandpur District, 1983-84, p.2.
3. Robert Reid, *History of the Frontier Areas Bordering Tribal Research Institute*, Aijawl, Reprinted, Aijawl, 1976.
4. J. Shakespeare; *The Lushai Kuki Clans*, Tribal Research Institute, Aijawl, Reprinted, Aijawl, 1976.
5. It refers to the 'economy' of the District.
6. A Study of the Land System of Manipur, Law Research Institute, Eastern Region, Gauhati High Court, Gauhati 1985 (sponsored by the North-Eastern Council, Shillong), p.45.
7. The chiefs of Chongkhojou, Mualkui, etc. enjoying grain-rent, etc.
8. A Study of the Land System of Manipur, op.cit., pp.45-46.
9. The chief of Chongkhojou, Mualkui, Saipum etc.
10. Chief's Union, Churachandpur District, Manipur State, Convention Press, Lamka, p.7.
11. Government of Manipur, Directorate of Survey and Settlement (Hill Survey) 1986-1987.
12. A Study of the Land System of Manipur, op.cit. p.30.
13. Sub-Deputy Collector, (Settlement), Churachandpur Sub-Divisional Officer, Churachandpur, dt. 20.10.1988.

14. Shri Rishang Keishing, Jainson Haokip and J.F. Rothangliana rose to the occasion and walked out of the House protesting against the amendment bill.
15. A Study of the Land System of Manipur, op.cit., p.144.
16. Government of India, Planning Commission, Report on Development of Tribal Areas - National Committee on the Development of Backward Areas, June, 1981, p.53.
17. Government of India, Planning Commission, Report on Development of N.E. Region, National Committee on Development of Backward Areas, November, 1981, p.19.
18. B.K. Roy Burman, *"Problems and Prospects of Tribal Development in N.E. India"*, Economic and Political Weekly, Vol. XXIV No.13 (Bombay April 1989), p. 696.
19. Arthur Young, quoted from Ruddar Butt & K.P.M. Sundharam's *"Indian Economy"*, Ravindra Printers, New Delhi, 1990, p. 440.
20. Handbook of Manipur (Village Authority in Hill Areas) Act, 1956, Government Press, Imphal, 1956.
21. Manipur Land Revenue and Land Reforms Act, 1960, (as amended from time to time) Directorate of Printing and Stationary, Manipur, 13 September, 1963.
22. The Manipur Hill Areas (Acquisition of Chief's Rights) Act, 1967, Directorate of Printing and Stationary, Manipur, Imphal, 1967.

21

Tribal Land Use System in Manipur (with reference to Liangmais)

- Kaikhamang Daimai

Land has since time immemorial been the economic guardian of the tribals. It is precious to them since it is their only source of livelihood. They use land in every aspect of life both at the time of sorrow and happiness. They do not have any written land laws as such, yet they have a long-practiced conventional system of land holding and utilisation. Land being the primary factor of production for the tribals, no one can forgo it.

Traditional Land Use System of the Liangmais

The traditional systems of land utilisation among the tribal communities are more or less the same. However, there may be certain variations from community to community. The general practice and traditional system of the Liangmais are briefly enumerated here. The whole village land is broadly classified into three categories. These are as follows:

(a) ***Kilong ram***: The area meant for the construction of houses for dwelling, barns and other sheds are called *kilong ram*. This includes an area for the kitchen garden as well. It is within the gates of the village. Every Liangmai village has two gates. The first gate is in the direction from which they first came to the village site at the time of settlement. The second gate may face any direction and is meant for exit.

(b) ***Rambow ram***: The area around the village is called *rambow ram*. It is a reserved land. Trees and other minor forest produce are all reserved and protected here. These trees are meant for protection of the village from wild fire and other natural calamities like heavy storms, etc. No one is allowed to cut any tree within this protected area. If one does so, he/she is fined. The village counci', i.e. the *pai*, imposes this fine on the wrongdoer. The fine is commonly in the form of a jar of locally brewed wine.

(c) ***Chalu ram***: The village land used for cultivation is called *chalu ram*. The entire land for cultivation is divided into a number of areas, locally known as *ramlong* or *charam* with proper schedule. Different individuals or clans own these areas. Within this portion of land or *ramlong*, there are a number of plots called *luphung*, i.e. cultivating fields. The owner of the *ramlong* is known as *charampou* and the owner of the plot is called *luphungpou*.

1. Payment on Land Utilisation

There are two kinds of payment for the utilisation of land in Liangmai community. The plot owners pay *rampon* to the owner of the *ramlong* once in every cultivating year. Those farmers who do not have a plot in a particular area have to hire the same in that year. The payment made for hire of the plot is called *lu-nge*. This *lu-nge* is paid by farmers who don't own any plot of land.

2. Utilisation of Land

Land is used only for jhum or shifting cultivation. In this method of cultivation, the farmers change the plot every year. They shift their field every year clearing the whole jungle for one year only. In certain cases, the plot can be cultivated for 2 to 3 years. In the olden days, the jhum cycle used to be between 10 to 15 years.

Second, land is also used as a gift from parents of a bride. A few well-to-do parents offer their fields for cultivation or *ramlong* at the time of their daughter's marriage.

Third, land is also used as a fine for homicide and other grave crimes such as adultery, etc.

3. *Land Ownership System*

The traditional pattern of the land holding system of the Liangmai is a rather complicated one. It may be termed as a trio system. In the first place the entire village land belongs to the chief or village community as a whole because the village administration protects the entire land at such time when there is an external attack or encroachment by any neighbouring villages. Second, as stated above, there are a number of areas known as *charam* owned by a few individuals. These are the real landowners in the eyes of the common people. Third, within a particular area of land, i.e. *charam,* there are a number of plots. These plots are owned by a large number of different families/individuals. These plot owners have certain rights over their plots. They can sell the plots without consulting the *charampou* if the sale is within the village. On the other hand, the *charampou* cannot sell his land without consulting the village administration. To sum up, the land ownership system of the Liangmais is a three-tier system. Above all, the village council holds supreme control over individual landowners. They settle any internal land disputes and protect land from outside encroachers.

Process of Land Acquisition/Ownership

In the days of yore, when the people first settled down in their respective villages at different points in time, they occupied uninhabited land. The area of land so occupied or earmarked became their village land. Their settlement was subject to any dream indications or omens they may have received, as by nature they are a superstitious people and believe in the powers of the supernatural. When a group of people come to a certain place to settle, the leader of the group always prays to Mother Earth to show some signs of approval if they are to settle there. If the leader sees a favourable indications or omen, they start making arrangements to settle down. Later, the leader of the group becomes the chief of the village. Before they physically occupy the site, they appease the gods and goddesses, rivers and mountains, and all creatures in it. They believe these creations possess the power to either grant them prosperity or misfortune. They offer animal sacrifices. At the time of sacrificing animals, they offer the following prayer:

(a) O, Mother Earth and Father Heaven, I will marry this land (put down powdered/sliced ginger in a hole followed by pouring rice beer/wine).

(b) O, Mother Earth, I have married you and you become my partner/friend;

(c) O, mountains and rivers, from today onwards, I have married you and we become friends;

(d) O, all animals, beasts, reptiles, poisonous or less poisonous, we become friends from today onwards as I have married this land.

After making this kind of appeasement, they enter the village site and physically occupy it. At the time of the first settlement, there was no individual landowner as such. The entire land belonged to the chief or village community. The animal sacrificed as an offer of appeasement had to be from the chief. The chief would then distribute areas of land to different clans. The central portion, i.e. the village site covering the *rambow*-homestead land is reserved for the chief. This was the beginning of land ownership in the village/society.

Once they settled in that site, there were still a number of taboos to be observed and rites to be performed. In every ritual, animals are sacrificed to the gods. In exchange for the sacrificial animals, the chief gave a portion of the land to the person who offered the animal to be sacrificed. This land may be a *ramlong* or *luphung* depending upon the size of the animal. This practice used to take place every year. This is the origin of individual landowners and plot owners. Otherwise, there was no private landowner at the time of the first settlement.

Ownership of land is acquired through purchase. Whenever a piece of land is sold, the ownership is transferred to the purchaser. The sale of land, however, is allowed only within the village. The ownership of cultivating fields does not change though the *ramlong* within which the field lies can be sold to another person.

The other way of acquiring the ownership of a piece of land is through gifts. Some parents of a rich family used to offer a *ramlong* or *luphung* (plots) as a gift at the time of their daughter's marriage. In such case, the ownership of that land is transferred to the groom's family.

When a piece of land is used as a fine for a grave crime committed such as homicide, adultery, etc. then too ownership of land is automatically transferred.

Need for Change in the Traditional System

In the days gone by and even in the recent past, the traditional pattern of land holding was good. There was respect and regard for one another. However, since everything in the world is transitional, there comes a time when the thought patterns of people change. They become aware of their rights. Today, landowners want to have some semblance of control over their lands. The traditional system, which held good at one time, becomes a bone of contention today in the absence of any written records. So, the basic system cannot be safeguarded. The understanding or good relationship that used to exist between landowner, villager and chief has become strange with the passing of time. Landowners start putting on a ban on bamboo, stone and other forest produce even among their own villagers. On the other hand, field owners also claim to have authority/power over their fields as they have paid for it. So, there are clashes of authority between landowners and field owners.

The age-old system no longer holds good for the people in present society. Everyone wants to own a piece of land. Since there are still some people who do not have land of their own, they are forced to hire a field for cultivation purposes on payment. As pointed out earlier, they pay 1 year's rent to the field owners. At the same time the cultivator does not know if he is the real owner of his plot. On the other hand, he is at the mercy of the landowner. If the landowner gets his land registered and starts fencing the area, the field/plot owner simply has to give up ownership rights. To prevent such incidents, the traditional system of land holding needs to be modified.

The heavy pressure on land is another factor that calls for modification of the old system of land holding. With the increasing population, every year there are hundreds of people more who depend on land as the only means of livelihood as there is no alternative occupation. While such is the pressure on land, the traditional system is limited to only a few owners. Thus, the need for redistribution of land arises. In the old system, people were afraid to set up any permanent establishment. They could set up a long-term project but when the project starts bearing fruit the landowners may simply reclaim the land. Because of this uncertainly, people do not wish to venture into long-term projects. As a consequence of this, the tribal economy lags far behind.

Suggestions for Improvements in the System

The following points could be a supplement to the age-old system of land holding among the tribals, particularly the Liangmais.

1. Common Land

As far as possible the land should be made common property. The existence of the landowner creates a division in society. In other words, individual ownership ought to be abolished. If necessary from a customary point of view, their control over the land should be restricted. They are not to have independent rights over the land. The village administration is to hold over-all control over the entire village land.

2. Redistribution of Land

As pointed out, there are a good number of people who do not have a piece of land of their own. Where land is abundantly available, it is unimaginable that there are people who do not have their own land in the tribal area. The existing plot system needs to be regularised therefore. Redistribution of land is to be done in such a way so that every household gets cultivating fields in every shifting year. The slogan, "land for the landless" is welcome even in tribal communities.

3. Terrace/Permanent Cultivation

The problem of land holding and redistribution of land can be, to some extent, solved through terrace or permanent farming. If in a village there are 100 households that depend on shifting cultivation, out of which some 20 households have terrace fields. They will not practice jhuming. When the jhum cycle comes in a particular area, 20 plots will be spared in that jhuming area. These 20 plots can be given to the growing population of families. In this way if 50% of the people in a village are engaged in terrace or permanent cultivation, there will be a big surplus of land. This method may facilitate the distribution of land more effectively.

In conclusion, the traditional land holding system of the Liangmais is a cohesive social and economic factor in the life of the people. The landowners and the field owners are inter-dependent. Landowners do not have absolute power. They cannot utilise their land independently. The selection of a jhuming area is decided upon by the village council (*pai*). Likewise, the field owners also cannot cultivate their land as they like. The village administration holds the final control as far as the utilisation of land is concerned.